Praise Page for
Optimizing the Power of Action Learning, 2nd Edition

"Action *and* learning are crucial to sustained organizational success. Mike Marquardt knows this and his book provides proven, practical, and useful thinking tools, techniques, and examples."

—*Mike Stonier, Senior Manager, University of Pretoria's Gordon Institute of Business Science, Johannesburg, South Africa*

"Marquardt's teachings have allowed Sony Music leaders to realize their greatest potential for solving problems: not by overwhelming a discussion with conflicted answers, but by asking powerful questions and reflecting on one's own leadership skills. That alone has made *Optimizing the Power of Action Learning* one of the most vital instruments of our leadership transformation success."

—*Kathy Chalmers, Executive Vice President & Chief Human Resources Officer, Sony Music Entertainment*

"A must read for anyone who wants to improve the effectiveness of people and organizations."

—*Doug Bryant, Director of Organizational Development, Honeywell Transportation Systems*

"Mike Marquardt is *the* key thought leader in action learning. In introducing this unique but simple process to our executive leaders, we have garnered huge benefits in problem definition and resolution, as well as in higher-level thinking and the acceleration of organizational learning."

—*Helen Goldson, VP Talent Management, Goodrich Corporation*

"As a certified action learning coach, I have found *Optimizing the Power of Action Learning* to be a valuable resource. The enhancements in the revised edition present practical and clear guidelines for implementing the six components of action learning in any organization. The illustrations provided in the case studies make the implementation of action learning even easier."

—*Dr. Jacqueline Villafañe, Manager, American Red Cross, Disaster Services Leadership Development*

"If you like turning problems into opportunities, this book is your solution. Marquardt's action learning techniques are not just process tools, they are mental repositioning systems and diagnostic organizational barometers."

—*Roland K. Yeo, Associate Professor of Organizational Behavior & International Business, Kuwait Maastricht Business School, and Adjunct Senior Researcher of Management, University of South Australia*

"To be a competent leader, continuous learning is the key contributing factor. This book shows how action learning can turn leaders from passive learners to active learners."

—*Dr. Florence Ho, Senior Lecturer, School of Professional Education & Executive Development, Hong Kong Polytechnic University, Hong Kong*

"As a writer and a scholar, Mike Marquardt has an uncanny ability to impart important and effective leadership strategies in a way that can be immediately acted upon by the reader. *Optimizing the Power of Action Learning, 2nd Edition*, is one more gem in Mike's repertoire of books, providing actionable knowledge and guidance to organizations seeking to solve complex problems."

—*A. Gidget Hopf, EdD, President and CEO, Goodwill of the Finger Lakes, Rochester, NY*

"In this era, the pressure to accelerate business outcomes, gain market share, and reduce cost is crushing. If your organization is looking to accelerate business outcomes, action learning is a powerful vehicle to make it happen. I know, because we've done it with the guidance of Dr. Marquardt."

—*Dr. Debra Gmelin, Corporate Director, Leadership Institute at Humana Inc.*

SECOND EDITION

Optimizing the Power of Action Learning

Real-Time Strategies for Developing Leaders, Building Teams, and Transforming Organizations

Michael J. Marquardt

Jennifer,
Best of success
with action learning!
Michael J. Marquardt

nb

NICHOLAS BREALEY
PUBLISHING

BOSTON · LONDON

This edition first published by Nicholas Brealey Publishing in 2011.

20 Park Plaza, Suite 1115A

Boston, MA 02116 USA

Tel: 617-523-3801

Fax: 617-523-3708

3-5 Spafield Street, Clerkenwell

London, EC1R 4QB, UK

Tel: +44-(0)-207-239-0360

Fax: +44-(0)-207-239-0370

www.nicholasbrealey.com

Printed in the United States of America

15   14   13   12   11   1   2   3   4   5

ISBN: 978-1-90483-833-3

Library of Congress Cataloging-in-Publication Data
Marquardt, Michael J.
 Optimizing the power of action learning : real-time strategies for developing leaders, building teams, and transforming organizations / Michael J. Marquardt. -- 2nd ed.
     p. cm.
 Rev. ed. of: Optimizing the power of action learning : solving problems and building leaders in real time. 1st ed. 2005.
 Includes bibliographical references and index.
 ISBN 978-1-90483-833-3
  1. Organizational learning. 2. Problem-based learning. 3. Active learning. 4. Leadership. I. Title. II. Title: Real-time strategies for developing leaders, building teams, and transforming organizations.
  HD58.82.M375 2011
  658.3'124--dc22

                                                           2011016209

CONTENTS

v

I recently conducted an action learning workshop for nearly fifty training directors from several departments of the U.S. government. Following a brief overview and demonstration of action learning, the directors formed eight randomly chosen groups and spent the next couple of hours working on problems introduced by members of the group. A volunteer in each group served as the action learning coach. To conclude the action learning workshop, I asked each problem presenter whether he or she had been helped. Every single one responded with an enthusiastic "yes." The volunteer learning coaches were then asked to summarize the activity of their group, and each seemed to outdo the other with wonderful testimonials on how well the group had worked on the problem and the valuable learnings that were shared. Finally, a training director from a table at the front of the room asked me, "Does action learning always work this perfectly?" My response to him and to all readers of this book is, "Yes, it can!"

Based on my experience with hundreds of action learning projects over the past fifteen years, I have become ever more and more confident that action learning has the power to always be successful. If the key elements of action learning described in this book are established and allowed to operate, action learning is amazing in its consistent capacity (a) to effectively and efficiently solve problems and challenges with truly breakthrough and sustaining strategies, (b) to develop the leadership skills and qualities needed by twenty-first-century managers, (c) to develop teams that continuously improve their capability to perform and adapt, and (d) to capture, transfer, and apply valuable knowledge at the individual, group, organization, and community levels.

Although action learning has been around since it was introduced by Reg Revans in the coal mines of Wales and England in the 1940s, it is only within the past ten years that it has begun sweeping across the world, emerging as the key problem-solving and leadership development program for many Global 100 giants such as Boeing, Sony, Toyota, Samsung, and Microsoft; for public institutions such as Helsinki City Government, Malaysian Ministry of Education, George Washington University, and the

U.S. Department of Agriculture; and for small firms and medium-sized firms all over the world.

Throughout this book you will discover how these and other organizations have flourished with action learning and are discovering how to optimize the power of action learning.

Requirements for Success in Action Learning

Briefly described, *action learning* is a remarkably simple program that involves a group of people working on real problems and learning while they do so. Optimizing the probability of success in action learning, however, involves some basic components and norms (ground rules), which form the substance of this book. These components include an important and urgent problem, a diverse group of four to eight people, a reflective inquiry process, implemented action, a commitment to learning, and the presence of an action learning coach. Norms include "questions before statements" and "learning before, during, and after action."

Action learning works well because it interweaves so thoroughly and seamlessly the principles and best practices of many theories from the fields of management science, psychology, education, political science, economics, sociology, and systems engineering. Action learning has great power because it synergizes and captures the best thinking of all group members and enriches their abilities.

Purpose of This Book

Over the past twenty years, I have had the opportunity to work with thousands of action learning groups around the world, as well as the good fortune of sharing ideas and best practices with many of the world's top action learning practitioners. The purpose of this book is to share what I have experienced and learned, the exhilaration as well as the challenges. Although action learning is a relatively simple process, the essence of which could fit on a three-by-five card, there are a number of key principles and practices that, as I have discovered, move action learning from good to great, that take it from being a solid organizational tool to a spectacular resource for transforming people, groups, organizations, and even entire communities.

This book describes each of the components of action learning and why they are necessary for action learning success. Through scores of stories and testimonials, the book clearly illustrates how many organizations have implemented and thrived with action learning. It also shows how any organization can simultaneously and effectively achieve the five primary benefits of action learning, namely, problem solving, leadership development, team building, organizational change, and professional learning.

This book presents the basic elements and principles of action learning as well as the more advanced, more recent innovations within the field of action learning, including the role and questions of the action learning coach, the balance between order and chaos for maximum creativity, and the step-by-step procedures for introducing and sustaining action learning within your organization.

Overview of Book

Chapter 1 provides an overview of action learning, the six basic components, and two key ground rules. It summarizes the five greatest challenges encountered by organizations in today's environment and how action learning enables organizations to respond effectively to those challenges. Chapter 1 also highlights the major contributions of action learning to organizations, groups, and individuals.

Chapters 2 through 7 explore in detail each of the six critical components of successful action learning programs. Chapter 2 identifies the criteria for an action learning *problem*, how it is best introduced and examined, and the differences between single-problem and multiple-problem groups. In Chapter 3 we explore the *group*, including diversity of membership, ideal size, continuity, roles, and characteristics. Chapter 4 introduces the reflective inquiry process and discusses the importance of *questions* as well as the group rule "statements only in response to questions." The problem-solving, goal-framing, strategy-development *action* is covered in Chapter 5, and Chapter 6 examines the individual, team, and organizational *learning* achieved through the action learning process. In Chapter 7, the roles and responsibilities, authority, and questions of the action learning coach are described. Chapter 8 presents the twelve steps for introducing, implementing, and sustaining action learning in the organization. Specific strategies for applying each step are offered.

Throughout the book are scores of case examples of groups around the world who have introduced action learning into their organizations. The challenges they faced as well as the successes they experienced are discussed. Finally, there are numerous checklists at the end of each chapter to guide readers in understanding and implementing action learning for themselves.

Action Learning: The Power Tool for the Twenty-first Century

Action learning is truly an exciting and awesome tool for individuals, teams, and organizations struggling for success in the twenty-first century. More and more of us have experienced the power and the benefit of action learning in our lives and in our organizations. It is my hope that many more will be able to share in the wonderful and amazing adventure of action learning. If you apply the principles and practices offered in this book, you too will see how action learning can, indeed, be powerful and successful every time. Good luck!

ACKNOWLEDGMENTS

I owe a deep debt of gratitude to so many people not only for this book, but for the action learning opportunities and experiences offered by them that made this book possible. First, I would like to recognize the founding pioneer of action learning, Reg Revans, who inspired me and thousands of others around the world about the power of action learning. Reg died in early 2003, and this book is dedicated to his memory.

There are many other giants in the field of action learning from whom I have learned so much, including Lex Dilworth, Charles Margerison, Victoria Marsick, Verna Willis, Gordon Wills, Richard Teare, Dick Gerdzen, and John Wicks. Special thanks go to my many colleagues and fellow coaches at the World Institute for Action Learning (WIAL)—Bea Carson, Skip Leonard, Ng Choon Seng, Garry Luxmoore, Billy Coop, Fumiyo Seimiya, Eric Sandelands, Barrie Oxtoby, John Sautelle, Arthur Freedman, Chuck Appleby, Cindy Phillips, Paulina Chu, Luiz Costa Leite, Cleo Wolff, Peter Loan, Shiowjiun Cheng, Kevin Hao, and Jennifer Whitcomb—who have worked with me to expand action learning around the world.

I am grateful to the many individuals who offered me the opportunity to develop and improve the action learning model presented in this book, especially to Nancy Stebbins at Boeing, Linda Raudenbush at the U.S. Department of Agriculture, Andy Cole and Beth Fennell at Fairfax County Public Schools, Trevor Chua at Fraser & Neave, Pierre Gheysens at Caterpillar, Harry Lenderman at Sodexho, Sabrina Shroff at Intelsat, Penti Sydanmaanlakka at Nokia, Kathy Chalmers at Sony Music, Frank Andracchi at Constellation, Shannon Banks and Shannon Wallis at Microsoft, Robert Kramer at American University, Helen Goodson and Christy Stringer at Goodrich, and Wendy Rodkey at Humana.

I would also like to acknowledge the students of my action learning classes who have taken the message of action learning back to their home countries: Antony Hii in Malaysia, Daisie Yip in Singapore, Viwe Mshontshi in South Africa, Rubens Pessanha in Brazil, Marisa Faccio in Italy, Mayuko Horimoto in Japan, Florence Ho and Sung Hae Kim in Hong Kong, Taebok

Lee and Sooyeon Choi in Korea, and my many students in the U.S., including Deborah, Terry, Colleen, Scot, Trenton, and Melissa.

Thanks as well go to friends and colleagues who have offered so much encouragement in my work and research in action learning: Ken Murrell, Frank Soffo, Neal Chalofsky, Howard Schuman, Clive Watkins, and Keith Halperin. Special thanks to the people at Nicholas Brealey Publishing who have patiently and competently helped in every stage of the development of this second edition, especially to Erika Heilman and Jennifer Delaney.

Finally, I would like to thank my family: my daughter Emily, who refers to her dad as the "traveling guru of action learning"; my daughter Catherine, who must face fellow teachers in Fairfax County Schools who have been trained by me in action learning; and to my daughter Stephanie, son Chris, and my wife, Eveline, for their wonderful love and support.

ABOUT THE AUTHOR

Michael Marquardt is Professor of Human Resource Development and International Affairs as well as Program Director of Overseas Programs at George Washington University. Mike also serves as President of the World Institute for Action Learning.

He has held a number of senior management, training, and marketing positions with organizations such as Grolier, American Society for Training and Development, Association Management Inc., Overseas Education Fund, TradeTec, and U.S. Office of Personnel Management. Dr. Marquardt has trained more than 95,000 managers in nearly 100 countries since beginning his international experience in Spain in 1969. Consulting assignments have included Marriott, Microsoft, Motorola, Nortel, Alcoa, Boeing, Caterpillar, United Nations Development Program, Xerox, Nokia, Constellation, Samsung, Organization of American States, and Singapore Airlines as well as the governments of Indonesia, Laos, Ethiopia, Zambia, Egypt, Kuwait, Saudi Arabia, Turkey, Russia, Jamaica, Honduras, and Swaziland.

Mike is the author of twenty-two books and more than one hundred professional articles in the fields of leadership, learning, globalization, and organizational change, including *Action Learning for Developing Leaders and Organizations*, *Leading with Questions*, *Building the Learning Organization* (selected as Book of the Year by the Academy of HRD), *The Global Advantage*, *Action Learning in Action*, *Global Leaders for the 21st Century*, *Global Human Resource Development*, *Technology-Based Learning*, and *Global Teams*. Over one million copies of his publications have been sold in nearly a dozen languages worldwide. Dr. Marquardt also served as the Editor of the UNESCO Encyclopedia volume on Human Resources. He has been a keynote speaker at international conferences in Australia, Japan, Philippines, Malaysia, South Africa, Singapore, and India, as well as throughout North America.

Dr. Marquardt's achievements and leadership have been recognized though numerous awards, including the International Practitioner of the Year Award from the American Society for Training and Development. He presently serves as a Senior Advisor for the United Nations Staff College in the areas of policy, technology, and learning systems. Mike is a Fellow of the National Academy for Human Resource Development and a co-founder of the Asian Learning Organization Network. His writings and accomplishments in action learning have earned him honorary doctoral degrees from universities in Asia, Europe, and North America.

Emergence of the Power of Action Learning

Action learning has quickly emerged as a tool used by organizations for solving their critical and complex problems. It has concurrently become a primary methodology utilized by companies around the world for developing leaders, building teams, and improving corporate capabilities. Action learning programs have become instrumental in creating thousands of new products and services, saving billions of dollars, reducing production and delivery times, expanding customer bases, improving service quality, and positively changing organizational cultures (Marquardt, Leonard, Freedman and Hill, 2009; Boshyk and Dilworth, 2010). Recent surveys by the American Society for Training and Development indicate that two-thirds of executive leadership programs in the United States used action learning. A 2009 study by the Corporate Executive Board noted that 77 percent of learning executives identified action learning as the top driver of leadership bench strength. *Businessweek* identified action learning as the "latest and fastest growing organizational tool for leadership development" (Byrnes, 2005, p. 71).

Since Reg Revans introduced action learning in the 1940s, there have been multiple variations of the concept, but all forms of action learning share the elements of real people resolving and taking action on real problems in real time and learning while doing so. The great attraction of action learning is its unique power to simultaneously solve difficult challenges and develop people and organizations at minimal costs to the institutions. The rapidly changing environment and unpredictable global challenges require organizations and individuals to both act and learn at the same time.

Global Leadership Development with Action Learning at Boeing

The Boeing Company, the world's leading aerospace company, is a global market leader in missile defense, human space flight, and launch services, with customers in 145 countries, employees in more than 60 countries, and operations in 26 states. Boeing adopted action learning as the methodology for its Global Leadership Program, since action learning enabled the company to build critical global competencies while solving its most critical problems. Action learning has successfully produced a forum for senior-level executives to learn while being challenged with real corporate issues related to the international environment in which they were placed.

What Is Action Learning?

Briefly defined, action learning is a powerful problem-solving tool that has the amazing capacity to simultaneously build successful leaders, teams, and organizations. It is a process that involves a small group working on real problems, taking action, and learning as individuals, as a team, and as an organization while doing so. Action learning has six components, each of which is described briefly here and presented in greater detail over the next six chapters of this book.

- ▶ *A problem (project, challenge, opportunity, issue, or task).* Action learning centers on a problem, project, challenge, opportunity, issue, or task, the resolution of which is of high importance to an individual, team, and/or organization. The problem should be significant and urgent and should be the responsibility of the team to solve. It should also provide an opportunity for the group to generate learning opportunities, to build knowledge, and to develop individual, team, and organizational skills. Groups may focus on a single problem of the organization or multiple problems introduced by individual group members.
- ▶ *An action learning group or team.* The core entity in action learning is the action learning group. The group is ideally composed of four to eight individuals who examine an organizational problem that has no

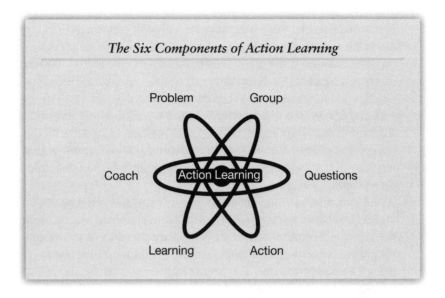

The Six Components of Action Learning

Problem   Group

Coach   Action Learning   Questions

Learning   Action

easily identifiable solution. Ideally, the group should have members with diversity of background and experience so as to acquire various perspectives and to encourage fresh viewpoints. Depending on the action learning problem, group members may be volunteers or be appointed, may be from various functions or departments, may include individuals from other organizations or professions, and may involve suppliers as well as customers.

▶ *A working process of insightful questioning and reflective listening.* Action learning emphasizes questions and reflection above statements and opinions. By focusing on the right questions rather than the right answers, action learning groups become aware of what they do not know as well as what they do know. Questions build group cohesiveness, generate innovative and systems thinking, and enhance learning results. Leadership skills are built and implemented through questions and reflection. Insightful questions enable a group to first clarify the exact nature of the problem before jumping to solutions. Action learning groups recognize that great solutions will be contained within the seeds of great questions.

▶ *Actions taken on the problem.* Action learning requires that the group be able to take action on the problem it is working on. Members of the action learning group must have the power to take action themselves or be assured that their recommendations will be implemented (barring any significant change in the environment or the group's lacking essential information). If the group only makes recommendations, it loses its energy, creativity, and commitment. There is no real meaningful or practical learning until action is taken and reflected on, for one is never sure an idea or plan will be effective until it has been implemented. Action enhances learning because it provides a basis and anchor for the critical dimension of reflection. The action of action learning begins with reframing the problem and determining the goal, and only then determining strategies and taking action.

▶ *A commitment to learning.* Unless the group learns, it may not be able to creatively solve a complex problem. And although solving an organizational problem provides immediate, short-term benefits to the company, the greater, longer-term, multiplier benefits are the long-term learnings gained by each group member and the group as a whole, as well as how those learnings are applied on a systems-wide basis throughout the organization. Thus, the learning that occurs in action learning may have greater strategic value for the organization than what is gained by the immediate tactical advantage of solving the immediate problem. Accordingly, action learning places the same emphasis on the learning and development of individuals and the team as it does on the solving of problems, for the smarter the group becomes, the quicker and better will be its decision-making and action-taking capabilities.

▶ *An action learning coach.* Coaching is necessary for the group to focus on the important (i.e., the learnings) as well as the urgent (i.e., resolving the problem). The action learning coach helps the team members reflect on both what they are learning and how they are solving problems. Through selective interventions and insightful questions, the coach enables group members to improve their performance and develop their leadership skills. The coach helps the group to reflect on how they listen, how they may have reframed the problem, how they give each other feedback, how they are planning and working, and what assumptions may be shaping their beliefs and actions. The learning coach also helps the team focus on what they are achieving, what they are finding difficult, what processes they are employing, and the implications of these processes.

Action learning power is at its peak when all six of these components are in operation, that is, when there is both learning and action. Unfortunately, much of what is called action learning involves only action (Cho and Egan, 2010; Raelin, 2008). Although these so-called action learning groups may be provided real-life problems, there are no structures or systems that ensure that time and effort is spent in learning, and thus little or no learning occurs. To the extent that organizations employ variations of action learning that do not utilize all six components, they lose much of the potential of action learning, not only in the strategic actions developed but also in the individual, team, and organizational development aspects. Neglecting or omitting any of the six components will result in little or no learning and/or little or no action.

Leadership Development at Shell Through Action Learning

Shell utilizes action learning programs to improve the abilities and thinking of leaders in three specific skill areas:

- ▶ Skills in business-oriented thinking, change management, and implementing change
- ▶ Team skills, including how to create and manage effective teams
- ▶ Analytical and synthesizing skills in areas such as finance, marketing, and operations

---

Single-Problem and Multiple-Problem Action Learning Groups

Action learning groups may be formed for the purpose of handling either a single problem or several problems. Table 1 provides an overview of the distinction between single-problem (also referred to as in-company action learning) and multiple-problem (often called open group or "classic" action learning) programs. Organizations may choose either or both types of action learning approaches, although the single-problem form of action learning is much more popular in corporate settings. The multiple-problem approach tends to be used when individuals from many different environments voluntarily choose to come together to help one another.

In the single-problem group, all the group members focus their energies on solving a single problem. In this type of action learning, both the group membership and the problem are determined by the organization. The primary purpose of the group is to solve the problem proposed to them by the organization. The group may disband after handling just one problem or may continue for a longer, indefinite period of time and work on a series of challenges submitted to them by the organization. Membership in the action

TABLE 1
Two Types of Action Learning Programs

Single-problem or in-company programs	Multiple-problem (open-group) programs
Entire group works on single problem	Group works on multiple problems
Problem determined by organization	Problems selected by members
Organization commits to take action	Individuals commit to take action
Membership determined by organization	Members self-select
Membership remains intact until strategies recommended and/or implemented	Members who depart may be replaced
Reflective inquiry process is used	Reflective inquiry process is used
Focus is on both action and learning	Focus is on both action and learning
Group recommends and/or implements	Individual implements the action
Coach is permanent and ideally certified	Coach is usually rotated among members

learning group is determined by the organization and is based on the type of problem and the aims of the program. For example, if the organization is seeking to create networks across certain business units, members from those units will be appointed. If the development of high potential leaders is the goal, then such leaders will be placed in these action learning programs. If the issue is more focused, then participants may be selected according to their interests, experience, and/or knowledge. In some in-company action learning programs, individuals may be allowed to volunteer, but the organization reserves the right to confirm or not confirm the final composition of an action learning group. The group remains intact until recommendations are made to the top management. In some cases, the group is also tasked to implement the strategies they have recommended. Coaches in single problem action learning are generally permanent, have received special training, and are ideally certified.

In multiple-problem (open-group or "classic" action learning) sets, each member brings his or her problem, task, or project to the group to be solved with the help of fellow group members. Individuals self-select to join the group and support and assist each other with the problems they bring. During action learning sessions, each member is allocated time for the group to work on his or her problem. Thus, a six-member group that meets for three hours would devote approximately thirty minutes to each person's problem. In open-group action learning, the members may meet on a monthly basis for a few months or a few years. Open-group action learning is usually voluntary and has more limited funding. Thus the groups often meet on their own time and rotate the coaching role among themselves. Over a period of time, new members may join as current members withdraw. The members are usually from a variety of organizations as well as independent consultants and people who are no longer in the workplace.

Balancing Chaos and Order in Action Learning

Fully optimizing the power of action learning involves capturing both the flexibility and chaos of action learning (elements such as diversity of membership, complex challenges, creative questions, lack of familiarity with problem and/or context) and the practical, time-urgent structure and order of action learning (elements such as real problems, accountability and responsibility, careful listening, testing, and action). Action learning allows for a wide latitude of processes that encourage innovation while maintaining minimal, but crucial, guidelines, norms, and group ground rules that produce sound, practical, and workable results.

Organizational theorists have discovered the importance of what is called the "edge of chaos," or "a natural state between order and chaos, a grand compromise between structure and surprise" (Collier and Esteban, 1999). It is the place where maximum creativity and possibility exist and learning best occurs, where a team or organization is optimally responsive to the complexity of the environment but still structured sufficiently to succeed. Fulmer (2000) argues that for a team to succeed, it needs to walk the fine line between stability and change, that is, to stay poised on the edge of chaos.

Successful action learning teams blend limited structure around responsibilities and priorities with extensive communication (listening carefully, asking questions, hearing all perspectives, and so on) and design freedom. Limited structure helps group members make sense of complex problems and operate within a complicated environment. Clear autonomy, communications, and responsibilities enable the group to move forward and apply appropriate solutions (Sanders, 2010). To stay at the edge of chaos, the team needs a few simple rules and a minimum set of norms or guidance. The rules should be simple but also adaptable (Olson and Eoyang, 2001).

Action learning seeks to avoid too much structure, which would lead to rigidity, constraint, and suppression of needed information and would constrict innovation and the team's ability to adapt. On the other hand, providing too little structure will lead to disorder, lack of focus, and fragmentation, and the group may become too permeable to disruptive input, making the group and its projects too difficult to coordinate.

At the first meeting of the action learning group, norms and group ground rules, which provide clear responsibilities and priorities, are established. The structure and stability in action learning come about as a result of the six components of all action learning programs and the group ground rules (norms established for all action learning groups). This structure is counterbalanced by the group's freedom and flexibility, the encouragement of fresh questions, the use of diverse people with and without familiarity with the problem or context. As Dixon (1996) notes, a few firm, clear rules and structure agreed to up front allow for great flexibility later on.

Applying Creative Ideas and People with Action Learning at Heineken

GERARD VAN SCHAIK, FORMER CHAIRMAN OF EXECUTIVE BOARD

Real progress in business is achieved only by corporations and individuals trying out creative ideas and making them work, by pooling talent and, most of all, by learning while doing. Action learning has become our vehicle for achieving this.

Two Group Norms/Ground Rules That Empower Action Learning

The need to balance chaos and order explains why action learning, with its great flexibility and search for innovation, needs clarity and stability. Since the power of action learning is based on two key behaviors—reflective inquiry and continuous learning—establishing the following two ground rules to help ensure that these fundamental tenets of action learning are practiced is critical for success.

Ground Rule 1: Statements Should Be Made Only in Response to Questions

Questions provide many valuable benefits to the action learning group, including (a) building group cohesiveness, (b) developing dialogue, (c) generating creativity, (d) developing leadership competencies, and (e) encouraging systems thinking. It is extremely valuable to immediately have the group transition from its initial impulse of advocating to the much more powerful force of practicing reflective inquiry. Thus the presentation of this ground rule: "Statements can be made only in response to questions."

This ground rule does not prohibit the use of statements; as a matter of fact, there will still be more statements than questions during the action learning meetings, since every question asked may generate one or more responses from each of the other members of the group, or up to five to ten statements per question. However, requiring people to think in terms of "questions first" transforms the dynamics of the group. The natural impulse to make statements and judgments gives way to listening and reflecting.

Once the problem or task has been introduced to the group, the members first ask questions to clarify the problem before jumping into statements to solve the problem. In action learning, we recognize that there is almost a direct correlation between the number and quality of questions and the eventual final quality of the actions and learnings. Balancing the number of questions and the number of statements leads to dialogue, which is a proper balance between advocating and inquiring. Questions do not slow down the problem-solving process, but generate quicker and more powerful ideas that are understood and committed to by group members.

Ground Rule 2: The Action Learning Coach Has Power to Intervene to Improve the Performance and Learning of the Group

Action learning coaches focus all their energy and attention on helping the group as a whole and each individual to learn and thereby improve the quality and speed of their actions. Coaches do not become involved in working on the problem. Rather, they look for opportunities to enhance the learnings so that the group increases its ability to solve the problem and develop innovative action strategies. The well-known axiom that says the "urgent drowns out the important" (also called the "tyranny of the urgent") underscores the necessity of ensuring that the *importance of the learning* will not be neglected because of the *urgency of the action*.

Experience and research have clearly demonstrated that if power is not provided to the person who is focusing on the learning, the urgency of the problem will always cause the group to push back and/or ignore the person who is focused on the importance of the learning. To ensure that learning is maximized for the group, action learning coaches are therefore given the power to intervene when they see an opportunity for the group to learn, to improve on what it is doing, and to develop the individual and group skills that will enable them to be better able to solve the problem and develop breakthrough strategies and actions.

This ground rule indicates that when the action learning coach decides to intervene, the group will temporarily stop working on the problem, listen to the questions of the action learning coach (who only asks questions), and respond to those questions. And only when the learning coach has finished asking questions should the group resume working on the problem solving.

It is important that the action learning coach be careful and economical in the timing of and time taken for interventions. Coaches should be cognizant of the fact that group members will be subconsciously continuing to work on the problem during a coaching intervention and, when returning to the problem, will be rejuvenated and more creative than before the intervention.

The action learning coach also controls the ending of a session and thus lets the group know in advance when the time for the problem solving or action planning will end. The coach then uses the last ten minutes or so to capture the learnings of that session and how these learnings might be applied to individuals, a team, and the organization.

Once a group has been involved in action learning for a short time, the group members truly appreciate these two ground rules and quickly recognize the enormous benefit they provide to the group. These rules ensure that the important elements of learning and questioning occur and thus better enable the group to succeed with the urgency of the problem. In short, these two ground rules immensely enhance and expand the power of action learning.

Why Action Learning Works So Well

Action learning has an amazing capacity and power to solve complex problems and change individuals, teams, and organizations. What accounts for this marvelous capacity? Why does action learning work so well? Simply stated, action learning is successful and powerful because it has the unique ability to interweave a wide array of organizational, psychological, sociological, educational, and political theories that form a foundation and synergy unavailable in any other source. Action learning works so well because it integrates and builds on the best practices and principles of the following disciplines:

► *Management science.* Action learning incorporates the leadership principles and theories espoused by theorists and world-renowned authors such as Collins (2001), Drucker (2006), Goleman (2006), Peters (2010), and Bryant (2011). It integrates theories of organizational change and complex adaptive systems as well as the major management principles of McGregor, Maslow, and McClelland. As Mintzberg (2011) notes, leadership is best built by reflecting on one's own experiences rather than those of others (as in case studies).

► *Education.* Action learning capitalizes on the theories, principles, and practices of each of the five schools of adult learning, namely, the behavioral, cognitive, humanist, social learning, and constructivist schools (Waddill and Marquardt, 2003). Unlike most development programs, which tend to favor one approach or another to learning, action learning bridges these schools and builds from their best ideas and practices.

► *Psychology.* Action learning utilizes key aspects of individual, group, and social psychology, including the classic theories of Jung, Skinner, Rogers, Allport, and Mead, as well as more recent research in the field of industrial or organizational psychology.

► *Group dynamics.* Action learning incorporates the best and most applicable principles of group interaction, communications, cohesion, management of conflict, decision making, strategy development, and action implementation (Sundstrom et al. 1999; Levi, 2011).

► *Sociology.* Action learning taps into the principles of the field of sociology as advanced by leading sociologists such as Mead, Durkheim, Weber, and Parsons. Also, the benefits gained by having diversity in organizational rank, age, gender, education, and experience allow a group's action learning to be powerful (Weick, 2000).

► *Open systems and engineering (chaos theory).* Action learning avoids the limitations of Newtonian physics and uses the energy and chaos of open systems engineering. Action learning groups are deeply and naturally engaged in systems thinking via the questioning process, the decision-making in complex environments, and the diversity in membership.

► *Political science.* Action learning utilizes and balances the politics of power, distributing it throughout the group, and ensuring opportunities for all to participate and lead (Shively, 2009). For example, a key power in action learning is not necessarily the person with the highest rank or the most knowledge but rather the one who has the best questions (which may come from an administrative assistant as easily as a CEO).

▶ *Appreciative inquiry.* Action learning searches to uncover and build on the best and most positive elements of every situation. Groups explore first what is going well, what works, what can be done better, what the group wants to achieve—not what went wrong. The group moves quickly from the presenting problem to the reframed problem to what it is attempting to achieve (Cooperrider, Sorensen, and Yaeger, 2001).

▶ *Ethics.* In action learning, issues that are normally kept underneath the table and are used to keep the group from its optimum performance are brought above the table by the questions of the action learning coach. Hidden and political agendas are opened with dialogue rather than entrenched and enhanced with debate and power grabs. Respectfulness and fairness are engrained in the action learning process (Dean, 1998).

▶ *Biology and life science.* As an organism's environment becomes more complex and unpredictable, the organism must develop adaptive and transformative capabilities. The organism's own capabilities interact with the environment to produce a unique path of evolution. No change can happen that doesn't build on existing capacity. Organisms, like action learning teams, must have the ability to create their own breakthroughs. All parts of the organism must be mobilized for action as action learning carries its learnings to the organization (McLagan, 2003).

▶ *Anthropology.* Action learning is widely practiced and equally effective in cultures around the world because it builds on the universals of individual and group values (respect, reflection, causes of satisfaction) and yet is sensitive to each individual culture (Geertz, 1993; Hofstede, 2010; Marquardt, 2001a).

It is action learning's remarkable ability to harness the powers of each of the disparate disciplines that enables it to achieve the multiple purposes of problem solving, team building, organizational learning, leadership development, and professional improvement.

"I have found the answer that I have spent my business life searching for!"
—Malaysian CEO, upon completion of action learning project

Overview of the Stages of Action Learning

There are many different forms of action learning. Action learning groups may meet for one or several times over a few days or over several months, may handle one or many problems, and may meet for short periods or long periods. Generally, however, action learning occurs via the following stages and procedures:

▶ *Formation of group.* The group may be appointed or made up of volunteers and may be working on a single organizational problem or each other's individual problems. The group will continue for a predetermined amount of time and number of sessions, or it may determine these at the first meeting.

▶ *Presentation of problem or task to group.* The problem (or problems, if a multiproblem group) is briefly presented to the group. Members ask questions to gather more information about the problem or task.

▶ *Reframing the problem.* After a series of questions, the group, often with the guidance of the action learning coach, will reach a consensus as to the most critical and important problem that the group should work on and will establish the crux of the problem, which may differ from the original presenting problem.

▶ *Determining goals.* Once the key problem or issue has been identified, the group searches for the goal, the achievement of which would solve the reframed problem for the long term with positive rather than negative consequences for the individual, team, or organization.

▶ *Developing action strategies.* Much of the time and energy of the group will be spent on identifying and pilot testing possible action strategies. As in the preceding stages of action learning, strategies are developed via the reflective inquiry and dialogue mode.

▶ *Taking action.* Between action learning sessions, the group as a whole, as well as individual members, collects information, identifies status of support, and implements the strategies developed and agreed to by the group.

▶ *Capturing learnings.* Throughout and at any point during the session, the action learning coach may intervene to ask the group members questions that will enable them to reflect on their performance and to find ways to improve their functioning as a group and to apply their learnings to their organizations and/or lives.

Throughout the remaining chapters of the book, we will explore in much greater detail these stages and processes of action learning.

Action Learning at LG Electronics

TAEBOK LEE, LGE CONSULTANT, AND EUNJU PARK, LGE DIRECTOR

LG Electronics (LGE), a major global company specializing in electronics and telecommunications, has seventy-two subsidiaries around the world and more than 55,000 employees. The LGE Learning Center develops and conducts numerous programs to strengthen executive and employee competencies. Its "Global Marketer" program, which employs the action learning approach, seeks to develop global leaders in marketing as well as enable participants to acquire the capabilities to solve any possible problems that they may face in a complex and rapidly changing environment.

Each action learning team is composed of three LG managers, an MBA student from a foreign university, a Korean expert, a foreign expert, and an executive who has specific knowledge and experience. The teams are given a marketing task that has been sponsored by the organization. Examples of group projects include "how to improve brand equity" and "how to launch new products." The teams work on the tasks for two-and-a-half months—one-and-a-half months in Korea and one month overseas. Teams participate in seminars conducted by domestic and foreign experts as well as conduct on-site interviews and surveys with competitors, customers, suppliers, and best practice companies. At the end of the program, each team presents its recommendations to the sponsors and other executives for adoption or adaptation and then implementation. LGE sees action learning as a great success because it has contributed greatly to business performance as well as to the personal development of the participants, including developing their problem-solving and global leadership skills and reinforcing global perspectives.

Five Major Challenges Facing Organizations

Organizations are turning to action learning because of its unique and wonderful ability to respond to what most leaders consider to be the five greatest challenges facing organizations in the twenty-first century.

Increased Complexity of Organizational Problems

Today's world is marked by rapid globalization and fierce competition in the marketplace, with turbo-speed changes created by technology. The constant movement of people in and out of organizations has generated sometimes overwhelming complexity and chaos in the workplace. Problems are becoming ever more difficult, require greater innovation, and must be resolved in shorter time periods with larger networks of collaborators. The old ways of solving problems by the single leader or specialized task forces no longer work.

Need for New Leadership Attributes and Capabilities

A new kind of leadership is needed in this competitive, global, knowledge-driven time. Recent leadership theories (e.g., Drucker, Collins) point to a need for leaders with transformational abilities, strong learning skills, emotional intelligence, ethical standards, problem-solving and project management strengths, keen self-awareness, and humble yet confident capabilities. Few leaders possess all these skills, and traditional executive development programs are unable to offer training programs that build these competencies.

Increased Importance of Effective, High-Performing Teams

More and more of the work of organizations can be done only with teams, since only teams have the knowledge and resources to understand and develop the services and products needed by internal and external customers. Unfortunately, most teams in most organizations are dysfunctional and rarely develop and deliver within the limited times imposed by the marketplace.

Increased Need to Capture and Transfer Valued Knowledge

Knowledge is the most valuable asset of organizations today. Most knowledge, however, remains hidden with an individual or group, and is not transferred to other parts of the organization that can benefit from it. Companies are generally weak in their ability to learn from successes and failure, and knowledge and learning are rarely transmitted and applied in a comprehensive and systematic manner.

Greater Need for Learning and Less Time for It

The constant stream of new products, services, customers, alliances, suppliers, policies, technology, and legislation requires us to learn on a continuous basis. Although we need more and more learning and training, the irony is that we have less time to acquire it. When we do attend a training program or conference, we are so pressured to continue serving our customers or fellow workers that we must spend our coffee breaks and lunch times checking e-mails or answering phone messages. If we are absent from our desks and customers for more than a few hours, the cell phone begins ringing. We need to be constantly in action and working, yet constantly learning. We know that we need to drain the swamp (that is, develop our knowledge and abilities), but we are so busy fighting alligators (handling the day-to-day crises) that we never get time to do the draining. In short, we know that we need to learn so we can do our jobs more efficiently and effectively, but we are too busy to find the time to do so.

Action Learning Responds Effectively to These Challenges

Action learning has the matchless power to overcome each of these five major challenges in an effective and cost-efficient manner. To respond to the challenges, action learning enables organizations to simultaneously solve problems, develop leaders, build teams, create learning organizations, and increase the abilities of individuals to continuously learn and improve.

Problem Solving

Action learning begins with and builds around solving problems; the more complex and the more urgent, the better suited is action learning. The dynamic, interactive process used in action learning allows the group to see problems in new ways and to gain fresh perspectives on how to resolve them. Questioning from multiple perspectives creates solid systems thinking in which the group sees the whole rather than parts, relationships rather than linear cause-effect patterns, underlying structures rather than events, and profiles of changes rather than snapshots. The action learning process enables the group to look for underlying causes and leveraged actions rather than symptoms and short-term solutions. Action learning examines both macro and micro views so as to discover when and how to best implement the proposed actions. As a result of its fresh approach to problem solving, action learning generates "breakthrough" insights, solutions, and effective strategies.

Using Action Learning to Solve Problems for National Semiconductor and AT&T

Working in action learning teams is seen as a key to increasing productivity and creativity at National Semiconductor. When senior managers in the South Portland, Maine, plant saw that delivery performance was holding National Semiconductor back from providing quality service at AT&T, they decided to do something about it. Choosing eight people from different areas throughout the company, they created a Customer Request Improvement Team to deal with delivery performance. Team members were chosen from sales, marketing, engineering, manufacturing, and planning as well as from AT&T. Meeting for two days a month for three months, the team eventually came up with a list of almost forty ideas, which resulted in four key action initiatives:

> ▶ Analyzing in new ways the delivery misses
> ▶ Increasing frequencies of lead-time updates
> ▶ Creating critical device lists
> ▶ Developing pre-alert reports

Following the implementation of these initiatives, AT&T recognized National Semiconductor as one of its "world-class" suppliers.

Leadership Development

Most leadership development programs, whether corporate or academic, have been ineffective and expensive (Pfeffer and Fong, 2002). The weaknesses of traditional leadership development programs are caused by a number of factors, most notably: teachers rather than practitioners are the purveyors of knowledge; a separation exists between the learning and action; very little learning gets transferred to the workplace; the business environment is changing so fast that the knowledge gained from the programs comes too slowly and is inadequate; and there is an absence of reflective thinking in the education process. Typical executive development programs provide little of the social and interpersonal aspects of the organizations and tend to focus on tactical rather than strategic leadership.

Action learning differs from normal leadership training in that its "primary objective" is to ask appropriate questions in conditions of risk, rather than to find answers that have already been precisely defined by others— and that do not allow for ambiguous responses because the examiners have all the approved answers (Revans, 1982a). Action learning does not isolate any dimension from the context in which managers work; rather it develops the whole leader for the whole organization. What leaders learn and how they learn cannot be dissociated from one another, for how one learns necessarily influences what one learns (Dilworth, 1998).

Learning via traditional leadership programs that use case studies is like learning how to steer a boat by looking out the stern. Examining what happened yesterday will not drive change or make a company competitive. Success factors keep changing, and no company can stay on top by doing what it used to do. In action learning, we have the opportunity to grow as leaders because we are reflecting on what is urgent and important to us and because our assumptions are challenged. McGill and Beaty (1995) point out that action learning provides managers with the opportunity to take "appropriate levels of responsibility in discovering how to develop themselves" (p. 37).

Action Learning at Dow Chemical

LARRY WASHINGTON, VP, HUMAN RESOURCES

In today's fast-paced, highly competitive business world, having knowledgeable, competent leaders at every level is our only true competitive advantage. We have found that action learning is the best way to align and motivate our organization to leverage that knowledge for competitive advantage.

Building Teams

Action learning teams are extremely cohesive and high performing; they become more effective every time they meet because the action learning process focuses on how individually and collectively teams can become smarter and faster. A "teamthink and teamlearn" capability steadily emerges. The group shares clear responsibility and accountability on real problems, causing a need for deliberative team unity and success. The process of ongoing questioning and shared learning builds powerful caring and cohesion among the members. Developing consensus around problems and goals develops clearness of task, strong communications, collaboration, and commitment, during which powerful team synergy and learning emerges.

Using Action Learning for Building Teams at Siemens

PETER PRIBILLA, CORPORATE HUMAN RESOURCES

Building teams has become a key goal and achievement of action learning at Siemens. Action learning has helped the company maximize the entrepreneurial spirit and enhance team player qualities such as cooperation and free exchange of ideas. The teamwork and global networking are designed to reinforce our pro-customer orientation and to optimize knowledge sharing throughout the company. The quality of teams has resulted in more innovative ways of finding new solutions for customer requirements.

Creating Learning Organizations

A learning organization is constructed around four primary subsystems: (1) increased learning skills and capacities, (2) a transformed organizational culture and structure, (3) an involvement of the entire business chain in the learning process, and (4) enhanced ability to manage knowledge. Members of action learning groups transfer their experiences and new capabilities to their organizations in a number of ways.

First, action learning groups themselves are mini–learning organizations that model perfectly what a learning organization is and how it should operate. Action learning groups seek to learn continuously from all their actions and interactions. They adapt quickly to external and internal environmental changes. Learning and knowledge are continuously captured and transferred to other parts of the organization that could benefit from the experiences. Individuals who participate in action learning groups appreciate the tremendous benefit of questions and reflection in helping them to continuously improve when they return to their respective jobs. They are better learners as well as better leaders. As the action learning members resume their day-to-day activities, their new mind-sets and skills gradually affect the entire organization, resulting in a culture more likely to continuously learn, reward learning, and connect learning to all business activities.

Building a Learning Organization at WCB

The Workers Compensation Board (WCB) of Alberta is a quasi-judicial insurance company consisting of approximately 1,400 employees. Over the past several years, this organization has gone from having a large unfunded liability to one that has a considerable financial surplus.

The financial turnaround from deficit to surplus is regarded as an important milestone in the organization's history. However, financial success in an organization does not always translate into high employee morale. New programs were needed—programs to help break down some of the organizational hierarchy, to address morale and retention issues, and to help to build business literacy.

WCB's Leadership in Action Program was designed for managers and supervisors to learn and develop leadership capability through working and taking action on real work projects. Participants cascaded what they learned to colleagues and staff, and also publicized their own successes and the successes of the initiative. At the end of the program, action learning teams presented their achievements and what they had learned to senior management. This ceremonial close to the action learning program had an educational impact on the participants as well as on the audience. For the senior management audience, it was an opportunity to gain exposure to the full spectrum of the organization, as the program participants from all divisions gave five-minute presentations on their projects. The ceremonies also helped to bring about some culture change by providing a positive story in the organization. Learning was seen as an investment rather than as an expenditure. Action learning alumni continue to talk about the confidence they have gained as a result of the program and how they have seen the organization change.

Continuous Learning and Improvement

Weinstein (1995) notes that participants in action learning achieve learning at three different levels: (1) understanding something intellectually, (2) applying a newly acquired skill, and (3) experiencing and thereby undergoing an inner development that touches on beliefs and attitudes and leads to personal and professional development. Action learning is particularly effective at this third level since it provides the opportunity for internal dissonance, while the problem and/or action may provide the external trigger. In action learning we become more aware of our blind spots and weaknesses as well as our strengths; and we receive the feedback and help that we have requested. Action learning generates tremendous personal, intellectual, psychological, and social growth. Butterfield, Gold, and Willis (1998) observe that action learning participants experience "breakthrough learning" when they become aware of the need to reach beyond their conscious beliefs and to challenge their assumptions about their present worldviews. This readiness to change and grow is a prerequisite for development and continuous improvement. Some of the specific skills and abilities developed for those participating in action learning include:

- ► Critical reflection skills, which are key to transformative learning for the individual (Mezirow, 2000)
- ► Inquiry and questioning abilities, which allow the individual to do more than just advocate and push personal opinions
- ► Systems thinking, which helps individuals to see things in a less linear fashion
- ► Ability to adapt and change
- ► Active listening skills and greater self-awareness
- ► Empathy, the capacity to connect with others
- ► Problem-solving and strategy-selection skills
- ► Presentation and facilitation skills

Action learning has also been utilized as a highly valuable tool for examining and advancing one's personal career. For example, job seekers have effectively used action learning to help them better understand themselves, their career goals, their strengths, and the best resources for locating and landing a job.

Action Learning at National Sorghum Breweries in South Africa

National Sorghum Breweries was regarded by some as a sleepy, money losing state-owned brewer of traditional African beers. Through a companywide action learning program, the company improved the organization's vision, which revitalized and empowered the organization's employees. Key issues addressed by action learning were the social, political, and economic disadvantages for black South Africans in the wake of apartheid. Action learning groups developed a plan to turn National Sorghum Breweries into a successful company largely owned and managed by black people. The successful privatization of the enterprise and the pride it gave to the black community was seen as one of the early successes in the post-apartheid era.

Action Learning Differs from Other Problem-Solving Methods

Problem-solving groups are similar to action learning groups in that both involve a group of people who work on a problem and try to solve it. Similarly, we could say that a caterpillar and a butterfly are alike in that they are composed of the same organic elements. We all would agree, however, that there are great differences between the butterfly and caterpillar. Through a metamorphosis, the caterpillar has transformed those organic elements into a new organism that has much greater power and capabilities that allow it to fly up and down, backward and forward, fast and slow. Through this transformation, the butterfly survives and succeeds. In a similar vein, action learning, with its speed and power and intelligence, completely transforms the capability of the problem-solving process and group.

By focusing on the learning (especially through the two ground rules) as well as action, the action learning process metamorphoses a typical "caterpillar group" so that it becomes a "butterfly group." Here's how each of the six components of action learning together creates a powerful team and weaves a new kind of problem-solving power.

Problem

The problems in action learning are critical, complex, and urgent to the organization, team, or individual. They are not case studies or unimportant problems, but challenges needing real actionable results. Complicated problems are presented briefly so as to allow the action learning process to identify the most strategic problem to be resolved.

Group

The membership size is fixed between four and eight (not the ten or more found in some groups). Members are sought for their diverse perspectives and characteristics rather than for their expertise or rank in the organization. Diversity is deemed more valuable than expertise for solving complex problems and developing new individual, team, and organizational knowledge and competencies.

Questions

Most problem-solving groups begin with various members offering solutions. Questions are rarely heard, but statements and advocacy are rampant. In action learning, questions and reflection are the mainstays of working on and solving the problem. Finding the great question is the key task and skill of the group. Reflective inquiry more quickly leads to systems thinking, consensus, and quality of actions.

Action

Action learning groups exist for the purpose of determining actions that they or the organization will be taking. They do not merely make recommendations. Because they are the only people working on the particular problem, they are accountable and responsible for achieving a breakthrough solution. Reframing the problem precedes identification of strategies. Action is not only important for its own sake, but also to provide additional opportunities for learning.

Learning

In action learning, the learning is as important as, if not more important than, the successful solution of the problem. Time and energy are spent at all sessions to capture individual, team, and organizational learnings. Everyone in the group has acknowledged that he or she must seek to learn and help others to learn. The more the group learns, the quicker and better it will be able to solve the problem.

Coach

To ensure that learning receives its proper level and time, a person is designated whose only responsibility is to assist and enable the group to capture and leverage its learnings. When this person intervenes, the group pauses to examine its progress and learnings and to identify what will make the group more effective as a team as well as how the individuals and the organization can better learn.

Action Learning at Oxford University Press

Oxford University Press (OUP) has been in existence for more than five hundred years and employs some five hundred people. The new UK Publishing Services managing director, David Fry, was particularly concerned to open up the OUP culture, to sharpen up service provision, and to reduce costs—but not necessarily at the expense of people while increasing revenues. The challenge was to find a tool that would include cultural change, people development, and a bottom-line contribution to OUP, a tool that would not just tinker with processes, but would bring about significant long-term change. OUP discovered and applied action learning, which accomplished the following:

- ▶ Helped managers learn the skills they needed to manage a real business-related project with clearly defined deliverables
- ▶ Encouraged the delegation of tasks and empowerment of staff
- ▶ Identified tangible rewards and satisfaction plus measurable financial gains in completing the projects

► Promoted teamwork and encouraged cross-functional work

► Spread knowledge of the company's aims and objectives

► Created a positive—not a blame—culture

Remarkable Successes with Action Learning

Action learning is a magic-like tool that has revolutionized how organizations around the world solve problems and handle crises. It has become the methodology of choice for developing leaders and building high-performance teams. Organizations have transformed their culture and their systems through action learning programs. Individuals have transformed the manner in which they work and live their lives.

Yet this remarkable tool is so basic and simple and built on common sense that it is easily able to be applied by individuals and teams to every corner of our organizational and professional lives. Six basic components and two key ground rules create all the necessary conditions for innovatively solving problems and developing people. Action learning groups can be oriented and operational within an hour. Action learning coaches can be trained to ask effective questions that enable groups to understand complex problems and generate breakthrough strategies while maintaining positive, supportive group cohesiveness.

Many of the success stories told in this book were achieved the first time the organization initiated an action learning program. The following chapters of the book will highlight and exemplify how you can use action learning to reach similar heights of success in your organization.

Applying the Six Components of Action Learning

The Problem

The starting point for action learning is the problem (also referred to as a project, challenge, opportunity, issue, or task), the resolution of which is of high importance to an individual, team, and/or organization. Simply put, without the problem, there can be no action learning. The problem should be important, urgent, significant, and within the responsibility of the team, and should provide an opportunity for the group to learn. The more complicated the problem, the more innovative becomes the action learning solution and the greater the degree of learning.

With action learning, problems are seen not only as a challenge, but also as an opportunity for learning and for developing individual, team, and organizational abilities. Problems are not burdens, but occasions to sharpen the wit as well as develop the skills of the people facing the problems. A fundamental premise of action learning is that we learn best when undertaking an action, which we then reflect on and learn from. The problem or project gives the group something to focus on that is real, important, and relevant; it means something to the group. It offers an opportunity to test stored-up knowledge and create new knowledge.

Using the Term *Problem*

Problem is a word with many different meanings—*difficulty, quandary, trouble, dilemma, crisis,* and *predicament* are among the synonyms listed in a thesaurus. Some people use *challenge, task, project,* or *opportunity* instead. Although these words do convey what the group is working on, action learning leaders prefer the term *problem* because it better captures a sense of urgency and a critical need for action. A problem generates a healthy pressure on the group, which leads to greater thinking, action, and learning, all of which are essential to action learning. Although *issue* or *challenge* or *opportunity* may imply an interesting and important matter, these words may not give the group a feeling of seriousness and significance. The excitement and commitment of the group thereby suffer, as does the quality of the solution and learning.

Criteria for Choosing the Problem

Not just any problem should be chosen as an action learning problem. The best or ideal action learning problems have a number of attributes that optimize the power and value of action learning.

Importance

First and foremost, the problem must be important and critical to the individual or organization that is posing it to the group. Solving the problem should make a significant difference and provide valuable benefits. The

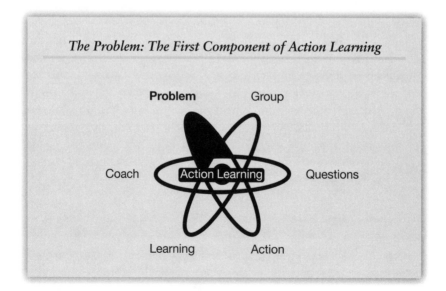

The Problem: The First Component of Action Learning

more important the problem, the greater will be the interest and commitment of the group to solve it. If the problem is unimportant or too simple (or perceived as such), the group will not put as much effort and energy into solving it, and their capacity to be an effective problem-solving team will not be tested. In addition, the group may feel that the organization or individual does not have a great deal of confidence or trust in the group. As a result, the time and resources of the group will not be well used, nor will their potential be fully tapped.

Urgency

There must be some degree of urgency to the problem. There should be a real time frame in which the problem needs to be solved and strategies developed and action taken. The group must know that its ideas and strategies will be acted upon in the immediate future. The members should be informed that the organization has high expectations and that they will be accountable and rewarded for the quality of their decisions.

Importance of Problem/Task Urgency

Perhaps no dimension is more critical to the success of action learning than the urgency of the problem. If the group senses that the problem is not urgent, they quickly lose their enthusiasm, energy, creativity, and commitment to working on the problem. If the problem is not urgent, the organization or individual can easily decide not to take any action on the strategies proposed, thus damaging group interest in or commitment to future action learning projects.

No Existing Solution

The problem should not be hypothetical or one that someone or some other organization has. Nor should the problem be merely a puzzle (a problem that has a single correct answer, which has probably already been determined by top management and which the group is expected to reinforce). It must be a true problem, one that has no existing solution and for which different people might come up with different solutions and strategies. And, of course, it should not be a case study, which, according to Revans (1982a), means "edited descriptions by unknown authors of inaccessible conditions for which members cannot deploy the talent of observation."

Feasibility

The problem must be feasible, that is, within the purview or the capability of the organization as well as within the competence of one or more members of the group to understand the problem or the context. If the problem is too complex for the time and resources available or overcomplicated, with too many variables, it will overwhelm rather than challenge the group.

Familiarity

There should be some familiarity for one or more members of the group with the problem and the context of the problem. However, just as it is desirable that someone be familiar with the problem, it is also advisable that not everyone be familiar with it. Total group familiarity can result in less innovative thinking. In addition, there may be less challenging of each other's basic assumptions about the problem. The fewer the members of the group who are familiar with the problem and its context, the greater the likelihood that there will be more innovative solutions. A person unfamiliar with a problem and/or the context in which the problem takes place will be forced to ask fresh questions, which, in turn, will stretch the thinking of the group and ultimately lead to breakthrough solutions. Greater challenges generally generate greater learnings.

Significance

The problem must be important and significant to one or more members of the group. In multiple problem sets, of course, this should not be an issue. In single problem sets, however, it would be possible for this criterion not to be met. However, if the top management has indicated to the entire group or to one or more individuals in the group that their careers, salary, reputation, and/or future opportunities depend on the success of the group's strategies in solving the problem, then the problem will have obvious significance.

Learning Opportunity

The best action learning problems also provide excellent and important learning opportunities for the group, especially learning about issues and skills that are critical to the organization. For example, if the organization would like the group members to learn about some content area such as customer relations, a problem related to that area should be presented to the group. If the development of leadership or team skills (which should be a learning aspect of all action learning groups) is what the organization seeks for the group members, then a problem that would develop those skills should be chosen. If a problem provides few opportunities for significant learning, an important benefit of the action learning process will have been lost. Also, it is important for the individual, team, and/or organization to realize that the greater the challenge in solving the problem, the greater will be the learning opportunities.

Group Authority

Finally, the problem should be one in which the group has been given the authority and power to solve and/or to implement action. If the group is unable to take actions between sessions, group members will not know if their ideas, strategies, and learnings really work. If the group has been notified that it will be making recommendations that the organization will implement, the group will know they have authority to develop strategic actions. However, if they do not have this assurance, the group's energy level will be low, members will be less creative, frustration and/or apathy may arise, and members may skip meetings and not undertake agreed-upon tasks.

Problem Choosing at Boeing

NANCY STEBBINS, DIRECTOR OF ACTION LEARNING PROGRAMS

For the Global Leadership Program, careful effort is made to choose real business issues and problems, the resolution of which are essential to Boeing. It is important that we not choose some interesting but unimportant topic around which no action may be taken. Problems chosen should include an array of complexity and challenges that provide greater opportunities for the selected managers to develop an array of leadership competencies. Thus, finding problems with greater learning opportunities is important.

Initially, the HR people chose the action learning projects. It was interesting to note that when the Executive Council saw the innovative and powerful strategies developed by the Boeing Action Learning Teams, the members of the Council decided that they themselves would choose future problems that were the big, critical worldwide problems faced by the organization.

Types of Problems Facing Organizations

Many of the problems faced by organizations today are more complex than the problems encountered five or fifteen years ago. The twenty first-century workplace involves a wide array of rapidly changing socioeconomic trends and markets, highly innovative competitors, mergers among disparate corporate cultures and industries, continually new distribution channels, and the globalization of business. In confronting these complex challenges, leaders will not find ready-made solutions. Problems have become ever more confusing and difficult to identify, much less solve. And solving problems can no longer be the domain of a single person or leader—there is simply too much information to incorporate and too many implications to be considered. The imagination, perspectives, and talents of many people need to be accessed to find the answers to today's overwhelming dilemmas. No one person, however prescient, will be able to fully understand the problem; nor can any group composed of people with similar backgrounds and perspectives generate the innovative answers that are needed.

Heifetz, Linsky, and Grashow (2009) make a distinction between the problems that were common to the twentieth century and those that are most prevalent and important in the twenty-first century, that is, problems that are *technical* as opposed to problems that are *adaptive* in nature and context.

Technical problems (those more common in the twentieth century) are those in which the necessary knowledge to solve the problem already exists in a legitimized form or set of procedures. The challenge in solving such problems requires the acquisition and application of knowledge in an efficient and rational—or Newtonian—way. Technical problems have linear, logical solutions, with precedents within or outside the organization; they are like puzzles, with single right answers.

Adaptive problems (more and more frequent in the twenty-first century) are problems for which no satisfactory response has yet been developed and no technical expertise is fully adequate. The challenge is to mobilize the people with the problem to make painful adjustments in their attitudes, work habits, basic assumptions, and other aspects of their lives, while at the same time they are learning their way into the creation of something that does not yet exist. Adaptive problems have no ready solutions. Technical expertise is not enough. They require people collectively to apply their intelligence and skills to the work only they can do. They also require people to unlearn the habits of a managerial lifetime, to learn to meet challenges for which current skills are insufficient, and to explore and understand the competing values that are at stake. Adaptive problems are difficult to define and resolve because they require the efforts of people throughout the organization.

This is not to say that technical problems are unimportant or easy to solve. But they are called *technical* because the information and knowledge needed to resolve them already exist, and those in authority have a concrete set of procedures or guidelines to follow as they work through the issues at hand. As the workplace continues to become more complex, however, strategic and operational problems will require more than a technical response. Action learning groups will be faced with learning more adaptive approaches in order to solve problems for which no plan of action has yet been developed and current technical expertise is not fully adequate.

Solving Problems with Action Learning at Fairfax County Public Schools

BETH FENNELL, DEPARTMENT OF HUMAN RESOURCES

Over the past several years, the principals and assistant principals of Fairfax County Public Schools in Virginia have worked in action learning teams and explored and developed powerful and effective strategies for numerous challenges. Examples of problems tackled include:

- ► How to deal with angry, demanding parents
- ► How to implement standards of learning (SOL) throughout the school system
- ► How to handle and supervise ineffective teachers
- ► How to develop key aspects of leadership at the FCPS Leadership Institute
- ► How to keep a balance between personal and professional lives
- ► How to deal with continuous "gotta minute" requests and yet stay on top of key management responsibilities
- ► How to make disciplinary decisions, especially when a "good" kid might benefit from alternative consequences as opposed to those imposed by standard school policies

Examples of Action Learning Problems

Since Reg Revans first began applying action learning to solve problems in the coal mines of Wales and England, action learning teams have overcome a wide array of difficult problems over the past sixty years. Individuals and organizations of all backgrounds and from every part of the world have achieved marvelous successes in handling challenges from marketing to management, from quality to quasars, from training to technology. Examples of problems posed to action learning groups include:

- ► How to create a billion-dollar service- and solutions-based business
- ► How to cut $100 million in costs using Six Sigma
- ► How to recruit and retain high-tech workers
- ► How to teach a French curriculum
- ► How to get an employee to work on time
- ► How to double business in Latin America by 2015
- ► How to overcome regulatory barriers to global growth
- ► How to identify alliance partners and acquisitions
- ► How to capitalize on the network computing phenomenon to reassert leadership and growth
- ► How to develop a risk management strategy for emerging markets
- ► How to better leverage a company's technology to create value for customers
- ► How to improve customer service
- ► How to simplify the manufacturing process by 25 percent
- ► How to resolve conflicts between business units

These and thousands of other types of problems both large and small—and always of significance—represent the potential value of action learning to organizations, groups, and individuals.

Problems and Action Learning at Deutsche Bank

In the late 1990s, Deutsche Bank faced tremendous changes in its business and staff structure, with critical implications for corporate culture. Organizational change was critical, and the following steps were considered:

- ► Reconfiguration along divisional product lines
- ► Shift from regional to global operational structure
- ► Shift from multinational to global leadership structure

► Acquisition of several U.S. entities and their leadership model

► Change in corporate language from German to English

Developing leadership skills and solving these problems was critical. Deutsche Bank recognized, however, that existing leadership development courses were focused on self-development and not on solving the problems of the organization. As a result, little knowledge was transferred to the workplace, nor were new skills applied to business challenges. In addition, the cost of off-the-job training and development was high and climbing. In searching for a tool that would develop leaders while simultaneously resolving these challenges, Deutsche Bank chose action learning because of its just-in-time learning and self-managed learning efficiency.

Key business challenges were identified and a six-month action learning program was begun. The CEO, program director, and/or program manager selected the problems best suited for Deutsche Bank and for the action learning participants. Each problem had to meet four criteria:

► Of strategic importance to the bank

► Potential source of significant organizational change

► Strategic—not tactical—in nature, to "stretch" participants

► Broad in scope, offering rich learning opportunities

Twenty participants were selected. Following a two-day introduction to action learning, the four groups met over a period of six to eight weeks on a part-time basis to work on their problems. The final two days of the program included the presentation of actions taken as well as the capturing of learning that could be applied throughout Deutsche Bank. The program was considered a great success, having attained innovative and cost-effective actions for each of the company's problems.

Single Versus Multiple Problems in an Action Learning Group

Action learning groups may be formed for the purpose of handling either a single problem or several problems. In the single-problem group (also referred to as in-company action learning), all group members focus all their energies on solving that problem. In multiple problem sets, each individual brings his or her problem to the group for fellow members to help solve. Organizations tend to choose the single-problem approach, whereas the multiple-problem approach (also referred to as the open-group or "classic" approach) is much more common when individuals from many different environments voluntarily choose to come together to help one another. In Chapter 1, we introduced some of the key distinctions between the two types of action learning. Let us explore in more depth the characteristics and benefits of these two approaches to action learning.

Single-Problem Action Learning

Single-problem action learning groups work on one common problem for the duration of their existence. This problem is generally selected by the organization, which has probably also appointed the membership of the action learning group. The group as a whole is not only responsible for reframing the problem and developing action strategies, but may also be designated to implement the solutions the group has developed. The organization "sponsors" the project/problem and ensures that the organization will be committed to taking action. The single-problem type of action learning offers numerous benefits to the participants and to the organization:

- ▶ A key, critical organizational problem is being handled in a highly effective way with a wide array of skills and focused energy.
- ▶ The impact on the organization will be significant, since a number of people from different parts of the organization will develop skills, knowledge, and ways of thinking and working as a team that will have a major impact on the culture of the organization, a foundational step in building a learning organization.
- ▶ Silos and barriers that might exist in the organization will be broken down as people from several business units who normally do not work together now strive jointly to resolve a critical organizational issue. New and strong networks and collaboration will emerge within the organization.
- ▶ Group members have the opportunity to demonstrate their leadership potential and other capabilities to the organization, and thus benefit their career advancements as well as the organization's future staffing requirements.
- ▶ The group skills developed can be applied to the multiple groups that the individual members participate in on a daily basis within the organization. Future staff meetings, for example, will become more productive and efficient.
- ▶ The problem-solving skills that will be developed will be a valuable asset to the organization for years in the future.

▶ The ability of individuals to continuously reflect and learn while on the job will produce immense dividends in every aspect of organizational life.

Action Learning at New York City Transit

New York City Transit used action learning to handle three major problems of the subway system: increased ridership, unintelligible announcements, and lack of teamwork. Action learning groups composed of the widest possible diversity based on job function, gender, ethnicity, and age were formed. Each action learning group identified five to ten possible solutions, and all but two were implemented. The action learning teams not only solved the problems, but began to change the organizational culture as well.

Multiple-Problem Action Learning

The multiple-problem action learning format is one in which each individual member brings his own problem/task/project to the group. The members may be from different departments of the same organization or from different organizations, or they may be simply individuals with a desire to help one another. For example, a group of people who are searching for jobs could help one another clarify career goals, job targets, strategies, and potential resources. In the multiple-problem format, each person serves as both a problem presenter/client and, in turn, as a resource/questioner to the other group members.

At the beginning of each action learning session, the group, with the help of the action learning coach, establishes the time frame so that each person has an agreed-upon time period to receive help and guidance on his or her problem. Generally the time is divided equally among the members, so that if there is a three-hour session, for example, with six members, each member would have approximately thirty minutes to be the focus. During this time, group members ask questions of, support, and challenge each other. Members decide together how often they will meet and where, and for how long a period they intend to work as a group.

At the first meeting members introduce their problems. Then they receive help reframing the problem and identifying action steps they would need to take to resolve the problem. At the end of his allocated time, the presenter is asked what action he intends to take. Following each individual's session, as well as at the end of the entire session, the action learning coach asks questions to enable the group to reflect on the decisions and interactions of the group and thereby helps the group improve its capabilities as a group. The coach also assists group members with identifying how their learnings can be applied to their respective organizations and/or lives.

At the next meeting, each person, during her allotted time, updates the group as to the actions taken and progress she has made on the problem, what the results were, what new difficulties may have arisen, and what further action she is considering. The group continues working on the problem through subsequent sessions until the individual declares that the problem has been resolved. If the individual's problem has been resolved or is no longer urgent to her, she may introduce a new problem to the group.

The role of the action learning coach may rotate among the individual members or may be taken by an outside person who serves in that role permanently, that is, someone who is not bringing a problem to the group. (See Chapter 7 for a thorough discussion of the roles and options for action learning coaching.)

Just as there are many advantages to the single-problem action learning project, so too are there numerous advantages for individuals and organizations that implement the multiple-problem type of action learning. First and most important, each individual receives undivided attention to his problem and, as a result, gains insights and ideas and solutions for his problem. The help given on this problem may be worth thousands of dollars and/or save hundreds of hours of doubt, frustration, and consternation.

When sharing problems with people who are not within her company or who are not her subordinates, the individual has a greater degree of comfort and freedom to share issues, concerns, personalities, and vulnerabilities than might be possible if the problem were discussed with company colleagues. Issues such as how to handle a subordinate, how to get a boss to recognize one's work, and whether or not to remain with a company are hardly problems that one would want to share inside the organization. Most of us are able to be more open and honest with people who are not working with or for us.

In multiple-problem groups in which members are from different organizations, there may be less hierarchical and fewer political issues to deal with as people work on each other's problems. In addition, when working with people from different organizations, individuals have the advantage of hearing different perspectives and approaches to problems and solutions. They also discover the various ways that other organizations react to and solve similar problems. This may cause individuals to change their mind-sets and set patterns for responding to issues and challenges.

The problems brought forth in multiple-problem sets are generally the personal, heartfelt, and urgent problems faced by individuals, who otherwise may feel alone in trying to resolve these issues. It is satisfying and fulfilling to help others with problems that are important and meaningful to them. Plus, sharing our individual problems with others often results in a meaningful insight—that my problem is not unique, that other people have the same or similar problems, and that I am not such a poor manager after all. This awareness provides us with great support and greater self-confidence.

Finally, as we help others with their problems and receive help in ours, we develop a number of important professional and personal competencies, such as how to give and receive feedback and help, how to solve problems, how to listen, how to do systems thinking, how to be more courageous, and how to take risks.

Action Learning at Novartis and Partners

Novartis is a world leader in health care, with core businesses in pharmaceuticals, consumer health, generics, eye care, and animal health. Headquartered in Basel, Switzerland, Novartis employs more than 100,000 people and operates in more than 140 countries around the world. Novartis recently formed a consortium of six noncompetitive companies from different sectors. Each company sends six to eight HR leaders to become part of a consortium action learning group. The resultant six to eight action learning groups (composed of a representative from each company) work as teams on business projects of importance to their respective companies. Each project has a business or HR sponsor from the company. The purposes of the action learning groups are threefold: to solve the business problems of the companies, to develop leaders, and to build organizational capacity. Leadership skills focus on developing a global mind-set, emotional intelligence, leadership style, and business acumen.

Who Presents the Problem?

In the single-problem action learning set, there are a number of possible options regarding who presents the problem and how it is presented to the group. In some situations, the presenter may be either the person who is the true owner of the problem or someone who has been designated by the organization, a person who will be responsible for having the strategies implemented and who will be a permanent member of the group.

There may be occasions when the true owner will be unable to be present at every meeting of the group (it is very important for each group member to be present at all meetings of the action learning group, as will be discussed in Chapter 3), or he may feel that his presence would lessen the spontaneity and courage of the group in seeking fresh answers or examining root causes to his problem. In these circumstances, the group may ask the problem owner to be present at the first meeting so that they can ask questions that will provide them with a clear picture of the problem as well as secure an understanding of the person's commitment and resources for implementing the group's decisions and strategies.

Sometimes the problem is one in which several or all of the members of the group are themselves currently enmeshed. The individuals who have knowledge of the situation and problem then serve as the resources for providing information the group will need to reframe the problem, develop goals, and plan actions.

A final option for single-problem groups is for the organization to prepare a document briefly summarizing the situations and/or desired goals, which are read by members of the action learning group prior to assembling for the first meeting. Instead of relying on an individual who presents the problem, the action learning coach will simply ask each person to write down the problem as each of them best understands it, and then the group proceeds with its questions.

In multiple-problem groups, the problem presentation is much simpler. Each person is responsible for presenting her problem to the group. New problems may be introduced in subsequent meetings if the earlier problem has been resolved or a newer, more urgent problem has arisen between sessions.

How to Present the Problem to an Action Learning Group

The initial presentation of the problem should be short, with an emphasis on the important points. Pedler (2008) suggests that problem presenters prepare themselves by examining the following questions.

- ▶ How can you describe your problem situation in a few sentences?
- ▶ Why is this problem important to you and/or the organization?
- ▶ How would you recognize progress on this problem?
- ▶ What are the difficulties you anticipate as you and/or the organization work through this problem?
- ▶ What will be the benefits if this problem is minimized or resolved?

There are a number of reasons for limiting the introductory presentation of the problem to a few minutes. First, it forces the group to get into the questioning mode, since there is so much information they still need before they can begin working on the problem. A short introduction of the problem also eliminates a lot of the unimportant and extraneous information that the presenter may believe is important, but that may or may not be vital for the group to know. The more voluminous the amount of information that the presenter provides, the more he will "box in" and limit the range of solutions and innovative options that may be possible. Sometimes presenters deliberately provide many details because they want the group to reach the same or a similar solution to the one they have in mind. Oftentimes, however, presenters unintentionally constrain the group. In action learning, the group will systematically and naturally ask the necessary questions and get the information that is essential for solving the problem. A final benefit of minimizing the initial presentation of the problem is that the questions coming from around the group begin to mold them together as a group, as they jointly uncover and discover the real problem.

It is important to note that although the questions will initially tend to be directed to the presenter(s), they should gradually be posed to other members of the group as the group becomes more and more familiar with the problem. Otherwise, the presenter may feel like he is part of an inquisition. The presenter can change this dynamic by doing any of the following: he may indicate that he is unable to answer a particular question at this time; he can say that he needs to reflect on it for a while; or, what is most valuable, he can begin asking questions of the group.

Using Action Learning to Solve the Problem of How to Sell the Lexus in Japan

The Lexus automobile was introduced in 1989 and soon became a global success with tremendous sales around the world. However, for a number of reasons, Toyota did not sell Lexus brand in Japan until 2004. Toyota decided to set up a large-scale action learning program in order to solve the problem of "how to best launch the sale of Lexus in Japan." A key initial decision was to emphasize not only the automobile, but also the concept of Lexus as being the best class brand for Japanese customers. Lexus also decided that the key to success would be the ability of their General Managers (GMs) to market and demonstrate a very high-class brand and to provide superb service.

A total of 160 Toyota General Managers from throughout Japan were selected by the distributors to participate in the Lexus action learning launch. Action learning projects began in September 2004 and continued until April 2005. In addition to developing a comprehensive marketing strategy for the Lexus, the action learning was also designed to create a new style of leadership for the leaders of Lexus, moving them from directive bosses to participative, team-oriented leaders.

Twenty teams of eight GMs participated in action learning projects for five days each month over the six-month period. Certified action learning coaches facilitated the work and learning of the groups. In addition to the action learning programs, a number of other leadership development and strategic activities were presented, including learning about customer service from the Ritz-Carlton Hotel, driving the Lexus, and taking a trip to the U.S. to explore how the Lexus had been successfully marketed there. A Lexus blog was also set up to enable the GMs to communicate with each other and to receive action learning support virtually from the action learning coaches.

The Lexus Action Learning Program led to a number of successes:

1. Sales within the first few months exceeded expectations, and by 2009 the HS 250h became the top-selling sedan in Japan.
2. Lexus Japan's network of 143 new dealerships became profitable in 2007.
3. The General Managers obtained a deep and insightful understanding of the Lexus brand.
4. A new and more powerful style of leadership emerged with the General Managers.
5. The General Managers created and communicated a brand concept of Lexus that enabled Lexus to successfully enter the Japanese marketplace.
6. Under the guidance of the GMs, strong Toyota teams were developed throughout Japan.

The Presented Problem May Not Be the Critical Problem

Organizational psychologists such as Block (2011) note that the problem originally presented is rarely the problem that is the most critical one for the group to work on; oftentimes it is only a symptom, and a more urgent and important problem emerges as the group works on the original problem. In action learning, groups carefully determine whether solving the original problem really resolves the situation. Gaining clarity and consensus on the real problem is thus the first and most important part of problem solving in action learning, for if we jump into solving the initial problem, we may end up solving the wrong problem.

"*The original problem is rarely the problem that ends up being addressed. There's something about action learning that allows people to uncover layers to an issue. Too often we apply solutions to surface problems. That's why so many of our problems don't remain solved. When we think we know what the problem is and try to provide a solution (because that is what is expected of us as leaders), we miss an opportunity to examine the issue in all its depth and complexity.*"

—Terry Carter, action learning participant

Biases in Presenting the Problem

When presenting a problem to a group, we should seek to be accurate and clear. If we do not, it becomes difficult for the group to correctly understand it or adequately resolve it. Many of us often unintentionally filter our presentation with biases and preconceptions such as the following.

- ▶ *Anchoring and adjustment.* What we choose to present does not come out of the air. It is usually built upon our values and basic assumptions, which determine what we believe is important in the problem and color how we present it.
- ▶ *Representativeness.* We tend to assess the likelihood of the cause of or the solution to the problem as matching a preexisting category (for example, these kinds of customers always act this way and cause these kinds of problems).
- ▶ *Recent and past occurrences.* We tend to assume that what has happened in the past will occur again and soon in the future relative to our problem.
- ▶ *Preconceptions.* We tend to have expectations about the problem and possible solutions that may have little to do with reality. Thus, it is important to be cognizant of the fact that both the problem presenters and the problem solvers have potential biases and preconceptions when one begins to ask questions about the problem or propose solutions for it.

Problems as Opportunities for Success and Growth

The Chinese word for *crisis* contains two symbols, one denoting danger and the other denoting opportunity. Action learning views problems in a similar light in that problems are indeed both a "hump to get over" and a tremendous opportunity to learn, to grow, to develop skills and competence, to practice, and to perform. The greatest and most significant learnings and achievements have occurred when individuals, teams, organizations, communities, and nations faced seemingly overwhelming problems, such as epidemics, or impossible challenges, such as reaching the moon in ten years. Action learning groups welcome these types of challenges because they are confident that the action learning process will lead to breakthrough solutions.

Checklist for Selection and Presentation of Action Learning Problems

► Is the problem significant and important to the organization and/or individual?

► Is the problem urgent?

► Is there a time frame for taking action?

► Is the problem within the scope and feasibility and understanding of one or more group members?

► Who should be presenting the problem?

► Do we know who will be responsible and accountable for taking the action?

► Is the group tasked with implementing the actions or only with offering the recommendations?

► Does the problem provide learning opportunities?

► Will the group be handling a single problem or multiple problems?

► Has the problem been presented in a brief manner?

► Do we acknowledge that the presented problem may not be the real or most important problem for the group to solve?

► Are we excited about the problem and eager to solve it?

The Group

The core entity in action learning is the action learning group (sometimes referred to as the "set" or team). The members of the action learning team become the people who are responsible for reframing the problem, assessing alternative actions, determining the most strategic goals, and recommending and/or implementing the strategies. The action learning group is ideally composed of four to eight individuals with diverse backgrounds and experiences; this diversity provides the wide array of perspectives and fresh viewpoints that ultimately lead to breakthrough thinking. Membership may include individuals from across functions or departments and, when possible and appropriate, from other organizations, professions, and even suppliers or customers.

Selection of Group Members

In determining who will be the members of an action learning group, there are a number of issues and criteria to be considered.

Commitment

Members should have a commitment to and stake in getting this problem solved and having the task completed. The problem should be one that individuals care about and/or that they recognize will accrue benefits to

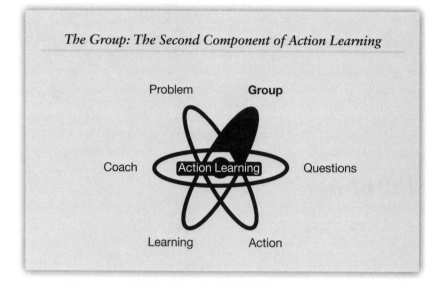

them if they are successful as a group. They should also understand that their participation will lead to personal and organizational growth and success as well as provide an opportunity to help others and build important networks and future support systems.

Knowledge

One or more members should have some knowledge and understanding of the problem and the organization. Although expertise may be sought from outside the group, it is advisable that there be some expertise and experience within the group. On the other hand, having some members with limited or no knowledge of the problem or the organization oftentimes results in fresh thinking as these members are less inhibited about asking fresh questions.

Power to Implement

Ideally the power to implement the actions should be within the power of one or more members of the group. If such a person cannot be part of the group because of other commitments, then it is important that the group members know that either (a) they have the power themselves to implement the strategies they develop or (b) the organization, business unit, and/or person with the power to implement action has assured the group that the strategies proposed by the group will be carried out.

Familiarity

One or more members should be familiar with the context in which the problem resides. There are benefits in having a mix of members in which some are familiar with the context and the problem and some are not. Those with familiarity can provide background and depth to the other members. Individuals who are familiar with the problem, however, may have a more difficult time seeing "outside the box." They often have preconceived ideas about the causes of the problem, what will or will not work, why some situations cannot change, and so on. They thus may too quickly reject the fresh ideas of members who have less familiarity with the context or problem. Members unfamiliar with the problem will need more time to "get up to speed," but once they grasp the situation, their new perspectives will result in more outside-the-box thinking and insights that might not have been possible otherwise.

Diversity

Group members may be chosen from all different hierarchical levels of the organization. One of the wonderful attributes of action learning is its potential for individuals of different ranks, education, and experience to work together effectively and on an equal basis. This occurs because asking good questions and listening well are central to action learning success. A janitor or customer or clerk may be able to ask better questions than a manager or CEO; thus, the reflective inquiry process "levels" the hierarchy.

Oftentimes, we are uncomfortable and impatient with outsiders as it takes so long to "bring them up to speed." However, since action learning is looking for questions rather than answers, an outsider may be able within a few minutes to ask a question that the insiders had never considered before, and enable the insiders to reach a new understanding of the problem and/or a great new strategy that they had never considered before. Also, what is inside and intrinsic thinking for one group of people (e.g., engineers) may be perceived as unusual, great outside-the-box thinking to another group (e.g., marketing people). Those new to action learning are often amazed at how quickly and easily people of different socioeconomic and academic backgrounds work smoothly and effectively together.

Five Departments Work Together to Solve Problem of Auto Decals

Prince William County, located in the suburbs of Washington, D.C., brought together an action learning team composed of directors of the various departments—police, library, human services, and fire—to work on the issue of auto decals. The solution was built on the system of how books are loaned by libraries, a solution offered by the librarian. The idea saved money, pleased citizens, and won the annual award for local governments in the State of Virginia.

Member Selection

If the organization selects members for action learning groups (as opposed to individuals volunteering), it is important that the company choose carefully and strategically. As Dilworth (1998) points out, membership is an important issue, and selection should not occur randomly. By selecting people from different departments, for example, the organization can not only gain a variety of perspectives and ideas, but also can build organizational learning and connectedness through the creation of networks that did not exist before.

Attendance

Members of an action learning group should be present at all the meetings of the group. The growth, workings, and cohesiveness of an action learning group are different from other types of problem-solving groups. It is much better to schedule fewer meetings when everyone can be present than more meetings when someone might be absent. Members of action learning groups, to amplify the metaphor mentioned in Chapter 1, metamorphose in a special way. Once the members have become butterflies, you do not want them to be joined by those still in the caterpillar phase. Therefore, before or at the first meeting, everyone should identify and commit to the dates and times for the action learning sessions so that all members can be present at all sessions.

Size of Action Learning Group

A group size of four to eight members is desirable because it provides sufficient diversity without too much complexity. Having more than eight members creates the following challenges:

▶ *Too little and/or too much participation.* In action learning, active participation by all members is desirable. In groups of more than eight, there is simply not enough time for everyone to remain involved. Individuals either will be aggressive to insert their views or ask their questions, or they will back away and become passive, particularly if their nature is not to be pushy. In large groups, members may not be happy with the options offered, but may feel there is not enough time to offer new choices. Individuals from cultures that value a respectful silence after someone speaks may never be heard when there are many members in the group.

▶ *Too much complexity of communications.* More than eight people create an enormous complexity of communication patterns. The difference between eight and ten people is not simply a difference of two people, but a difference of hundreds of more possible communication channels. Small-group conversations are likely to occur in large groups, with judgments and viewpoints being asserted outside the realm of the entire group.

▶ *Too much time needed to reach consensus.* As we know, many problems and tasks must be worked out and decided within a few hours or even less. The more people involved in making a decision, however, the more time is usually required to come to an agreement. Sometimes the group never reaches a consensus. Ultimately, those who have the most persistence or speak the loudest end up "winning" the decision.

On the other hand, if there are fewer than four people involved in the action learning group, it suffers from a number of other equally daunting challenges.

▶ *There will be a limited number of perspectives.* As a result, the solutions and strategies will not be as creative or innovative as they might be with a larger group.

▶ *The group may not fully understand the problem or the entire system.* It will be more difficult to see the many causes of the problem and the possible impact of proposed solutions.

▶ *There will be less challenging of each other's assumptions.* Fewer participants may result in less challenging of one another's basic assumptions and viewpoints.

▶ *A small group may feel overwhelmed and intimidated by the problem.* The energy of the group may slacken, and excitement may be lost, as one person can easily affect the attitude of the other two members.

▶ *There will be less feedback for each other.* There will be less information and examples given to each other in response to questions from the coach about individual, team, and organizational learnings and applications.

Expectations and Accountability of the Group

In action learning, as will be discussed in greater detail in Chapter 5, the groups are responsible and accountable for developing solid solutions to the problems or tasks assigned to them. The group members' careers, reputations, eventual leadership in the organization, salary increases, and/or future opportunities may well depend on how well they do as a group. Reg Revans called members of action learning groups "comrades in adversity."

As a result of these expectations, there should be much energy and commitment for members to "hang together" as they work through the problem and develop strategies; otherwise they may end up "hanging separately." Even those who may be unfamiliar with the context or have no stake in the outcome should also demonstrate some sense of accountability and support to those members who have a much greater stake in the outcome of the action learning project.

The intensity of working together to successfully develop action strategies is an important component of generating greater learnings as well as building stronger group cohesiveness and supportive behaviors. Of course, the quality of the resulting action is significantly higher when members are accountable for and rewarded for developing great strategies. The fact that the group will also be implementing the action plan enhances the quality of both the learning and the actions.

Learning at Fairfax County Public Schools, Virginia

DELORES A. HERNDON, CAREER DEVELOPMENT SPECIALIST

As part of Fairfax County's leadership program for support employees, an action learning group composed of a maintenance supervisor, two finance assistants, a customer service supervisor, and an administrative assistant was given the challenge of developing a comprehensive orientation program for individuals new to support services. The initial action taken was to survey the various offices in the Human Resources Department to determine the pertinent information needed for new employees. Also, a survey of support employees was taken to determine what information they would like to receive as new employees.

The action learning group developed and submitted to the school district's top leadership a comprehensive orientation program that would be beneficial to all employees, both support and instructional. With great enthusiasm, FCPS incorporated the group's recommendations into what is now the school district's New Employee Orientation program.

Some of the thoughts of participants of the leadership program's action learning groups are as follows:

"Action learning is one of the best tools for solving problems. Different people, ideas, backgrounds, experiences, careers, coming together for one purpose ... what power."
—Custodial supervisor

"A thinking, open-minded way to share ideas and brainstorm."
—Administrative assistant

"What an outstanding concept. I had fun ironing out team ideas as well as confrontations. I thoroughly enjoyed the experience."
—Maintenance supervisor

"What a great approach to team building and working as a team. My usual [previous] impulse was to get things done and cut off input, thereby reducing ownership of projects."
—Administrative assistant

Importance of Group Diversity

As individuals, we all have mind-sets and assumptions that limit the scope of ideas that we are able to generate. People with different perspectives will challenge our mind-sets and assumptions. The more difficult the problem, the less valuable is expertise and the more valuable is diversity. Therefore, whenever possible, we should try to balance levels of experience, business unit location, gender, age, and ethnicity to add diversity and richness to action learning groups.

Diversity of group membership contributes immensely to the power and success of action learning, especially when dealing with complex, adaptive problems (see Chapter 2). Weick (2000) notes that teams and organizations need "requisite variety" if they are going to be able to adequately understand and successfully adapt to the complex environment around them. Thus, the more complex the problem, the more important is diverse thinking. Various perspectives provide the opportunity of generating many, rather than just one or two, possible solutions.

Adding the element of reflective inquiry, as we do in action learning, to group diversity multiplies the group's creative powers and magnifies its ability to undertake systems thinking. The wide array of diverse questions forces the group to see problems and challenges with new eyes and in new ways.

"We do not see things as they are; we see them as we are."

—The Talmud

Roles of Action Learning Group Members

In action learning programs, there are a number of different roles that involve particular responsibilities. Some of these roles are enacted through-out all the sessions, whereas others may be carried out at the first or last session only or before, between, or after the sessions. Let's look at each of these roles.

Problem Presenter

In a multiple-problem group, each person becomes the presenter for an agreed-upon period of time. In single-problem groups, one person or the entire group may perform the role of problem presenter. There will also be occasions in action learning programs in which the person presenting the problem will be representing the entire business unit or the problem sponsor.

The problem should be presented in a way that shows that it is urgent and significant to the presenter. If the problem comes across as unimportant or trivial, the group will respond accordingly, that is, in a less than energetic and committed fashion. The person should present the problem clearly and concisely. A brief overview is all that is necessary, as the group members will, through their questions, acquire the essential information they need to reframe the problem and begin developing action strategies.

The problem presenter must be willing and must want to be helped. He should believe that the other members really want to assist him in a mutual exploration of problems. He should trust that the group is interested and is able to help. He should also trust the reflective inquiry process of action learning. It is important for the presenter to accept questions with openness and respond clearly and specifically to questions addressed to him. He should avoid answering questions not asked and should not add more detail than has been requested, as this slows down and can sidetrack the group.

The problem presenter should be honest and straightforward in responding to the questions addressed to him. If he receives a question for which he does not know the answer, he can simply say, "I don't know" or "I don't have that information." There may be some questions that he needs to reflect on and think about, and there may be some that he does not know how to respond to.

At any point, he can and should feel comfortable and free to ask questions of the group. Usually, the problem presenter may need to first feel confident in and comfortable with the group before he begins questioning other members. When he does begin questioning, the dynamics of the problem solving change immediately. Instead of feeling put on the spot, the presenter now senses that the process has become a group opportunity to share and learn. The problem is now transferred from the presenter to the group, and the group feels like the problem presenter truly trusts them. The individual's or organization's problem has become the group's problem. Real and effective group problem solving can now begin.

Many of us may find it difficult to ask for help or to answer questions in a way that might indicate some vulnerability on our part. We may feel that it is a flaw or weakness to admit we need help. However, when we come to an action learning session with a difficult problem, we are merely acknowledging that as an individual, business unit, or organization, we need new ideas and perspectives, and that we are willing to change, to grow, to learn. Only through our acceptance of being vulnerable are we able to capture the ideas and the resources needed to overcome the problem.

It is up to the problem presenter, particularly in multiple-problem sets, to manage the limited time that is available for her. In this way, she is assuming and developing leadership capabilities. By responding clearly, frankly, and reflectively, she enables the group to focus on the key issues and to identify the most powerful actions. When a person brings a problem to an action learning group, she should be committing to the group not only her willingness to answer questions, but also her commitment to take action between sessions. If the individual or organization does not take the promised action, the group will be less likely to listen and help in later sessions.

At subsequent meetings of the action learning group, the problem pre-senter will be expected to update the group as to what actions she has taken (or the organization has taken) since the previous meeting and the results of those actions. This serves as an important starting point for this session.

Action Learning Coach

The action learning coach is the member of the group who focuses on the learning and development of the individual members and the group, and not on the resolution of the problem. The action learning coach may be the same person throughout the action learning program, the role may be undertaken by other coaches, or the role may be rotated among the group, with a different person serving as the action learning coach at each meeting. The primary responsibility of the action learning coach is to help the team to learn and thereby become more competent in solving the problem. She also identifies opportunities to develop the individual leadership competen-cies of the individual members as well as the application of that learning throughout the organization or in the lives of the individuals.

As well, the action learning coach has a number of other logistical and orientation responsibilities. She coordinates and manages the sequencing and overall time frame of the action learning sessions so that each session has both learnings and actions. She may also handle administrative issues between sessions. The coach is responsible for orienting the group at its first meeting regarding the purposes and principles of action learning and the role of the action learning coach. She might serve as the link to top management, to the sponsor, and to the champion (of the problem). In some organizations, she may also be the action learning champion.

The more competent the coach is, the more quickly, smoothly, and effectively will the group function. Thus, a person who has been trained or certified will be more competent and confident in enabling the group to be successful. (See Chapter 7 for more details on action learning coach certification as well as a more detailed description of the roles and respon-sibilities of the coach.)

Members of the Action Learning Group

The members of the action learning group may have voluntarily joined or may have been appointed to the group to help solve the problem(s) submit-ted to them. They are also engaged in order to develop specific leadership, team, or individual skills as well as to generate better collaboration among departments, between staff and customers, or among other units.

The primary responsibility of each group member, including the problem presenter, is to ask questions and to respond to questions addressed to them in as clear and concise a manner as possible. Group members should ask questions that are helpful regarding the problem, rather than questions that serve one's own purposes (such as gaining information for oneself or making oneself look knowledgeable).

The focus is on the questions rather than on one's opinions. Group members should allow adequate time for everyone to ask questions. Sometimes individuals need to delay their own questions to allow active participation by all.

Individual members should remember that if they ask great questions, they will be doing their job (and doing it well). The questioning process will solve the problem. It is valuable for group members to also recognize that periods of silence can be liberating to all members, especially the problem presenter, who may sometimes feel overwhelmed by the questioning.

Group members should be willing to try new ways of doing things, to experiment, to take risks, to ask questions, and to reflect on their experiences. They should be active by word and by body language in supporting their fellow learners. Members should provide colleagues with genuine support, encouragement, and assistance and cultivate an attitude of empathy. Individuals build strong groups by listening to each other's questions and asking questions that show they have listened and thus care. The more people build trust, the more group members will feel comfortable taking risks.

When an individual becomes a member of an action learning group, it is important for that person to be present at every meeting and stay for the entire meeting. The powerful cohesiveness of an action learning group is unlike any other type of group. When someone is absent, valuable knowledge and companionship are lost. Teamwork, especially team thinking and team learning, requires participation by all members.

After the group has reached a consensus on the root and true problem, it then begins to ask questions that generate action plans and great strategies. It is important not to jump prematurely into solutions (usually the action learning coach will ask questions to confirm agreement before moving forward). Group members should avoid becoming impatient or defensive at such junctures.

Action learning members should be enthusiastic about the opportunities to learn, rather than frustrated that the time for learning seems to be taking time away from the urgent problem. They should pride themselves on being able to ask fresh questions and thereby contribute richness to resolving the problem. Individuals should bring forth their unique perspectives while at the same time examining their own assumptions and quality of participation. In action learning, everyone has the ability to contribute to forming an environment of mutual support in which there is rich dialogue that leads to great solutions and learnings.

At the end of each session, action steps will be identified, which may involve gathering information, testing a plan, or seeking resources or support. Group members are held accountable for carrying out actions that they commit to undertake, and these are to be presented at the subsequent action learning session.

In some cases the group members not only determine the true problem and develop the strategies, but also are tasked with the responsibility of implementing the action. At the first action learning session, group members should be informed as to whether they will be developing strategies that other members of the organization will be implementing, or whether they will also be the group that will be taking the actions.

Problem Sponsor

The organizational problem used in action learning generally has a sponsor who may or may not be a member of the group. The sponsor is someone who understands the nature of the problem, thinks it is important, and can be influential in helping the group gain access to necessary resources as well as power. The sponsor appoints himself or someone else to be available to the group. He also makes certain that the problem is given high visibility and acceptance and ensures that the organization will be committed to taking action.

If the problem sponsor or her representative is not able to be present in the group, she should make every effort to appear before the group at the first meeting to provide a brief background of the problem and answer questions raised by the action learning group before departing. There may be subsequent sessions in which she will be asked to appear again to answer more questions about the problem or to provide feedback relative to the strategies and actions being considered. It is important to note that a problem sponsor who is not a permanent member of the group should be there only to respond to questions, and not to assert her authority or prejudge the work of the group, unless the group asks for her thoughts or judgments.

Organization's Action Learning Champion

Many organizations that employ action learning identify someone who is the organization's action learning champion, someone who will support and seek support for all the action learning projects in the organization. Normally, the organization's action learning champion does not participate in the group meetings. However, there may be occasions when the action learning group determines that it needs information or special support and assistance from this person. Accordingly, the group may request his presence at an action learning session to respond to inquiries of the group. However, the major role and service that the champion provides to the group is to assure them of the company's overall commitment to action learning.

Success with Action Learning Groups at Baxter International

Baxter International, a $12 billion global pharmaceutical market leader, recently began a large-scale Leadership for Growth Action Learning Program. Baxter's action learning groups were composed of high-potential vice presidents selected by Human Resources and top business unit leaders. Each group had coaches, sponsors, and team members.

Baxter International sees the action learning program as an opportunity to develop a number of skills relative to business issues (e.g., strategic thinking, business knowledge, and customer insight) and leadership competencies (self-awareness, team leadership, and change leadership). Baxter's experience with action learning has resulted in a number of valuable lessons. First, the organization realized the value and importance of action learning coaches, not only during the sessions but also between sessions, when they also provided coaching assistance to the participants. The focus on learning and development as well as resolving problems also made the action learning extremely valuable. The organization also recognized the importance of wisely selecting who would be in the action learning groups and discovered that continuous feedback should be provided to the group members. Executive sponsorship proved to be important in implementing the following:

- ► Defining the business issue scope and deliverables with the team
- ► Providing political support
- ► Keeping top management informed about progress
- ► Monitoring the action plans of the action learning groups
- ► Ensuring follow-up on project decisions

Action Learning Members: Volunteers or Volunteered?

Action learning groups may be composed of volunteers, appointees of the organization, or some combination of the two. Depending on the specific goals of the action learning program, companies may request volunteers or appoint particular individuals to join the action learning group(s). For example, if there is a companywide initiative and corporate strategy to create a corporatewide culture, a cross section of staff members may be chosen to form the groups. If the issue is more focused, such as creating a new staff appraisal system, participants may either be selected according to interest and/or knowledge or be allowed to volunteer.

Individuals may volunteer to belong to an action learning group for a variety of reasons: because of their interest in the topic, their desire to work with this particular group of individuals, their wish to be recognized by top management as being committed to action learning, and/or their commitment to learn, practice, and develop new leadership and team capabilities and skills. Whether members are "volunteered" by the organization or volunteer themselves, it is important for action learning programs to avoid creating groups in which members form a clique or tend to think alike or simply enjoy being together. Such situations may provide ease and comfort to the members, but will probably result in limited innovation and breakthrough thinking.

Intactness of Group and Use of Outside Resources

In action learning groups, the intense learnings, deep sharing of personal perspectives, critical responsibility, and direct accountability all place high expectations on the group. The high level of teamwork that is created via the reflective inquiry process and the interventions of the coach create an important group solidarity. Once the membership of the group has been established, it should stay intact throughout its existence. Putnam (2000) notes that the most complex problems can be solved only by a group that has developed a strong social bonding. Therefore, it is much better that the group meets fewer times when everyone is present than more times when one or more of the members may be absent.

There may be occasions when an outsider is invited to join the group as a resource to respond to questions raised by the group. Outsiders might thus attend parts of a particular session or sessions. They should be invited when the group as a whole determines that they can be of help in providing information or support relative to the resolution of the problem. Of course, action learning groups will generally need to interact with outside people between action learning sessions as they seek information, identify resources, and test action strategies.

The Pizza Man Delivers Fresh Questions Worth $35 Million

An engineering consulting firm, commissioned to develop an innovative, cost-cutting process for a government department, quickly established a task force to work on the problem. The team leader, Bill, introduced the group to action learning and encouraged the engineers and scientists to use this approach. Progress, however, was slow and new breakthrough ideas were not emerging. And the final project was due within a week.

One day, as the group was working late into the evening, they decided to order out for pizza so they could continue wrestling with the project for a couple more hours. When the pizza man arrived, Bill made a startling request. Noting that his group was composed only of internal engineers who had similar experiences and viewpoints, he decided that a different, fresh perspective was needed. "How about joining us for the next hour and earning a big tip?" he asked the pizza man. "I will call your boss and get his approval. All you need to do is listen to what we are doing. If there is anything that you do not understand or you see wall charts that don't make sense to you, all you have to do is ask questions." This sounded good to the pizza man, although one can imagine the surprise and frustration felt by Bill's colleagues, who probably muttered, "We have only a couple more days to work on this project, and now we are going to waste an hour with a pizza man!?" The pizza man sat down. After several minutes of listening and observing, he decided he would have to earn his tip. He noticed a chart on the wall and asked why an arrow went from point A to point F. The person who drew the arrow gave an exasperated response, "For reasons 1 and 2." But then another member said, "Oh, I thought it was for reason 3." A third member chimed in, "Well, if reason 3 works, why don't we simply go from point A to point D?" The group realized that the pizza man's "dumb" question had caused them to examine some unchallenged assumptions they all had been making.

After the pizza man left, the group began with clean sheets of paper and a determination to look outside the box. Over the next couple days, they incorporated many new ideas that emerged from the fresh questions of the pizza man. Their breakthrough project was submitted to the government, which resulted in a $35 million savings over the life of the contract. Thanks to the pizza man!

Action Learning Engages All Types of Personalities

Because of the inquisitive and reflective nature of action learning groups as well as their commitment to both thinking and acting, all types of personalities can actively and effectively participate. As a result, both introverts and extroverts can excel in the action learning process, because the focus on questions levels the playing field. Those individuals who are quiet by nature are given the time and encouragement to verbalize their insights and ideas, so instead of sitting back and becoming frustrated by the outgoing personalities, they can more easily express themselves and contribute to the work of the group. On the other hand, the reflective inquiry process slows down the extroverts, forcing them to listen more carefully and contribute with more reflective substance.

For action learning to be at its most innovative, it needs the participation of reflective types as well as action-oriented individuals. Reflectors are critical, as they tend to raise questions more easily than the action-oriented people, who, on the other hand, will prevent the group from reaching "analysis paralysis." Pragmatists will emphasize the details and follow-up actions, while the theorists are valuable in seeking new solutions that are broad and systemic. Action learning requires and encourages both types; the group examines the present and what is working or not working but also is forced to seek innovative, untried systems-changing solutions. Those who need quick solutions are forced to ensure that the problem has been properly reframed and that the solutions will achieve the goal and not create other problems. This reassures those who feel constricted by structure and deadlines that decisions are not moving too fast. Action learning is not only concerned with strategic, logical solutions (which appeal to the rational, thinking types), but also with the quality of interaction and the growth and learning of the group and individuals (which appeals to the more feeling-based types).

Precautions with Subject-Matter Experts

One of the ways in which action learning differs from most problem solving groups is that action learning deliberately seeks group members who possess different perspectives rather than filling the group with individuals who possess expertise on the problem or the context. Research shows that solving complex problems demands diversity more than it requires expertise.

Experts can be detrimental to the success of problem-solving groups for a number of reasons. Although experts can provide valuable information, they can also think too much within the box—the natural tendency when one has become highly specialized in a subject area. With their superior knowledge, experts will tend to dominate the group's discussions. Those with less expertise, in turn, will become uncomfortable in making statements or even raising questions they fear will be perceived as "dumb" by the experts. The nonexperts may also hesitate to offer solutions, fearing them to be ideas that the experts may have long ago discarded.

Experts also create dependence and/or risk avoidance on the part of the other group members. We are all aware of the disasters that have occurred when only experts dominated the decision making and there was an absence of fresh questions from the nonexperts. Catastrophes such as the sinking of the *Titanic* and the failure of the *Challenger* shuttle have been attributed to the inability of nonexperts to challenge the experts in their groups. Experts can immobilize group members as well as decrease the development of individual and group confidence.

Thus, expertise in confronting problems is more valuable than expertise with the answers. Freedom to consider new ideas is essential if groups are to be innovative when working on problems and seeking fresh solutions. A key advantage of the action learning group is its ability to interpret or make sense of confusing information instead of having a scientific and easy answer.

Virtual Action Learning Groups at Lockheed Martin

An action learning group at Lockheed Martin was composed of leaders from geographical sites throughout the United States. As a result, members could only occasionally meet at the same physical site, and often met virtually. Lockheed Martin was very pleased with the successes of the group. To further develop the capability of future action learning groups at Lockheed Martin that would need to meet virtually, the group reflected on the following questions at their final session:

- ▶ What successes did we have while working virtually?
- ▶ What factors contributed to these?
- ▶ What were we not able to do?
- ▶ How are virtual teams different from physically intact teams?
- ▶ What are some learnings for future work in virtual teams?

Virtual Action Learning Groups

As more and more groups are required to work in virtual situations, many organizations are exploring the possibility of creating virtual action learning teams. Research shows that virtual groups, who share an interest but not the same space, can be more egalitarian, frank, and task oriented than groups that communicate face-to-face (Putnam, 2000). However, teams that work virtually rather than in person encounter a number of significant challenges.

Because of the paucity of social cues and communication, virtual groups will find it harder to reach consensus and may feel less solidarity with one another. When we meet face-to-face, we are effective at sensing nonverbal messages from one another, especially about emotions, cooperation, and trustworthiness. We lose that ability when we cannot see the other people with whom we are interacting. In addition, virtual groups often develop a sense of depersonalization and are less satisfied with the group's accomplishments.

Although virtual groups are quicker to reach an intellectual understanding of their shared problems, they are much worse at generating the trust and reciprocity necessary to implement that understanding (Putnam, 2000). In issues and situations that are clear and practical, virtual groups can function reasonably well. However, more serious difficulties and frustrations occur in situations of uncertainty and heavy accountability.

How can we develop the technology and adapt action learning to enhance social presence, feedback, and behavioral cues necessary for successful group problem solving? Virtual action learning, like face-to-face action learning, requires the competent intervention of the action learning coach. The coach should supplement the power and value of technology with her reflective questions to better enable the participants to share cues and feedback. As the group members gain comfort and confidence with the computer-mediated meeting, the coach can assist the group in reflecting about what is being learned and how the learning is occurring.

With end-user software becoming increasingly less difficult to navigate, action learning participants can more easily share both cognitive knowledge and social cues. As software developers build new e-commerce applications, action learning should be incorporated into the design so that these new applications can complement the elements of action learning. Waddill and Marquardt (2011) and other researchers continue to search for ways in which action learning principles can be applied to virtual work groups. A growing number of organizations, such as the U.S. Department of Agriculture and George Washington University, are using virtual action learning teams with increasing levels of success.

Virtual Action Learning for George Washington University Students

Six students in my action learning course at George Washington University participated in a virtual multiple-problem action learning set. On Wednesday evenings for six weeks, they each took a turn presenting a problem/task they faced. Capitalizing on chat and other online technologies, they asked questions and reflected on proposed strategies. The group rotated the role of the action learning coach. The group reported great success in that each individual was helped, and the team learned about leadership, groups, and themselves.

Cooperative Work Groups Are More Successful

Members in action learning teams seek to work in a highly cooperative and collaborative manner. The six components and two ground rules initiate and sustain the needed supportive and positive behaviors. Johnson and Johnson (1998), in their research on hundreds of work groups, concluded that cooperative work groups are much more successful than work groups in which members compete with one another. Their analysis identified four major advantages for cooperative work groups:

- ▶ Work groups that had collaborative norms and behavior had greater productivity.
- ▶ Such groups demonstrated a higher quality of reasoning strategies. Reasoning strategies include the ability of the group to integrate new information with prior knowledge, to identify concepts underlying data, to problem solve, to implement metaphoric reasoning, and to increase metacognition. Metacognition is critical for groups because it leads to the generalized improvement in learning capability.
- ▶ There is a better quality of work relations in cooperative work groups. New ideas and solutions are generated, which would not have occurred if individuals were working independently.
- ▶ Finally, in cooperative work groups, there is wider and better transfer of learning. With more complex understandings, cooperative situations produce greater transfer of the learnings back to the organization.

Characteristics of Effective Action Learning Groups

High-performance work groups exhibit a number of common character-istics that initiate and sustain their success. The principles, components, ground rules, and activities of action learning synergistically generate and reinforce the following key attributes of successful action learning teams.

A Shared Commitment to Solving the Problem

A critical ingredient for successful groups is the members' commitment to the work of the group. In action learning, the group has been brought together for the purpose of solving a single problem or problems that are important to one or all of the members. Group members realize that they must work together to succeed and, if successful, they will be rewarded as a group. An added dimension occurs with multiple-problem sets in that everyone helps each other with his or her specific problems; thus, there is a feeling that since you have helped me with my problem, I will make an effort and commitment to helping you to solve your problem.

Revans and Action Learning in the Coal Mines of Wales and England

Reg Revans's first job was HR director for mines in Wales and England. His first challenge was to increase the low productivity in the mines as well as to raise the low morale of the mine workers. Instead of seeking outside expertise, Reg decided to ask the miners themselves what could be done. The miners, of course, had lots of ideas. They were in the mines every day and saw things that worked and things that were just outright stupid. The miners were also strongly committed to identifying solutions that would increase safety as well as production, since they would need to return to the mines after their solutions had been implemented (unlike the consultants, who did not have to go down into the mines to see if their solutions were viable). The miners clearly had a common and strong commitment to solving the problems. As a result, the mines where Reg worked had productivity levels 30 percent above the other mines of Wales and England, and not surprisingly, morale was much higher.

Commitment to Developing a Clear, Common Purpose

Members of most groups assume that they all have a clear and common understanding and agreement as to their group's purpose. However, when they are asked to state what it is, there is invariably a wide array of opinions.

Even when a specific goal is presented to us at the same time and in the same location, each of us hears it differently. Why? Because our backgrounds and experiences cause us to interpret concepts quite differently. Thus, although we may think we are trying to accomplish the same thing, in reality, we are often working at cross purposes with our fellow group members. Therefore, an absolutely critical component for any group to maintain short-term and long-term success is for it to reach a consensus as to its purpose.

In action learning, we never assume that there is agreement on what the problem is or what the group is expected to do. Action learning groups begin by collaboratively reframing the problem and/or clarifying the goal. Research shows that consensus on a goal is possible only when the group members ask questions about the goal and each other's understanding of the goal. To confirm the consensus, the action learning coach checks with the group regularly before allowing group members to begin working on solutions. Most groups jump in quickly, trying to reach agreement on strategies when they do not have agreement on the goal, and thus many hours or days may be spent by members trying to force one another to accept their strategy. It is very difficult, however, to agree on strategy if we are striving for different goals. It is much easier to agree on strategies if everyone agrees on the goal.

Willingness to Work with Others to Develop Strategies

High-performing groups require members who are willing, committed, and even excited about working together. Action learning begins with a complex problem, one in which there is no known solution and a variety of options are possible. No one has all the information or resources or political power to resolve it. Thus the perspectives, knowledge, and experience of all group members are necessary. Members need each other's help to think through the ideas and to test them. In action learning groups, the members may have been thrust into problems and situations entirely new to them as the organization seeks individuals with fresh questions as well as individuals who have experience with the issue. Effective work groups must have members who are open to new ideas, who recognize that people with different perspectives will see things they don't see.

Courage to Question Others

For a group to be effective, its members must be able and willing to question each other, to challenge ideas and statements, no matter who the other members may be. In action learning, everyone is expected, even required, to ask questions of each other and the group. Consequently, members quickly develop the ability and confidence to ask questions, and they soon see the immense value of the questioning process. Many members also enjoy the fact that focusing on questions removes the burden of needing to have all the answers. Although it may in fact be difficult to ask good questions, most people soon realize that questioning is easier than having answers, and they jump into reflective inquiry with greater gusto and openness than they initially imagined they would.

Ability to Work with Clear Norms

High-performing groups need to have clear norms, whether they are imposed on the group or have been built by and agreed to by all the members. All action learning groups begin with the norms contained in the six components and two ground rules, namely, reflective inquiry, questions before statements, commitment to learning, confidentiality, focusing on problem solving and taking action, and the power of the action learning coach. Each group then establishes additional norms during the first intervention of the action learning coach when she asks the following questions: "How are we doing thus far as a group? What are we doing well? What could we do better?"

As each action learning group responds to these questions, its members are consciously and subconsciously establishing the norms that they will be adhering to during the rest of their time together. For example, if a member of the group says, "We have been listening well," the coach will ask for examples as well as the reasons the group members may have been listening well. This discussion imprints itself on the psyche and behavior of the group members. The group invariably continues to behave in the manner it has determined to be "good behavior." After responding to "What could be improved?" the group immediately begins to behave in the ways that it has suggested. Norms, therefore, are actually set as the group focuses on its responses to the questions. These norms are always positive, for example, listening, respecting, being creative, questioning, reflecting, committing, and so forth. Amazingly, these norms are so powerfully ingrained through the reflective discussions that it is very difficult for an individual member to step outside these group-created norms, and norms are thus rarely violated.

Why Action Learning Groups Can Skip Storming for Power

A remarkable characteristic of action learning groups is that, as a result of the norm "statements can be made only in response to questions" as well as the impact of learning as well as acting, action learning groups go through little or no "storming of personalities and power" (of course, storming of ideas is healthy and encouraged in action learning). As a result, instead of going through the typical stages of forming, storming, norming, and performing, action learning groups go immediately from forming/norming to performing (working on a specific problem—see table 2). The norms are in place before the group arrives in the room; they are explained before the group begins to perform. And, even more valuable, the norms are regularly raised through questions from the action learning coach such as "What are we doing well, and what can we do better?"

There is a direct correlation between the level of norms and the level of the performance. The higher the norms, the higher the performance. Many problem-solving groups have such a difficult storming phase that they never fully recover from the pain they inflicted on one another and, as a result, never perform very well. Members never truly enjoy being part of such groups. Action learning groups, on the other hand, are filled with fulfilling, successful, and enjoyable experiences.

Respect and Support for Others

Successful work groups are filled with members who are respectful of each other and interested to learn about others' perspectives and viewpoints. As a result of the interplay of the six components of action learning, particularly as members share their learnings and vulnerabilities through the interventions of the action learning coach, action learning members generate a positive and healthy self-regard for one another. In one group in which I served as the action learning coach, two of the participants

TABLE 2

Stages of Group Life

Typical Groups	Action Learning Groups
Forming	Norming
Storming	Performing
Norming	Norming
Performing	Performing

had worked together for more than fifteen years, could not tolerate each other, and certainly did not respect the talent or efforts of the other. Yet, amazingly, within sixty minutes of working together in an action learning group, they were questioning and listening to each other, sharing and respecting each other's ideas and strategies. After the session ended, one commented, "This is the first time in fifteen years that I really felt able to work with him, that he really had some commitment to our organization and wanted to contribute."

Willingness to Learn and to Help Others Learn

Successful groups need to have members who are willing to learn and develop themselves as well as help the members around them to learn and develop their competencies. When people join an action learning group, they are clearly informed that the group has two purposes: to work on the issue and to learn. They know that time and energy will be spent on developing individual and team capacities. Accepting the need to learn and help others learn engenders a helping, sharing attitude as well as a sense of humility among the group members. Such attitudes build not only powerful, but also sensitive and caring groups.

Cohesiveness and Trust

Action learning group members are tightly connected to each other as they work out the problem. As they jointly focus on reframing the problem and developing strategies, they are also building strong bonds. Interconnectedness is also built by the egalitarian nature of action learning groups, in which the quality of questions rather than the ability to provide answers is important. Finally, high levels of trust are built when people share their vulnerabilities, that is, that they have problems and they need to learn. As a result, action learning groups are energizing and enjoyable for the participants.

Focus on What Is Best for the Group versus Individual Glory

Members of successful action learning teams ask questions and seek answers that will be best for the project and for other members rather than what would be best for themselves. It is similar to the mindset that Japanese people employ when eating or enjoying some drinks at a restaurant. During these occasions, everyone is watching each other's cup of tea or glass of beer to ensure that it is full; and if it is empty or even partially empty, someone will fill that person's glass. One never needs to fill his own cup or glass, unlike in our culture in which we each take responsibility for our own glass. So too in action learning: everyone is constantly looking for opportunities to give other group members a chance to answer or ask a question. Not only is the process more enjoyable and relaxing, but it results in much better listening to and appreciation of each other's ideas.

Checklist for Action Learning Group Membership

► What are the criteria for membership in the action learning group?

► Are the group members from diverse backgrounds?

► Are members here by choice or by appointment?

► Is the size of groups between four and eight members?

► Will the groups operate full time or part time?

► Is there a balance between experts and nonexperts? Individuals familiar and unfamiliar with the problem and the context?

► Do we have members from outside the organization—customers, suppliers, dealers, other organizations?

► What is the level of accountability and responsibility for the group's results?

► Are all members committed to be present at all the meetings?

► Is there a sense of ownership of the problem?

► How will the group be recognized for their efforts and success?

► Do group members have the support of their supervisors in allowing them to attend all sessions and to be able to work on the actions between sessions?

► What access to outside resource people will be available?

► Are the dates and times established?

► Will there be any virtual meetings?

Questions and Reflection

Questions serve many purposes for action learning groups and offer numerous benefits. They enable members to understand, to clarify, and to open up new avenues of exploration, and to become more insightful in solving the problem and developing strategies. They generate the seeds for great ideas for strategic actions and potential paths for solutions. Questions build teamwork and better listening skills. Questions also serve as the foundation for individual, team, and organizational learning.

"The important thing is not to stop questioning."

—Albert Einstein

Focus on Questions in Action Learning

One of the primary ways in which action learning differs from other problem-solving approaches is by focusing on questions rather than on solutions. Action learning recognizes that only through questions can a group truly build and gain a common understanding of the problem, acquire a sense of each other's potential strategies, and achieve innovative, breakthrough strategies and solutions.

Questions, when asked at the right time in the right way, provide the glue that holds the group together. The seeds of the answer are contained in the kernels of the questions. Thus, the better the questions, the better

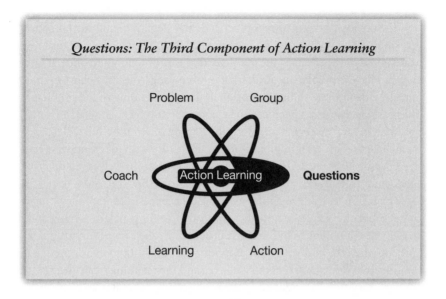

Questions: The Third Component of Action Learning

will be the solutions as well as the learnings; the deeper the reflection, the greater the development of individual and team competencies.

Action learning recognizes that problem solving must begin by first diverging, through the use of inquiry, and only then should the narrowing and converging occur. First the group must gain the big picture of the problem—see the "entire elephant"—before determining possible goals and specific strategies (see the sidebar titled "Seven Blind Men and the Elephant"). The acquisition of a wide, helicopter view of the problem can be accomplished only by openly and freshly questioning each other and then reflecting on the responses. A central aspect of action learning is the reflective inquiry process and the resulting group environment that allows for and encourages people to ask "dumb" or, more accurately, "fresh" questions.

Seven Blind Men and the Elephant

A well-known Hindu fable tells the story of the seven blind men who encounter an elephant for the first time. The man who felt the ear said, "This is a large leaf." The man who grabbed a leg said, "No, this is a tree trunk." The man who felt the tail said, "It is a thick rope," and the man who touched the elephant's flank declared it to be a wall. "No, it is a snake," said the man who touched the trunk. The sixth man said it was a bag as he felt the elephant's mouth. Touching the tusk, the seventh man declared that it was a spear.

The obvious, but not always practiced, first step in solving any problem is to be sure you know what the problem is. Most of us assume, because we heard about or experienced the problem, that we now know and understand exactly what the problem is. And, what is more dangerous, we believe everyone else now has the same perception and understanding of the problem. The reality is that seven people who hear about or even experience the same problem, in fact, discern it and describe it quite differently. Why? Because we all, like the seven blind men, come to the reality with different perspectives, perspectives created by our previous experiences as well as our diverse ages, genders, cultures, and social and educational backgrounds.

For action learning proponents, these differences, although they cause some initial challenges, are positive and valuable for problem solving and strategy development. Why? Because problems by their nature are complex and complicated, and proposed solutions can affect the environment in innumerable ways. Different perspectives and the resulting fresh questions are necessary to fully understand the problem (e.g., that it is an elephant), and only when there is agreement that it is indeed an elephant, can workable strategies (e.g., pulling the trunk) emerge that will enable us to move the elephant.

Power of Questions

Questions will always be more powerful than statements in solving problems and developing concerted actions. The key to the power of action learning resides in the quality and flow of questions. Accordingly, action learning places a high priority on group members asking good, challenging questions. Asking the right question is not an easy task, especially when the group is struggling with an overwhelming problem (fighting the alligators). Revans (1982a) notes, "The capacity to ask fresh questions in conditions of ignorance, risk, and confusion, when nobody knows what to do next" is at the heart of action learning. John Morris (1991), a leading pioneer in action learning, remarked that only "through constant questioning do we see more clearly just who we really are, and what remarkable resources we have access to. We will also see more clearly what is really facing us, and we will become more capable of accepting and responding to change."

In action learning, we focus on the right questions rather than on the right answers, because we know that the right questions will lead us to the right answer and that the beginnings to the answer will lie in the questions. Questions help the group to recognize and reorganize their knowledge. As group members are engaged in asking questions of each other, they gradually gain a group consensus on answers and strategies, since they now more clearly see the others' perspectives and have greater clarity on their own.

Questions, especially challenging ones, cause us to think and to learn. Questions create energy and vitality in the group, since they trigger a need to listen, to seek a common truth, and to justify opinions and viewpoints. Questions generate a dialogue in which people begin to leave their individual limitations to find a new wholeness.

An interesting phenomenon occurs as we ask questions about someone else's problem. The questioning process causes us to become more interested in the problem as well as in the other person. And when we listen to someone respond to our question, we appreciate their efforts and their attention. Group members will find the truth more easily through listening to each other's questions and reflections than by being forced to listen to opinions and statements that are based on assumptions. Truth does not emerge from opinions but from the free movement of open minds. Questioning causes us to view each other as learning resources.

The *Titanic*, the Bay of Pigs, and the *Challenger*

What do the sinking of the *Titanic*, the Bay of Pigs incident, and the *Challenger* disaster have in common? According to historians who have carefully examined the background and details of these three events, the common element was the inability or unwillingness of participants to raise questions about their concerns. Some group members were fearful that they were the only ones who had a particular concern (when, in fact, it was later discovered that many people in the group had similar concerns). Others felt that their question had already been answered in the mind of the group; if they asked, it would be considered a dumb question. But because individuals did not ask questions, lives were lost in each of these tragedies. Thus, an important tenet of action learning is to create a structure and environment in which people are encouraged to ask what they might think of as "dumb" questions. Often it is the "dumb" question that is really the great "fresh" question that ultimately solves the problem and perhaps saves the company.

Four Major Benefits of Questions

Questions provide four powerful benefits to the action learning process, namely, problem solving, team building, leadership development, and learning enhancement. Let's examine each of these.

Innovative Problem Solving Through Questions

In action learning, questions are asked not just to seek answers, but to understand, to respond to what is being asked, to force us to think. The focus is not on a quest for solutions only, but also to generate opportunities to explore and to learn. For purposes of problem exploration and solving, research shows that questions are always more powerful than statements in clarifying, in gaining mutual agreement, and in gaining a consensus of perspective (Cooperrider, Sorensen, and Yaeger, 2001; Marquardt, 2005). Questioning forces us to listen carefully in order to stay in the game.

Questions and reflection allow time for the minds of all the members to be working. This simultaneous learning, a type of "team thinking," is much faster than talking, especially talking that is interrupted by more talking. Being responsible for asking good questions takes the burden off individuals to solve the problem. No one needs to be defensive or take sole responsibility for finding the answers.

Responding to questions enables the group to become aware of inconsistencies as well as consistencies. Responding to questions causes the problem presenter to "talk out loud" his thoughts, thereby creating clarity and insights not possible when he contains the process in his own mind. Weick (2009) describes the process as constructive insight, or "How can I know what I'm thinking until I hear what I've said?"

Einstein and Questions

All inventions in the history of the world came as a result of the inventor asking a question that no one had asked before. Einstein, who created the most powerful formula/solution in the world ($E = MC^2$), indicated that what made him so creative was that he could still ask questions like a child. He further stated that if he had an hour of time, he would spend the first fifty-nine minutes coming up with a question.

Team Building Through Questions

Questions build strong and cohesive teams because of the many positive effects they have on a group of people. Questions require us to listen to other people and can affect how we feel toward other group members. For example, we tend to reconstruct how we perceive and value someone who is asking us for our knowledge and opinions. Questions tend to make the person being questioned feel important. It gives the other person an opportunity to "shine," to demonstrate her worth to others and to herself. The person being asked a question thinks, "Maybe the person asking me questions is a pretty nice person since he recognizes my intelligence and values my perspectives."

When everyone is expected to focus on questioning and the primary form of communication is questions, it is very difficult, if not impossible, for one person to dominate the discussion. People can participate in the interactions only through the asking of questions or the answering of someone else's question. If the question posed is not useful, the group may move on to another person's inquiry.

Questions also have the power to build strong group cohesion. Inquiries go to the center of the table, and the focus is on the question rather than on the person asking or answering the question. Synergy and togetherness grow as people work on what has now become the group's question, as members develop group solutions. When the group develops innovative insights and solutions as a result of the questions, ever stronger bonds and support are generated. Questions, by their very nature, also cause individuals and teams to be more receptive to adapting, changing, and growing.

Leadership Development Through Questions

What is the most important skill of a leader? Vaill (1996), Senge (2006), and many other management theorists, as well as globally recognized leaders such as Ollila (Nokia), Gates (Microsoft), and Chambers (Cisco Systems), cite the ability to ask great questions. Throughout history, from Socrates to Senge, asking the right question has been seen as a mark of the wise man. Kotter (1998), a noted Harvard University business professor, stated that the primary difference between a leader and a manager is that leaders are those who can ask the right questions, and managers are those tasked to answer them. Asking the right questions enables us to discover the right response, and the right response enables us to take the right action.

In action learning, everyone receives ample time to practice and demonstrate the art of asking questions. With the guidance of the action learning coach, the group reflects on the quality and impact of the group's questions. In action learning, we believe that finding the right question is more important than answering well the wrong question. As Drucker (2006) notes, the leader of the past was one who had the answers; the leader of the future is one who has the great questions.

As a matter of fact, can you think of any leadership skill that cannot be demonstrated through the use of a great question? Great questions show others that we have been listening and reflecting. They demonstrate our ability to empathize and care about others. They generate creativity and energy in others and in ourselves. Questions can build great teams. Questions can motivate more than exhortatory statements. And perhaps most important for leadership, questions cause the people around us to think, to learn, and to grow.

Individual and Team Learning and Growth

Seminal education theorists, such as Bruner, Bandura, and Knowles, all state that deep and significant learning occurs only as a result of reflection, and they recognize that reflection is not possible without a question—whether the question is from an external source or from within one's own mind. Thus the central action learning process of reflective inquiry presents the best and ultimately only way to optimize individual and team learning.

Questions also have a physiological impact on the synapses of our brain. The synapses open wider and make more connections because of the body's need to deal with the question. To demonstrate this, take a heading in this or any book and convert it into a question. For example, look at the statement "Action learning helps us to learn." If you simply ask yourself, "How does action learning help us to learn?" you will be surprised at how much more you will learn and retain of what you read in that section.

In action learning we learn not only about what directly causes the problem or what solution may work (which is single-loop learning), but we also seek to discover and learn what might be the underlying causes and solutions (double-loop learning) as well as the culture and the mind-set that create these causes and solutions (triple-loop learning).

A final way in which action learning helps people to learn is through the supportive, creative environment of the group. When people respond in a positive way to the questions you ask (as occurs frequently), it gives you confidence, a feeling of self-worth and importance, and an appreciation of the learning environment, all of which contribute to your learning mentality and success.

"When in an epoch of change, when tomorrow is necessarily different from yesterday, new ways of thinking must emerge. New questions need to be asked before solutions are sought. Action learning's primary objec-

tive is to learn how to ask appropriate questions under conditions of risk rather than find answers to questions that have already been defined by others. We have to act ourselves into a new way of thinking rather than think ourselves into a new way of acting."

—Reg Revans

First Ground Rule of Action Learning: Make Statements Only in Response to Questions

This is the first ground rule of action learning. Questions are at the heart of action learning and contribute immensely to the success of action learning. As we have discussed, much of the potency of action learning is built upon questions that generate reflective inquiry. Because questions are so important and powerful in solving problems, generating learning, and building leaders and teams, it is critical to ensure that questions rather than statements are the primary means of communication in action learning. Therefore, we strongly encourage action learning groups and the action learning coach to establish this ground rule: *Statements can be made only in response to questions.*

This ground rule does not prohibit the use of statements; as a matter of fact, there may still be more statements than questions during the action learning meetings since questions asked may generate one or many responses from other members of the group. By requiring people to think "questions first," the dynamics and thinking of the group is significantly transformed. The natural impulse to make statements and judgments begins to give way to listening and reflecting.

Once the problem or task has been introduced to the group, members should begin by asking questions to clarify the problem before jumping into statements to solve the problem. In action learning, we recognize that there is a correlation between the number and quality of questions and the speed and quality of the resulting actions and learnings. Balancing the number of questions and the number of statements leads to dialogue, which is a proper balance between advocating and inquiring.

This ground rule provides tremendous value to the action learning group. First, it forces everyone in the group to think about asking questions, about inquiring rather than making statements or advocating. Questions tend to unite; statements can cause divisions. An environment in which questions are valued requires people to listen to each other. Questions prevent domination by a single person and instead create cohesion. Questions may slow down the rapid flow of communication, but in action learning this is seen as positive, as it forces members to be reflective and creative, to listen first.

Will some people manipulate this rule, raising their voices at the end of statements to convert them to questions? This is certainly possible, but once any statement is converted into a question, the power then moves to the respondents, who may choose to agree or not agree, to reflect upon the question or to respond with a more open question.

It is amazing how quickly group members become comfortable and competent in this approach to communications. As action learning groups experience the tremendous benefits of questioning, they gladly embrace this precept. It recaptures their natural way of communicating and learning as young children before the impulse was inhibited by adults telling them to "stop asking so many questions." The quality of the group's work and the comfort of the interactions often cause members to apply this ground rule in other parts of organizational life.

Asking Great Questions and Improving Customer Service at the National Bank of Dominica

The National Bank of Dominica has built a sound reputation as an excellent corporate citizen over the years. In 2009, the Bank was recognized by the Eastern Caribbean Central Bank (Bank Regulator for the Eastern Caribbean) as the "Best Corporate Citizen" among member territory banks. The award was based on the bank's sponsorship and support for education, health, sports, culture, and community development and its reputation of being the employer of choice in its market.

In 2009, action learning was introduced to the bank by Vow Mourillon, Executive Manager for Human Resource and Organizational Development. A number of challenges were selected, one being the need for the bank to become more customer-focused. A Customer Service Action Learning group was formed, which worked over a period of several months, asking great questions, reflecting, and asking more great questions. Ultimately, the group identified some 50 strategies/actions on how to better treat bank customers, all of which were implemented.

The results: there are many more smiles on the faces of the customers as well as the customer service workers! Mourillon notes a "buzz of excitement" about customer service in the bank. Employees throughout the bank, although initially skeptical about the work of another problem-solving group, saw how the action learning group analyzed the problem more systematically and provided comprehensive attention to many factors throughout the bank's system. Mourillon observes how "action learning has dramatically changed the culture of the National Bank of Dominica. We are more creative, committed, and excited about both our present and our future as a result of action learning."

Questions Identify and Integrate Knowledge

In most problem-solving situations, only the knowledge that is brought into the group by its members is utilized. This knowledge (which action learning refers to as programmed knowledge, or "P") allows for an incremental, narrowly focused understanding and mediocre solution to the problem but rarely generates the quantum improvements or spectacular leaps in knowledge necessary to solve today's more complex problems. The knowledge that individual group members have when entering an action learning group is never sufficient enough to solve difficult, complex problems. The group must increase its knowledge and skills in order to fully understand the problem and solve it in a fully systems-based way.

Only through questions and reflection (that is, the reflective inquiry process of action learning) can a group generate a holistic broad-based perspective. By seeing each other as learners and learning resources, members of an action learning group anticipate the generation of new knowledge within the group. Questioning builds on the knowledge that people bring into the group while at the same time constructing new knowledge and learning.

By beginning with questioning rather than using past knowledge as the reference point, the group can gauge whether the present available information is adequate and relevant to the situation. The key to problem solving is to start with fresh questions, not constructs and assumptions from the past. Questions enable groups to unpeel the layers around the problem and uncover the core elements of knowledge necessary to discover the solution.

Judging versus Learning Mind-set in Asking Questions

All too often, questions are limited, incorrect, or simplistic. Ineffective questions lead to detours, missed goals, and costly mistakes. Marilee Adams (2004) notes that, depending on how the person asks a question, it can be perceived as "an invitation, a request, or a missile." She emphasizes how our mind-set frames how we see the world. It simultaneously programs what we believe to be our personal limitations as well as our possibilities. Mind-sets define the parameters of our actions and interactions and affect, either explicitly or implicitly, outcomes in any area of focus. They are a determinant in deciding the types of questions we ask ourselves and others. In addition, our mind-set determines how we observe, understand, and accept ourselves and others.

The attitude in which questions are asked is very important in action learning. Questions should be asked for the purpose of enabling the group members to broaden and deepen their view of the situation or issue they are addressing. Thus it is important that the action learning members adjust their style from that of eliciting/interrogating to that of enabling (McGill and Beaty, 1995).

Adams (2004) refers to two types of mind-sets that may reside in the questioner: (1) learner and (2) judge. In the learner mind-set, the questioner seeks to be responsive to life's circumstances, and is thus more likely to think objectively and strategically. The learner mind-set constantly searches for and creates solutions, and relates to others in a win-win manner. Group members with the learning mind-set tend to be more optimistic and search for new possibilities. They exude optimism, possibilities, and hope. They are thoughtful, flexible, and accepting.

Group members who have a learning mind-set when asking questions are more open to new possibilities, and less attached to their own opinions and the need to be right. According to Adams, the learning mind-set leads to much greater effectiveness, breakthroughs, and transformations. Although it is sometimes more difficult and challenging to operate within a learner mind-set, it is much more rewarding for everyone involved. Learning mind-sets lead to thinking objectively, creating solutions, and relating in a win-win way. Group members with learner mind-sets ask genuine questions, that is, questions to which they don't already know the answers.

The judge mind-set, on the other hand, is reactive. People who ask questions with the judging mind-set tend to be more automatic and absolute in their actions; they tend to emphasize negativity, pessimism, stress, and limited possibilities. Judging questions are inflexible and judgmental. For the judger, questions are more likely to be reactive to the situation, and thereby lead to automatic reactions, limitations, and negativity. Judging questions result in win-lose relating as they all too often operate in an "attack or defend" paradigm.

Some examples of questions asked from the learning mind-set would include:

▸ What's good or useful about this circumstance?
▸ What possibilities does this situation open up?
▸ What can we do about this?

- ▸ How can we stay on track?
- ▸ What can we learn from this?

Examples of judging questions, on the other hand, include:

- ▸ What are we doing wrong?
- ▸ Why don't we do it my way?
- ▸ How could you not see the consequences of this strategy?

Questions that are learning questions enable the action learning group to be more creative, build more trust and openness, cause each other to listen and learn from one another, and make the action learning experience enjoyable as well as successful.

Open and Closed Types of Questions

There are several types of questions that can be asked in action learning sessions, all of which build the group's capacity to understand and reframe the problem, to build common goals, to develop potential strategies, and to take effective actions. Questions not only build a deeper and better understanding of the problem and possible solutions, but also construct better working relations among the problem solvers. Here are some examples of questions that members should be encouraged to utilize in action learning sessions.

Open questions. These are questions that give the person or group a high
  degree of freedom in deciding how to respond; for example, "What
  would be the best results if we took that action?"

Affective questions. Such questions invite members to share feelings about
  an issue: "How do you feel about leaving this job?"

Reflective questions. These encourage more elaboration; for example, "You
  said there are difficulties with your manager; what do you think causes
  these difficulties?"

Probing questions. These questions cause the person or group to go into
  more depth or breadth on a topic: "Why is this happening?"

Fresh questions. Such questions challenge basic assumptions; for example,
  "Why must it be that way?" "What do you always ... ?" "Has this ever
  been tried?"

Questions that create connections. These help to create a systems perspective; for example, "What are the consequences of these actions?"

Clarifying questions. These are questions that result in further descriptions and explanations, such as, "Are you saying that … ?" "Could you explain more about this situation?"

Explorative questions. These open up new avenues and insights and lead to new explorations: "Have you explored/thought of … ?" "Would such a source help?"

Analytical questions. Such questions examine causes and not just symptoms; for example, "Why has this happened?"

Closed questions. These can be answered by "yes" or "no," or a quantitative response. They can be useful to clarify or seek further understanding and quickly move the group forward; for example, "How many people will be affected?" "Did you agree with this decision?"

The types of questions that are not helpful in action learning are *leading* (i.e., *judging*) *questions*, those that force or encourage the person or group to respond in the way intended by the questioner (for example, "You wanted to do it by yourself, didn't you?"), and *multiple questions*, a string of questions put together to meet the needs of the questioner but confusing to the responder.

"You look at what's there and say, Why? I dream about what isn't there and ask, Why not?"

—George Bernard Shaw

What Makes a Good Question?

In action learning, group members continuously strive to ask good questions, even great questions. The better the question, the greater will be the insight gained and solution attained. Often, the best, easiest, and most effective way to ask a good question is simply to build on a previous question or the response to that question. The art and science of careful listening and then generating an open, creative question will quickly and constructively move the group to problem reframing and then strategy development.

What makes a good question? There is no single correct answer to this question, but action learning proponents believe there are a number of essential ingredients to good and powerful questions. Superb questions accomplish a number of wonderful results, as they

- ► Cause us to focus and/or to stretch
- ► Create deep reflection
- ► Challenge taken-for-granted assumptions that prevent us from acting in new and forceful ways
- ► Are difficult to answer and may take courage to ask
- ► Lead to breakthrough thinking
- ► Contain the keys that open the door to great solutions
- ► Are supportive, insightful, and challenging
- ► Are unpresumptuous and offered in a sharing spirit
- ► Are selfless, not asked to illustrate the cleverness of the questioner or to generate information or an interesting response for the questioner
- ► Open up the problem owner's view of the situation
- ► Open doors in the mind and get people to think more deeply
- ► Test assumptions and cause people to explore why and how they act
- ► Generate positive and powerful action

Great questions are asked at the time when they will generate the most reflection and learning. "Why" questions are valuable and frequently used in action learning, as they cause us to reflect and to perhaps see things in fresh, unpredictable ways. Questions such as "Why do you think that?" or "Why did this work?" can help the group examine old issues in new, original ways. Other examples of questions that could produce rich responses include the following.

- ► Can that be done in any other way?
- ► What other options can we think of?
- ► What resources have we never used?
- ► What do we expect to happen if we do that?
- ► What would happen if you did nothing at all?
- ► What other options do you have?
- ► What is stopping us?
- ► What happens if … ?
- ► Have we ever thought of … ?

Action learning groups will know and feel when a great question has been asked. One or more members will spontaneously say, "That's a great question!" Great questions cause us to expressively respond in those or similar words. When a group generates one or more such questions, it can move forward with great confidence that it will reach greater clarity of understanding and imaginative solutions.

"A good question is never fully answered. It is not a bolt to be tightened into place, but a seed to be planted and to bear more seed toward the hope of greening the landscape of ideas."

—John Ciardi

Who Asks the Questions?

Everyone! In action learning, questions are not limited to only those with the most expertise or prestige. Questions are asked, and need to be asked, by all members of the group, each of whom has unique perspectives and experiences, each of whom can help the group gain a comprehensive and systemic overview of the problem that allows the group to reframe it and then begin developing the most strategic and innovative solutions.

The problem presenter should also ask questions. If she only responds to questions, she will feel like she is at an inquisition. Of course, it is natural that the initial questions be addressed to the problem presenter, as she is the source of vital information needed by the group. However, as soon as possible, the presenter should begin asking questions of the other group members. This is important because it demonstrates to the group that the problem presenter now has sufficient confidence in the group to seek members' ideas, and that she has not predetermined a solution.

By asking questions of the group, the problem presenter changes the communication dynamics from a wheel hub (presenter) with spokes (other group members who interact only with the hub) to an interaction in which everyone interacts with everyone else. It is generally at this juncture that the problem moves from the presenter to the entire group. The problem is now in the center of the table for everyone to examine rather than in the mind of the problem presenter. Once group ownership is achieved, greater energy, commitment, and creativity in solving the problem will occur.

"The ability to process new experiences, to find their meaning and to integrate them into one's life, is the signature skill of leaders and, indeed, of anyone who finds ways to live fully and well."

—William Bennis

Reflection and Reflective Inquiry

The quiet time between questions and responses provides opportunities for group members to examine assumptions and to find common perspectives. For reflective inquiry to occur, there must be space for people to stand back and to unfreeze their presuppositions and basic assumptions. Reflection does not come easily or naturally. In most group settings, attempts to create reflection fail. In action learning groups, however, reflection is continuous and natural.

Action learning deliberately carves out the time and creates the conditions for reflecting and listening. The expectation on all members to ask questions and to carefully listen to the responses develops the habit of reflective inquiry within the group as well as in individuals' lives.

Reflection involves recalling, thinking about, pulling apart, making sense, and trying to understand. Reflective inquiry challenges one's programmed knowledge, or what Schein (2010) refers to as "theories in use." This type of inquiry does not deny the importance of programmed knowledge, but it does provide the opportunity for group members to introduce new knowledge. Mezirow (1991) points out that reflection involves bringing one's assumptions, premises, criteria, and schemata into consciousness and vigorously critiquing them.

Reflective inquiry generates mutual support for group members, as they need to listen intently to one another. It is the key to transformative learning. Schön (1986) describes the elements of reflection: (a) diagnosis (ability to frame or make sense of a problem), (b) testing (engaging in experimentation and reflection to test alternative solutions), and (c) the courage to act and to be responsible for one's actions. Reflection plays a role in all stages of the learning cycle described by Kolb (1984), as shown in figure 1.

Hammer and Stanton (2009) note that organizations and groups can fail in a variety of ways, but these failures all share one underlying cause: a failure to reflect. Authors such as Mintzberg (2011) and Kouzes and Posner (2002) see reflection as indispensable for leadership development, noting that leaders learn much more by reflecting on their own experiences rather than the experiences of others (e.g., via case studies).

Dialogue and Reflective Inquiry

Dialogue is a special kind of communication in which listening and learning are prized above talking, persuading, and selling. In dialogue, there is a

FIGURE 1
Reflection in the Learning Cycle

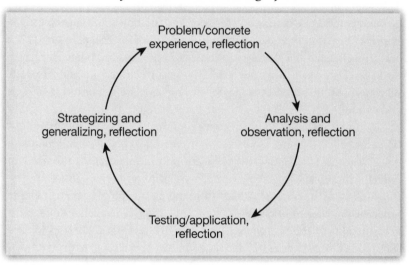

balance between advocacy and inquiry. Advocacy is our natural tendency to push our agenda, whereas inquiry is our attempt through questions to identify the assumptions and perspectives of others. Dialogue encourages win-win situations and does not focus on trying to convince others. Dialogue is very different from debate or discussion, as table 3 shows.

Dialogue allows the group to tap the collective wisdom of its members and to see the situation more as a whole than as fragmented parts. In dialogue there is an emphasis on asking questions rather than posing solutions, on gaining shared meaning rather than imposing one's own meaning.

TABLE 3
Dialogue Versus Debate/Discussion

Dialogue	Debate/Discussion
Seeing the whole among the parts; seeking the connections between the parts	Breaking issues/problems into parts; seeing distinctions between the parts
Inquiring into assumptions	Justifying/defending assumptions
Learning through inquiry and disclosure	Persuading, selling, telling
Creating shared meaning among many	Gaining agreement on one meaning

In dialogue, every person's ideas are listened to and respected by other members of the group. There is a common pool of information. Dialogue is a special form of conversation that affirms the person-to-person relationship between discussants and acknowledges their collective right and intellectual capacity to make sense of the world. Out of this social sharing of knowledge emerge the seeds of innovation, of some new and imaginative insights that may lead to unexpected but valuable ideas.

Dialogue involves the suspension of opinions and criticism, and instead promotes a creative exploration of issues and problems. Dialogue promotes collective thinking, a positive "teamthink" process. The group now has the potential to co-create meaning as a common understanding is developed. Dialogue brings people to a new way of perceiving an issue that may be of concern to all. That new understanding might include an identification of what actions should be taken or decisions made individually and collectively.

Dialogue involves a relationship. Central to the concept of dialogue is the idea that through the interaction, people acknowledge the wholeness, not just the utility, of others. The focus is on acquiring greater understanding and attaining shared meaning. Dialogue is based on the principle that the human mind is capable of using logic and reason to understand the world, rather than having to rely on the interpretation of someone who claims authority through force, tradition, superior intellect, or divine rights.

Dialogue is an affirmation of the intellectual capability not only of the individual, but also of the collective. It acknowledges that everyone is blind to his or her own tacit assumptions and needs the help of others to see them. It acknowledges that each person, no matter how smart or capable, sees the world from a particular perspective and that there are other legitimate perspectives that could inform that view.

Isaacs (1993) notes that dialogue is more than a set of techniques for improving organizations, enhancing communications, building consensus, or solving problems. It is based on the principle that conception and implementation are intimately linked, with a core of common meaning. During the dialogue process, "people learn to think together—not just in the sense of analyzing a shared problem or creating new pieces of shared knowledge, but in the sense of occupying a collective sensibility, in which the thoughts, emotions, and resulting actions belong not to one individual, but to all of them together" (p. 25). Through dialogue people can begin to move into coordinated patterns of action and start to act in an aligned way. They can begin to see how to fit parts into a larger whole.

Dialogue and Innovative Thinking in Action Learning

Dialogue is a critical part of the action learning process because it joins people with diverse perspectives; it helps to connect possible solutions to the problem and possible actions with the learning. It is not easy for a group to engage in dialogue, as most people find it difficult to hear an assumption that contradicts their own. Holding on to and defending assumptions gets in the way of dialogue. Action learning's insistence on the use of questions and the reflective inquiry process enables individuals to more easily and effectively engage in dialogue. Dialogue helps remove barriers among participants, as people genuinely seek to engage in open, honest communication.

The practice of dialogue requires a group climate that is open and respectful of individuals and in which information is shared. In an action learning environment, members are free from coercion, and everyone has equal opportunity to challenge the ideas of others. Without such a climate, it is unlikely that the group members would expend the energy or incur the necessary risks to effectively and innovatively solve the problem.

Dialogue is particularly important with the kinds of tough issues often faced by action learning groups. When there is tension or a difficult dilemma to resolve, people are like electrons at high temperatures. They collide and move at cross-purposes. Dialogue, on the other hand, seeks to produce a cooler, shared environment by refocusing the group's attention. Groups tend to go through several stages on their way to achieving dialogue.

1. The *invitation stage* occurs when a group comes together. At this stage, the individuals bring with them a wide range of tacit, unexpressed differences in perspectives (similar to the blind men with the elephant).
2. At the *conversation stage*, the people begin to interact. The word *conversation* is derived from the Latin word *conversare*, "to turn together." In action learning, this is the stage in which the group "turns together" to seek a common understanding of the problem in an effort to reframe it.
3. The *deliberation stage* begins at the point when the group seeks to make choices.
4. The *suspension stage* requires group members to suspend their views and thereby loosen the grip of their certainty about all views, including their own. At this stage, the group begins to question assumptions.

5. The *dialogue stage* (*dialogue* is a Greek word translated as "the flow of meaning") occurs when the group chooses to live in chaos rather than certainty. During this stage, the group may feel like it is in a giant washing machine. Certainty and conclusions are difficult to manage. However, the group recognizes that there is no need to panic, and if it listens and inquires, clarity will emerge from the chaos, and creativity will occur in the decisions that need to be made by the group.

Asking Questions in Other Cultures

ISABEL RIMANOCY

I have had two very different experiences with cultures not accustomed to accepting questions. In Thailand, questions can be seen as challenging the opinion of another person, and rule number one is that no one should "lose face." My experience led me to reframe the question as a gift for someone, as a sign of interest and curiosity. This reframing totally changed the perception of the question, and the group easily adopted the questioning process. In northern Europe, I was working with pragmatic engineers who initially were upset that they would get questions instead of answers and solutions. I trusted the action learning process and by the end of the second session, I was surprised to hear participants saying that "my life is divided into before and after this program, before and after I started using questions." A deep transformational impact had taken place in those individuals.

The Poetry and Art of Asking Great Questions

The ability to ask powerful and challenging questions is an art as well as a science. The science is simply to listen carefully to the preceding question and/or response(s) to that question and build on it (rather than focus on your own interests). The art is to create questions that are truly open and fresh. Walt Disney referred to questions as "uncontaminated wonder."

Like a great poem, the question may be interpreted in a way not intended by the questioner, but may lead to ideas not considered by either party. The seeds to great solutions are thus contained in the words of those great questions. And like great poetry, great questions require time and openness to be truly appreciated. Action learning, through the questioning and reflective processes, taps the best of science and the best of art to generate practical but innovative and imaginative questions that lead to breakthrough solutions to difficult, complex problems.

Checklist for Questions and Reflection

- ▶ Are we using open, reflective, and probing questions?
- ▶ Are our questions fresh, clarifying, timely, and supportive?
- ▶ Do we avoid closed, multiple, and leading questions?
- ▶ Is everyone involved in the questioning?
- ▶ Did we jump to solutions before framing the problem via questions?
- ▶ Are we questioning to solve the problem or to impress?
- ▶ Which questions have evoked the greatest actions? The greatest learnings?
- ▶ Is there reflective time between questions and comments?
- ▶ Is listening attentive and open, or is it evaluative and inattentive?
- ▶ Are we filtering out what the person is saying?
- ▶ Do we listen without interruption?
- ▶ How do we encourage others to ask "fresh" questions?
- ▶ Are we viewing each other as learning resources?
- ▶ Do we give an interpretation of what is said rather than an accurate response?
- ▶ Do we make and convey assumptions beyond what is said?
- ▶ What is the level of interest in listening to each other and to oneself?
- ▶ Are we open to new ways of doing things?
- ▶ Are new insights arising, and are people making connections with the diversity of questions and opinions being offered?

Action Strategies

An essential part of action learning groups is for them to take action and to learn from that action. Actions involve what occurs within the action learning sessions (problem reframing, establishing goals, developing strategies) as well as what occurs outside of the action learning sessions (testing, gaining support and resources, getting additional information, pilot testing, implementing strategies). Unless action is taken, the group can never be sure that its strategies and ideas are effective and that the members have, in fact, learned while they were working as a team.

"One must learn by doing the thing, for though you think you know it, you have no certainty until you try."

—Aristotle

Learning is significant only if we take some type of action as a result of that learning (thus the action learning axiom of "there is no real learning without action, just as there should be no action without learning"). Accordingly, one or more members of the action learning group must have the power to take action themselves or be assured that their recommendations will be implemented (barring any significant change in the environment or the group's lack of essential information).

Increasing the quality and scope of knowledge and learning is an inherent part of the action learning process. Organizations should make every effort to afford action learning teams the opportunities to learn from their strategizing, pilot testing, and implementing of plans. Action enhances individual and group learning because it provides a basis and anchor for additional questioning and reflection. As the group assesses and reflects on its actions both within and outside the group, it can determine its level of success and improve the group's knowledge as well as future actions. The learnings gained from the actions should be applied not only to the present problem, but to future tasks and challenges as well.

"To know something, but not to use it, is not knowing."

—Buddhist proverb

Approaches to Problem Solving

Groups and individuals may choose between two contrasting approaches to problem solving: *analytic/rationalistic* and *integrative*. Proponents of the *analytic/rationalistic* type of problem solving believe that there is one right solution to a problem. The group should develop a strategy based on a careful analysis of the situation and then determine in a logical fashion the causes of the problem and the solutions to it.

Advocates of the *integrative* approach, on the other hand, believe that there may be multiple right answers. Learning while taking action and

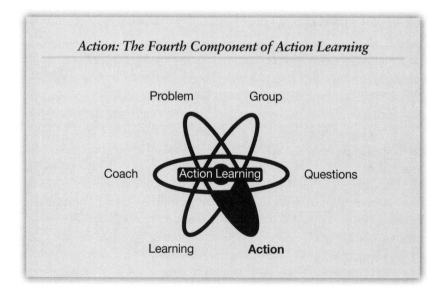

Action: The Fourth Component of Action Learning

Problem   Group

Coach   Action Learning   Questions

Learning   **Action**

acting out the thinking and learning are both equally important. Solving the problem is only part of the goal; learning from the opportunity is also a goal. The group attempts to collect a variety of insights in a holistic manner and to integrate the various possibilities. Intuition, open questions, and free associations are all tools of the integrative process of problem solving. Finding interrelationships between problems and solutions is valuable not only for this problem, but for future problems as well. Table 4 summarizes the differences in these two approaches.

Systems Thinking in Problem Solving

Effective and long-lasting problem solving and strategy setting must be built on the foundation and benefits of systems thinking. Systems thinking, in contrast to linear thinking, is based on a conceptual framework that allows us to see patterns and to discover how to effectively change those patterns. Based within the field of chaos theory, systems thinking focuses on seeing the whole picture (using holistic thinking). It provides a framework for seeing interrelationships rather than linear cause-effect chains, for noticing underlying structures rather than events, for discovering patterns of change rather than snapshots (Senge, 2006).

Systems thinking recognizes that what affects one part of an organization affects other parts in both planned and unplanned ways with sometimes

TABLE 4

Approaches to Problem Solving

Analytic/Linear	Integrative/Systems
One right solution	Multiple great solutions
Thinking is separate from action	Thinking requires/exists in action
Goal is to solve problems	Goal is great strategies and great learning
Clear problem definition—hypothesis and linear causality	Diffuse problem definition—issues and multiple causalities
Analysis of factions, reductionist; elimination of possibilities, specific questions; deterministic and sequential	Collecting insights, holistic; integration of possibilities; open questions; associative, intuitive; synchronistic
Objective: find the solution; quality of the answer	Objective: discovery of interrelationships; quality of understanding

surprising and unpredictable consequences. Thus, small, well-focused actions can produce significant, sustainable changes when these actions occur at the right time, in the right place, and with sufficient leverage (Gharajedaghi, 2005).

Whereas systems thinking is based on quantum physics, linear thinking is built on Newtonian physics. Linear thinking is much more mechanical, slow, and narrowly focused. Problems are treated as if the environment were predictable and cause and effect could be identified and isolated.

A key to action learning's power is its employment of systems thinking. Action learning acknowledges what scientists proved nearly a hundred years ago, namely, that Newtonian physics does not and cannot explain reality. Action learning recognizes that the old way of thinking and solving problems does not work, especially in today's rapidly changing environment. Action learning therefore utilizes quantum physics, chaos theory, and systems thinking.

Diverse group members who utilize reflective inquiry to work on complex problems are the perfect embodiment of a systems thinking approach to solving problems and developing powerful and positive action strategies. The questioning process and diverse perspectives create a natural systems way of responding to complexity. Asking layers of questions and reflecting on responses to those questions forces group members to think beyond symptoms to root causes, to explore a wide array of perspectives. As a result, action learning is much more holistic and comprehensive in its approach.

Quantum Physics and Action Learning

For nearly three centuries, the world and the workplace have been built on Newtonian physics— the physics of cause and effect, of predictability and certainty, of distinct wholes and parts, of reality being what is seen. Newtonian physics is a science of quantifiable determinism, of linear thinking and a controllable future—in sum, a world that does not change too fast or in unexpected ways. In the Newtonian mind-set, people engage in complex planning for a world that they believe is predictable. They continually search for better methods of objectively perceiving the world. This mechanistic and reductionist way of thinking and acting dominates our lives, even though it was disproved by Albert Einstein and others who introduced the scientific community to quantum physics in the 1920s. Margaret Wheatley (2006), author of *Leadership and the New Science*, notes that this old, disproved mind-set in today's world is "unempowering and disabling for all of us."

Quantum physics, on the other hand, deals with the world at the subatomic level, examining the intricate patterns out of which seemingly discrete events arise. Quantum physics recognizes that the universe and every object in it are, in reality, vast empty spaces that are filled with fields and movements that are the basic substance of the universe. Thus relationships between objects and between observers and objects determine reality. The quantum universe is an environment rich in relationships; it is a world of chaos, of process, and not just of objects and things. Quantum physics deals with waves and holograms, of surprises rather than predictions. With an understanding of quantum physics, organizations and teams realize that they cannot predict with certainty, that chaos is part and parcel of reality. The actuality of quantum physics requires us to change the way we think and the way we attempt to solve problems as well as the way we deal with order versus change, autonomy versus control, structure versus flexibility, planning versus flowing.

Clear and Compact Time Frame for Problem Solving

The problem or task assigned to the action learning group is one that should be real and urgent and thus require a clear time frame for the group. Since action learning groups face real time constraints, the opportunity to resolve the issue may exist for only a limited period. Action learning groups should therefore move quickly and judiciously to complete their work.

Depending on external forces as well as internal expectations, the decision or strategy might need to be initiated within a few hours or within a few months. The group therefore might meet only one time for thirty minutes or for three hours. If the target time is a week away and the problem is complex, the group may need to meet eight hours a day for a full week. On the other hand, if the decision point is not imminent (e.g., cut costs by 10 percent by the end of the fiscal year) or the decision and strategy are complex and involve many internal and external players, the group may be able to meet on a part-time basis over several months, perhaps once a week for a few hours. Thus, depending on the circumstances, action learning groups may meet either full time or part time, for a single session or for multiple sessions over several months.

Full-Time Versus Part-Time Programs

Meeting full time allows action learning groups to quickly respond to the problem or crisis assigned to them. They are less likely to be interrupted by other job responsibilities. Top management should seek ways to delay or delegate members' other commitments so that members can concentrate their energies and efforts on solving the problem and developing strategies. Two disadvantages of full-time action learning groups are that (a) there may be insufficient time between or during sessions to collect and confirm needed information, to create and/or maintain necessary support from within the organization, or to test the strategies; and (b) there may not be sufficient time or opportunity for individual members to apply their learnings or to see the personal growth in their leadership and professional competencies.

Part-time action learning groups, on the other hand, have somewhat contrasting benefits and disadvantages. The significant benefit of meeting on a part-time basis is that actions can be taken between sessions and progress can be reported. Difficulties and setbacks can be learned, and new strategies for tackling the problem can be developed. Also, reflections on learnings can occur over a longer period of time. Members will be better able to see the progress/changes in learnings and confidence occurring within themselves, the team, and/or the organization. The disadvantages of part-time groups include (a) membership or enthusiasm is lost over time, (b) the problem is not adequately reframed and resolved within the available time frame, and (c) the context has changed and the organization or individual no longer sees the issue as urgent.

Optimizing the Success of Action Learning at General Electric

To optimize the success of problem solving at General Electric, the following criteria are established for any action learning project.

1. Each action learning project needs to have consistent, high-level champions; otherwise, we will not work on it.

2. Each action learning group should have a real business problem or opportunity that is well-defined and scoped.

3. Quality planning time is critical to final outcome and success of each action learning group.

4. There must be a strong commitment for action learning from GE leaders and action learning members.

5. Follow-up is critical throughout the action learning project.

6. It is important to keep employees involved in implementation, and there must be an established process with checkpoints.

7. Leaders must ensure that employees have the support needed to implement the action plans.

8. We must ensure that there is no overlap or duplication with other ongoing work in the organization.
9. Sponsors should respond positively to the recommendations made by the action learning group unless they are illegal, unethical, or out of bounds, in which case the sponsors should modify the recommendations.
10. Before tasking the action learning group, there should be clear boundaries on what is open to change and what is not (financial, head count, technology enhancements, customers, etc.).
11. Top management should have a clear understanding and orientation on how action learning works.

Stages in Action Learning Problem Solving

In action learning, the group goes through four stages from the point of examining the problem to the final implementing of the strategies. The first two stages make up the diagnostic phase, during which the group is exploring questions about what needs to be accomplished, what is preventing the organization from achieving its objective, and how to overcome obstacles. The final two stages represent the strategy and implementation phases. The learning that occurs after each of the four stages, and how the tested and implemented actions can be applied to other parts of the organization, are discussed in Chapter 6.

Stage 1: Understanding and reframing the problem

Stage 2: Framing and formulating the goal

Stage 3: Developing and testing strategies

Stage 4: Taking action and reflecting on the action

"It is better to first put your finger on the problem before sticking your nose in it."

—Anonymous

Stage 1: Understanding and Reframing the Problem

Understanding the problem is the most important step in problem solving (what value is it to come up with great solutions to the wrong problem?), yet most individuals and groups rush into the search for the answers. This is a natural and normal impulse, as most people are uncomfortable with and do not like to spend too much time in ambiguity. As a result, most groups neglect the problem clarification stage and end up either disagreeing over solutions because they have internally diagnosed the problem differently or correctly solving a wrong or less important issue. Both can lead to disastrous results for the individual, team, and/or organization. Thus, it is important that we take time to get agreement on the problem; otherwise, we can never get true agreement on the solutions.

Action learning, through its clear insistence on questioning and gaining consensus on what the problem is, forces the group to spend important time on understanding the problem and its context and conditions. The coach does not allow the group to proceed to the problem solution and strategy development stages until the members have questioned the problem thoroughly and reached an agreement on the real, true problem.

In action learning, we recognize that the presenting problem may be neither the real problem nor the most important problem. Members must be open to this possibility. Block (2011) notes that the original problem is rarely the one that is most crucial, and therefore groups who merely accept the initial problem often end up solving a surface problem—one that is unimportant and, if solved, does not resolve the situation. The systems thinking and diverse perspectives approach used in action learning allows groups to thoroughly uncover the layers that surround or camouflage the true problem.

Action learning also recognizes that problems can be understood and agreed to as a group only through the questioning process. The initially presented problem inevitably contains assumptions, expectations, biases, symptoms, and limited perspectives on the part of both the presenter and the group members. Through questions and reflection, the individuals gradually join together in agreeing on the critical problem and related goal on which the group should spend its energies. Questioning rather than debating results in clear understandings and agreements, in enabling individuals to see the full problem in a similar way.

Experienced problem solvers recognize that in the process of clarifying the presenting problem and moving to the critical problem, we must diverge before we converge—we must see the whole forest (the big picture) before examining the individual trees. To properly explore the problem, we should examine possible causes and consequences to find the basic roots as well as the observable symptoms.

The ground rule "questions before statements" is critical at this stage of problem solving. Asking questions rather than immediately offering solutions unfreezes the group and defuses defensiveness on the part of the problem presenter. Understanding the problem is not solely the burden of the presenter, but is everybody's primary task. Questions help reveal the problem and give the group a systems perspective of both the content and context of the problem. When the problem is still unclear and nobody is ready with solutions, asking questions sparks new ideas and possible strategies. The seeds of potential solutions are unconsciously being sown. Thus, we are birthing solutions while we are inquiring about the problem. As the problem becomes more clearly defined, possible insights and solutions will naturally emerge.

As a result of the entire group questioning the problem as originally presented, the group gradually begins to reframe the problem. Reframing, according to Dilt (2006), helps people to reinterpret problems and find solutions by changing the frame in which the problems are being perceived. Reframing transforms the meaning of the problem by putting it into a new context. By observing a problem from different angles, we can thus reinterpret it. This is important in helping us solve the real problem, so that once it is solved, it can stay solved.

There are two types of approaches to reframing. The first—the *content* approach—changes the meaning of the way a person experiences a situation. Reframing the *context*, on the other hand, helps us to perceive and evaluate the same situation in a different way as we change the meaning of external stimuli.

The action learning coach is often quite active during the problem reframing stage. At the beginning of the session, or at the beginning of each person's problem presentation in multiple-problem sets, she will ask the problem presenter to take just a few minutes to describe the problem as he sees and feels it. Later on, before allowing the group to move to setting goals and developing strategies, the coach will check to see if everyone agrees on what is the real problem. She does this by asking each person to write down what he or she believes the problem to be. Members are then asked to state the problem as they understand it, with the problem presenter being the last person to speak. If the group believes there is agreement, they can then move on to the next stage; if not, they continue working on identifying and reframing the problem until consensus has been reached.

The problem presenter's perspective on the problem is not necessarily any better than group members who are hearing the problem for the first time. As a matter of fact, it is oftentimes the problem presenter who least understands the real problem as he is so immersed in the muddy details that it is hard for him to get a clear, clean view.

Also, it is important to note that the organization and/or problem presenter should authorize and empower the action learning group to be able to redefine the problem after a systematic examination of it. Consequently, the group members have the responsibility to solve the real and most critical problem rather than merely and meekly accepting the problem initially presented to them.

Using Action Learning to Fund and Develop Training Programs for Public School Principals

Eight staff members of Fairfax County Public Schools (FCPS), including some principals, teachers, and HR staff, had only two hours to meet and to develop a long-term training program for principals and assistant principals. Despite the impatience of some members during the initial stages of the action learning session, the group persisted and kept focusing on determining the real problem and the real goals. It took more than sixty minutes to reach an agreement about the true problem and the most important goals. But in the final thirty minutes, the group identified four strategies they all agreed to, and developed the outlines of a project that ultimately led to a five-million-dollar grant from the Reader's Digest Foundation for leadership development in FCPS.

Stage 2: Framing and Formulating the Goal

After the group has reached consensus on the problem, it should determine the goal, that is, what the group, the organization, or the individual is striving to achieve (although some action learning groups are given the goal, and thus their initial efforts are to go back to what may be the obstacles that prevent the organization or individual from achieving that goal).

Freedman (2011) refers to the goal as the desired state versus the problem, which is the current state. It should be noted that if the problem is different from what it was originally thought to be, then the target goal or objectives to solve that problem will be different from what was originally expected.

With the confidence gained from determining and reaching consensus on the problem, the group is ready to move from the reframed problem to the desired or possible goal(s). Remaining focused on the problem will not get the organization where it needs to go. The problem is what provides urgency for the group, but it can ultimately generate negative and dissipating energy unless or until the group begins to focus on the desired future, which creates positive energy (Cooperrider, Sorensen, and Yaeger, 2001).

Framing the goal causes the group to shift in three ways: from a problem frame to an outcome frame, from an "it is impossible" frame to an as-if frame, and from a failure frame to a feedback frame. When we move to the goal statement, we move from what is wrong to what we want, from what caused it to what resources we have, from what is too expensive to what is affordable, from "what a waste of time" to "how can we use available resources wisely," from a feeling that our ideas will never work to looking at how we can implement our ideas, and from an unrealistic plan to how we can make the plan more tangible and concrete.

The group should be courageous in selecting a goal it believes is most strategic, has the most staying power, and will solve the real problem with best-to-leverage results. If the group simply accepts the given problem or task (sometimes we mistakenly do so even when top leadership is expecting us to utilize the time, wisdom, and perspectives of the group), it ends up providing a disservice to the organization by not identifying the needed long-term goal. Likewise, there is a disservice to the group members themselves because they have missed an opportunity to examine the true issue and goal in its depth, and learn from it.

Goals Should Be High Level and SMART

Oftentimes the organization may give the group a modest, not-so-much-above-the-current-status goal, or the group may establish a similar low-level objective. These types of goals are not very challenging and do not test the ability of the group to achieve quantum levels of improvement to the current status. Low-level goals do not lead to long-term sustainability, and they often create unintended problems in other parts of the system.

High-level goals, on the other hand, are inspiring and challenging. They positively impact more parts of the entire system. High-level goals expand the possibilities for ideas and actions. They enlarge the creative space and elevate the thinking of the group beyond obvious, linear first answers. High-level goals generate a greater focus on the future, and thereby create more energy and a longer-range mindset.

An example of a low-level and high-level goal that demonstrate the differences in strategies and results would be the goal chosen by a teacher in an elementary school classroom. Say a fourth-grade teacher has a poor-performing, disruptive student in her classroom, and she decides that her goal will be to change this student into a higher-performing, better-behaved student. She considers a number of strategies, such as spending more time with this student and his parents, rewarding this student for modest improvements, establishing tougher discipline in the classroom, and so on. In a few months, she is pleased that she has met her goal of improving the academic and behavioral level of this student. But what else has probably happened? The other students in the classroom have become upset, even angered, by the fact that poor grades and behavior is getting more attention than good grades and behavior. They may resist the new rules that curtail their freedom and fun. They may complain to their parents, who bombard the teacher with how their child is complaining about the classroom learning.

Now what if the teacher instead establishes a high-level goal, such as "making the classroom a great learning environment for all of my students." This is a much more inspiring goal, creates many more resources (such as the students helping each other), encourages new teaching methodologies, and so on. And the long-term impact will extend positively outside of the classroom and into the other parts of the students' and the teacher's lives.

Thus are the power and benefits of high-level goals. Action learning groups, when moving to the goal stage, should be asking questions about what the ideal future would look like, what great success would be like, and so on. These are the great questions. Remember, in action learning, we do not need the answers immediately because we know that great questions will always lead to great ideas, learnings, and actions.

Also, it is important to recognize that the best and final goal may not be clearly and fully defined at this stage. It may become more refined as the action learning group works on strategies or reconsiders the problems and obstacles—this is what problem solving is all about in a system, unlike the linear approach of moving directly in a straight line from problem to goal to strategy to action.

When more final goals are set, the group should try to establish goals that are "SMART," that is, specific, measurable, achievable, realistic, and time bounded. We should also seek goals that are exciting and meaningful to the group and to the organization. As the group develops and agrees on such types of goals, the creativity and cohesiveness of the group will ever grow stronger.

"Without power to discard beliefs shown to be wrong, one cannot intro-duce actions known to be right."

—Reg Revans

A $36 Million Action Learning Solution for Downer Group in Australia

Downer Group is a market-leading supplier of services to the infrastructure, mining, metals, and energy sectors in New Zealand, Australia, the Asia-Pacific region, and the United Kingdom. With over 10,000 employees worldwide, Downer provides a comprehensive range of services to its clients across the whole life cycle of their physical infrastructure assets, from "front end" consulting and design through to the creation, operation, maintenance, upgrade/expansion, and final decommissioning.

An action learning project was built around the issue of fuel burn before and after road haul improvement at one of the company's sites. Low fuel burn could be caused by poor road haul conditions or the dump trucks not reaching their maximum speed or low payloads. Upon analysis by the action learning group, it was discovered that trucks were not carrying maximum loose material density weight. However, it was also evident that truck trays were not capable of carrying more load material since it was already falling out of the back and side of the truck trays. More questioning and reflection revealed that by altering the angle of repose (the angle the material can reach before it rolls down or spreads out) and creating larger sides to the trucks, the average loose cubic meter tonnage per truck could be increased significantly. This was a major breakthrough for the action learning project.

Consequently, a Road Analysis Control (RAC) system was established, which measures haul road improvement and efficiencies, and tells the digger operators instantly how much weight each load is carrying, thus ensuring the maximum payload is reached on each truckload. This allowed the payload per truck to be increased significantly, and the total loading costs decreased accordingly. Payload could be improved by 13 percent per payload, which, when extrapolated across Downer's various mining projects, has resulted in higher payloads per truck and a greater return on investment. The benefit to Downer—calculated to be over $36 million and growing!

Stage 3: Developing and Testing Strategies

During this stage, the action learning group develops both strategic (what things to do) and tactical (how to do it) strategies. Gaining consensus on strategies is much easier if the group has reached agreement on the problem and the goal during stages 1 and 2.

In stage 2, we identified the goal, that is, what we wanted or needed to do. During stage 3 the group becomes more specific and begins exploring questions such as, What will probably work best and why? What resources will we need? What will be the impact of this action? Revans (1983) describes this stage of action learning as the point at which no one knows the right answer, but all are obliged to find it.

In forming an action plan, there are two distinct areas of concern: Is the action appropriate to the problem? Is the action doable in the time available? Strategies will simply not get implemented if they are not appropriate or doable. They also will not get implemented if we do not identify the people "who know what we need to know, who can get it implemented, and who care about getting it done." In other words, who are the people who have the information and possible insights to ensure that the best steps are being taken; who have the power to ensure that agreed-upon strategies are in fact implemented; and who have the passion and commitment to follow up on the strategies that have been developed? These are the people who know, who care, and who can. These are the folks who are critical in implementing and supporting the strategies developed by the group. If the group's plan is not appropriate and doable, the plan will forever remain a plan.

In examining the strategies, the group should identify the obstacles preventing the individual, team, or organization from achieving its goal(s). The group considers which obstacles are most critical, and which, if overcome, will provide the greatest benefit and leverage. Which ones are changeable and which ones can be left alone? It is important that they be examined in a systems-oriented manner.

Many groups use brainstorming to identify a variety of options for resources and application. This approach, however, is built on the Newtonian way of strategizing. It usually results in a long list of possibilities, most of which are totally impractical or absurd, result in a lot of busy work, and require a considerable amount of time just to painstakingly examine and discard. On the other hand, the action learning approach of developing strategies by building on each other's questions is based on chaos theory and systems thinking. This approach is more robust, is less time consuming, and systematically starts with good to great possibilities and moves to great and greater strategies, strategies that are built on understanding the complexity within the chaos and examining both the content and the context of the problem.

Another dynamic that occurs frequently as groups seek to solve problems is the tendency of various individuals to provide anecdotes and examples of their experiences and successes or failures. In action learning, we seek to move people from anecdotal to analytical communications for two reasons: the anecdotal approach slows down the group, and it puts attention on the person with the story rather than on the problem.

Often more than one strategy will need to be developed and then tested. Multiple alternatives will increase the possibilities of better actions and results. As the various alternatives are considered, the action learning group should carefully examine issues such as how realistic and cost-effective each alternative may be, what new problems are created by the alternative, and which ones have the most passion, power, and knowledge to lead to a successful, strategic result.

Most problem-solving groups tend to use what Revans called *programmed knowledge* (the knowledge they brought with them into the group) as they begin considering and developing action strategies. Programmed knowledge is often embedded in the past and is therefore not likely to match precisely the unique needs of the new problem or situation. The action learning process, however, immediately builds on the programmed knowledge of each member with the new knowledge and skills created by the questions within the group. This creative new knowledge is what enables action learning groups to be more successful in developing innovative, high-impact strategies that respond specifically and strategically to the problem being addressed.

Plans and strategies, whenever possible, should be tested to determine their impact and effectiveness. Strategies should be selected that provide optimum leverage at the least cost to the individual, group, or organization. If systems thinking is applied, small, well-focused actions result in significant, enduring improvements (e.g., adjusting the direction of a space shuttle by a few millimeters before liftoff causes more directional change than an adjustment thousands of miles in space).

High-leverage changes, however, are often not obvious to individuals within the environment in which they are operating. Thus we tend to choose strategies that are closer to us in time and space. Testing strategies within the action learning group or between sessions allows for final opportunities to adapt or develop new plans at subsequent sessions.

Pilot actions will enable the group to gain greater assurance of ultimate success in the actions taken as well as provide higher levels of learning. Of course, there will be occasional risks in action learning, but they are prudent risks because they are taken with much more information about the possible consequences of the action. Action learning holds that the most significant learning occurs when members reflect on the results of their actions and not just on their planning. In action learning, we recognize that actions are also learning opportunities. Only by testing their ideas in practice will members know whether the proposed strategies are effective and practical, whether any issues have been overlooked, what questions should have been asked, and what they can learn and apply to this and other projects and activities.

Action Learning Successes at an Elementary School

JAN FUNK, PRINCIPAL

Action learning has served as a wonderful vehicle to assist the staff at William Halley Elementary School in solving a number of important problems. One major concern related to improving SOL test scores, which is necessary to ensure state accreditation. Over a four-month period, the staff met in vertical teams (teams that included teachers and staff) to determine what was going well and where change needed to occur in order to raise test scores. From this continuous dialogue, eight learning teams were created to research a variety of programs, models, and strategies. At the end of the year, each team shared the outcomes of its research with the entire staff, and we selected the following two challenges as being most critical and strategic.

► Fragmentation. In grades five and six, fragmentation, or "time to teach," was a major issue. With all of the pull-out programs—band, strings, chorus, gifted/talented, peer mediation, patrols, and SCA—there were few blocks of teaching time during which the entire class was present. Classroom management took a significant amount of time from instruction. Two action learning teams were created to determine how to resolve these concerns. Volunteers met during the summer to puzzle over the creation of a schedule to reduce fragmentation. After several days and sessions, a block schedule emerged that now gives the teachers more than four hours of uninterrupted teaching time.

► Positive classroom behavior. Another action learning team tackled the concern of maintaining positive classroom behavior. With the help of a grant from Johns Hopkins University, the action learning team developed a schoolwide Positive Discipline Program. This program provides teachers with strategies and techniques that are unified throughout the school. A Behavior Support Team works with teachers who need additional assistance with difficult students. Students and parents were made aware of the program through a handbook designed by the team. As a result of this action learning project, discipline referrals have been tremendously reduced.

At Halley Elementary, not only did action learning successfully address two major concerns, but also teacher leaders began to emerge, and everyone felt part of a culture of learners. Teacher fulfillment as well as SOL scores improved, and Halley enjoys recognition as one of the top elementary schools in the State of Virginia.

Stage 4: Taking Action and Reflecting on the Action

Taking action is an important element of any action learning group's work. Although some groups may be tasked with just developing recommendations that will be presented to the corporate sponsor at the end of their work, they still will be taking actions between each and every action learning session, as well as making decisions (that is, taking action) during every action learning session. If the individuals (in multiple-problem sets) or the group members (in single-problem programs) do not take action between sessions, the group may feel that the problem is not urgent and that they are wasting their time. At subsequent sessions, the group will be less enthusiastic when working on the problem and less creative in developing action strategies.

Action after every session is important, for if the group does not regularly take actions, the result will be diminished commitment as well as diminished learning. Revans (1983) notes that just as one cannot learn how to serve a tennis ball unless he hits it, an individual or group cannot learn unless there is the opportunity to implement. Thus, at the end of each session, the group agrees to take concrete, specific actions. The steps developed include the specifics of who, what, where, and when, as well as the measurable, the visible, and the worthwhile. These actions should be recorded and then referred to at the beginning of the subsequent session of the action learning group.

The strategies must take into account the overall impact of the various alternatives being considered so that the actions do not create greater problems. This is why action learning groups should consider the option of pilot testing possible strategies to study the effects of those strategies and to learn from them. Throughout the problem reframing and strategy developing, the group examines and taps potential sources of power, passion, and knowledge so that the plan, when fully completed, will be implemented, rather than remain a great idea only. Outside company resources and links may need to be identified as well.

To ensure that the individual or group will develop actions before the end of the session, the coach reminds the group how much more time they have to work before he will ask the individual or the group what actions they will be taking. If the coach senses that the group may be running out of time, she will remind the group of the necessity of generating action before concluding the session. It is important that every session ends with specific actions decided on and agreed to. Otherwise, the group will not be able to act or to learn from those actions between sessions. Lost opportunities for learnings will occur, and subsequent improvements will not occur if there are no actions.

Building Open Government with Action Learning

U.S. government agencies were recently requested to develop strategies on how to become more open, to be more "transparent, participatory, and collaborative, ... to become better at sharing data and information, hearing and implementing ideas, and engaging in ongoing conversation with employees and the public." An action learning group established at the Office of Personnel Management (OPM) quickly developed a comprehensive strategy that was ultimately ranked in the top five by non-government stakeholders. The plan received a White House Leading Practice Award as well. Mary Volz Peacock, a member of the OPM action learning group, notes that another great result was that OPM began collaborating immediately through action learning—both across the agency and with external stakeholders—rather than just "planning" to collaborate.

Systems and Tools for Solving Problems and Developing Strategies

The context for problem solving in action learning, according to Revans (1982a), involves what he refers to as *Systems Alpha, Beta,* and *Gamma.*

- ▶ *System Alpha* is analogous to situation analysis. Group members need to understand the system within which the problem resides. They must be involved in examining the nature of the value systems, both the external system that affects the decisions being made and the internal system in which the manager works.

▶ *System Beta* refers to the negotiation and implementation of a solution and involves (a) survey, (b) hypothesis, (c) experiment, (d) audit, and (e) review. This system is equated to learning systems of recognition, prima facie acceptance, rehearsal, verification, and conviction.

▶ *System Gamma* refers to the mental predisposition that the individual, group, or organization brings to the situation. Individuals and groups must continually check their expectations of what should be happening against what is actually happening. Insofar as they are able to identify the discrepancies between what they first took to be the condition and what experience suggests the condition actually was, and insofar as they are able to change this perception accordingly, we may say that they are learning.

Although action learning does not encourage a profusion of problem-solving tools, there certainly are occasions when they should be utilized. Such tools could include rational analysis, audit methods, double-Q diagrams, Pareto charts, force field analysis, and mind mapping.

Cutting the Costs of Moving at a Malaysian Business College

A budget of $100,000 had been established to move all the equipment and other furnishings from the current site to new buildings across the city of Kuala Lumpur. An action learning group composed of teachers, students, and administrative personnel explored a variety of options and eventually decided that much of the moving could be done by themselves. A careful, item-by-item plan was developed. Over a weekend, the entire move was completed for less than $20,000, in a shorter period of time, and with new cross-functional teams and greater collegiality among all the people of the college.

Distribution of Time in the Four Stages of Action Learning

Every action learning group and every problem has its own unique dynamics and flow, complexity, and challenge. Thus, the amount of time and energy devoted to each of the stages will vary. Normally, especially when the group is first formed, stages 1 and 2—reframing the problem and framing the goal—will consume much of the first meeting. The group naturally needs to gather information and seek clarification of the problem before it can begin searching for the most powerful purpose. At subsequent meetings the group may need to spend only a few minutes to reconfirm the problem and goal, mainly to check that no new forces or circumstances have altered the situation, thereby creating new and different problems, which may then necessitate changes in the goal. Generally, the bulk of time at subsequent meetings will be spent working on stage 3, namely, the development of strategies.

Many problem-solving groups follow these same four stages. Action learning groups, however, devote more effort and time in stage 1 than other groups might. In action learning, we recognize that if we can first agree on the problem, then it is much easier to agree on solutions. For example, if a group has a total of sixty minutes to work on the first three stages, up to forty-five minutes may be devoted to gaining consensus as to what the real problem is.

Typically, groups are rushed into developing strategies (stage 3) and may spend forty-five minutes (or hours) advocating a strategy based on members' understanding of the problem. But if everyone understands the problem in a slightly different way, it is difficult, if not impossible, to get agreement on the goal, much less on the strategies to achieve that goal. Whereas, if there is agreement on the problem, then agreement on strategies becomes easier and less painful.

Questions During the Problem Solving Process

All types of questions (see chapter 4) are asked throughout the four stages of problem reframing, goal clarification, strategy development, and action implementation. However, as can be seen in figure 2, certain types of questions occur more frequently and naturally during each of the stages. For example, during stages 1 and 3, when the group is attempting to identify the real problem and when the group is beginning to identify possible great strategies, the question will be more divergent and tend to be less judging and more open-ended, imaginative, creative, and intuitive. In stage 2, the later phases of stage 3, and in stage 4, the questions will become more convergent, require more judging, and be more analytical and closed-ended.

Successes at Oxford University Press

Action learning projects have resulted in a number of important and valuable changes in operations at Oxford University Press, including a reduction in information contract costs, a better use of security, an improvement of journal dispatch turnaround, and a reduction in printer maintenance, all of which were implemented within the six-month time frame of the action learning project.

FIGURE 2
Questions in the Problem Solving Process

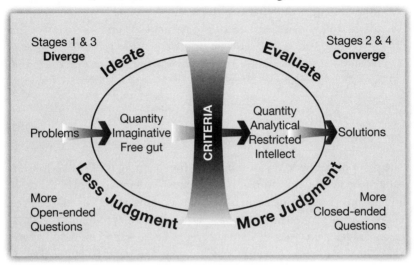

An Action Framework for Action Learning

Smith (2001) has developed a framework to assist action learning teams to systematically and carefully plan action strategies. He proposes that performance systems in action learning be based on three elements—*focus, will,* and *capability.* The resulting performance level achieved by the systems depends on the interactions and interdependencies of these elements. *Focus* represents a clear understanding of the problem and the performance proposed. Focus deals with the question "What are we trying to accomplish?" as well as information-gathering questions that ask what, how, who, where, when, and why. *Will* represents the strength of intent to take action on the performance determined in focus. It is associated with attitudes, emotions, beliefs, and mind-sets, the "Who cares?" question. *Capability* represents the wherewithal to transform into reality the performance defined in the focus. Capability is associated with resources such as skills, infrastructure, budgets, tools, and physical assets. In exemplifying this action learning model, Smith provides the following two examples.

- ▶ At an organizational level, *focus* might represent the firm's strategic plans to enter a market; *will* would reflect the organization's cultural potential to support the new initiative, and *capability* would relate to the firm's asset position on entering that market.

► In marketing, *focus* might represent dividing up a sales territory; *will* would be associated with how the participants and members of the sales organization at large would feel about the proposed new segmentation; and *capability* would address the skill requirement and infrastructure required for the newly segmented sales force to function adequately.

The Power of Action in Action Learning

The proof of the pudding for users of action learning is the quality of the solutions generated by action learning groups. As demonstrated by the cases and endorsements throughout this book, action learning has indeed produced innovative strategies that have saved companies millions of dollars, expanded global markets, developed new products and processes, and solved complex management issues. From Chicago to Cairo and from Bangkok to Boston, action learning has provided amazing results for organizations such as Unilever, British Airways, Boeing, Caterpillar, Novartis, DuPont, Nokia, the Canadian Royal Mounted Police, and the U.S. Army. The power of action learning will continue to generate successes as more companies employ the dynamics and elements of the four stages of action learning.

Checklist for Problem Reframing, Goal Formulation, Strategy Development, and Action Taking

Problem reframing

► What is the quality of the problem solving?

► Has the problem been reframed?

► Is it a technical or adaptive problem?

► Did we ask fresh questions?

► Is the presenting problem the real problem or only a symptom of the problem?

► Have we identified the true problem?

► What is the level of commitment to solving the problem?

Goal formulation

- ► Will achieving this goal or objective solve the real problem?
- ► Will this goal keep the problem solved?
- ► What is the leverage gained and impact achieved by this goal?
- ► Will the goal stretch the individual, team, and/or organization?
- ► Does the goal complement and support other goals of the organization?

Strategy development

- ► Have the obstacles been identified?
- ► Are we being creative, practicing innovation, and thinking outside-the-box?
- ► Are we committed to innovative, high-quality solutions and strategies rather than quick solutions?
- ► Have we tapped the sources of power, passion, and knowledge?
- ► Have outside resources and links that may be needed been identified?
- ► Have the impact and consequences of the strategies been carefully considered?
- ► Are these the best-leveraged and most strategic possibilities?

Action taking

- ► Are actions to be taken a part of each meeting?
- ► Are the actions clear as to who, what, and when?
- ► Are they recorded and then reviewed at the next meeting?
- ► Are the strategies being tested and implemented?
- ► How do we handle situations when members do not carry out actions agreed to?
- ► Have we gained learnings from actions taken?

Individual, Team, and Organizational Learning

Organizations and leaders around the world now recognize that learning is their most important competency and that knowledge is their most valuable asset in this competitive and unpredictable global environment in which complex problems need to be solved with new leadership and team skills. Thus programs and means that can create knowledge and encourage rapid, relevant, and critical learnings will appeal to any company that is concerned about both its short-term survival and long-term success.

The power and attractiveness of action learning lie in action learning's ability to increase and expand the knowledge of an organization at the same time that it is solving critical, urgent, and complex problems. Solving problems provides immediate short-term benefits to an organization, team, or individual (and is important in getting organizational buy-in for setting up company-based action learning programs), but the greater, long-term value of action learning to the company is the application of new learnings on a systemwide basis—throughout the organization and in the professional lives of the participants.

Dilworth (1998) notes that the learning that occurs in action learning has greater strategic value for the organization than the immediate tactical advantage of solving a problem. In action learning, we recognize that learning is ultimately much more valuable than solving the problem itself; for example, solving a particular reengineering problem may be worth $1 million; applying that knowledge throughout the organization may be worth $10 million. Then applying the new leadership and team skills developed in the action learning program by the group members may be worth $100 million as each person applies the new skills over the course of his or her career with the organization. The collective application of the developed competencies in one organization thus has a multiplying and leveraging impact that can transform the company and enable it to make quantum leaps with its powerful competitive advantage. Accordingly, learning as an individual, as a group, and as an organization leverages tremendous, value-laden knowledge throughout the enterprise.

Action learning creates a special, valuable kind of knowledge and learning. The degree and quality of learning are not unexpected, because they develop via real people working with each other on real problems, searching for knowledge that will effect positive change. Learning is emphasized continuously in the action learning process, since it is the increased learning of the team that ultimately makes it more effective in problem solving and decision making.

"In times of change, the learners will inherit the world while the knowers will remain well-prepared for a world that no longer exists."

—Eric Hoffer

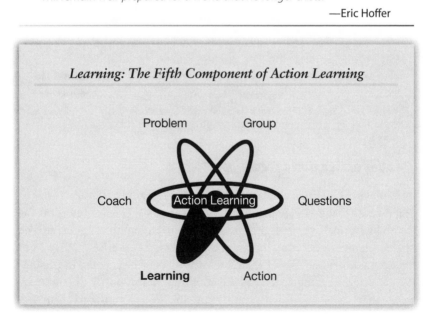

Learning: The Fifth Component of Action Learning

Problem Group

Coach Action Learning Questions

Learning Action

Responsibility and Benefits of Learning

Because of the value of learning, members in action learning groups are advised at the very first session that their learning will be as important to the group and to the organization as solving the problem. If they become smarter as individuals and as a team, they will become capable of achieving breakthrough thinking and groundbreaking solutions. Thus, as a critical part of membership in the action learning program, individuals accept responsibility for their own, the group's, and the organization's learning. The group is informed that time will be set aside specifically for learning, and a person (the coach) will carve out and manage these times for learning.

Dilworth (1998), one of the early pioneers in action learning, frequently emphasized the importance of learning for building long-term capabilities. He wrote, "Fresh thinking and new learning are needed if we are to avoid responding to today's problems with yesterday's solutions while tomorrow's challenges engulf us" (p. 35).

"We had the experience, but missed the meaning."

—T. S. Eliot

Speeding Work and Learning at Siemens

PETER PRIBILLA, HEAD OF CORPORATE HUMAN RESOURCES

The speed at which a corporation can learn and employ new knowledge is a decisive factor in corporate success. It is not enough to learn and to work. Learning and work must be integrated. Action learning addresses this challenge very efficiently.

Creating and Capturing Learning

A number of conditions and circumstances are created in the action learning process that generate high levels of learning. Of greatest impact is the carefully planned, created, and sustained environment that is generated by the six elements of action learning, especially the reflective inquiry from group members and from the action learning coach. As noted in Chapter 1, the action learning coach has the authority and responsibility to intervene whenever she senses an opportunity for the group to learn. Through a series of reflective questions (as noted in greater detail in Chapter 7), she guides the group in its learning process. The coach enables group members to become more conscious of and competent in several areas: gaining new knowledge and information; reasoning differently; behaving more effectively in groups; gaining greater understanding of their motives; altering beliefs, values, and basic assumptions; becoming creative; sensing systems; and learning how to learn.

The coach provides a safe environment or "practice field" in which reflecting and learning can occur. Within the group, it is safe to be vulnerable, to learn, and to take risks. Failures within the group or in solving a problem are seen as wonderful opportunities to learn rather than events that must be hidden or ignored. Members are encouraged to recognize the potential of all situations to provide learning opportunities. Individuals are provided the time to reflect on their effectiveness and helpfulness to the group. Problems and crises become valuable occasions for learning and development.

Since individuals in the group know they are there to learn as well as to solve the problem, there is an expectant mood and a disposition to learn. Learning is rewarded through recognition and improved skills. Members are expected to contribute to each other's learning. The urgent and important problem serves as an energizing impetus to build our learning capabilities.

The questioning process creates the physiological and psychological conditions for learning and thus augments learning opportunities. In addition, the requirement for the group to take action forces members to test their ideas and theories in reality. Since everyone is expected and encouraged to learn, the group environment is conducive to change and growth. As Sandelands (1998) observes, learning is synergistically effective with a group of colleagues who are responsible together.

Action learning encourages self-critical reflection and feedback from frank and honest fellow group members. Group learning is generated as members discuss, share, and pool their ambitions and experiences, thus creating a gestalt in which the benefits of group synergy can be reaped (Smith, 2001).

How Action Learning Generates Continuous Reflection and Learning

Learning is continuous and pervasive in action learning—it takes place throughout the whole action learning process. Opportunities to question,

Cycles of Learning

FIGURE 3
Kolb Learning Model, Level 1

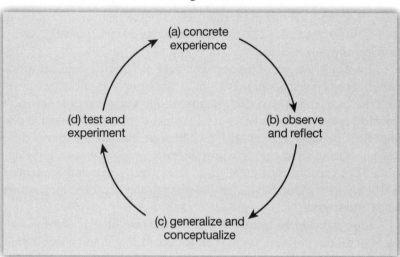

FIGURE 4
Internal Action Learning Model, Level 2

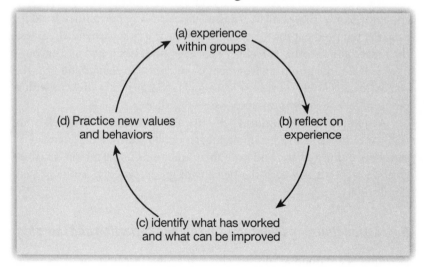

reflect, and learn occur during each of the stages described by Kolb (1984), both as the group works on the problem (figure 3) and while the group reflects on its interactions and activities (figure 4). In action learning, we create knowledge through concrete experience, observing and reflecting on this experience, forming generalizations from experiences, and testing the implications of those generalizations in new experiences. Let's examine the learning at each of the four stages and at each of the two levels.

Concrete Experience

Level 1: The concrete experience of the group is the problem or task that the group must resolve. One or all of the members may have actually been working on the problem before joining the group. The problem has become urgent and important to them as the organization (or individual in a multiple-problem set) is depending on the group to develop a strategy to overcome the problem.

Level 2: All of the members create a new, real group experience as they jointly reframe the problem, frame the goals, develop strategies, and take action. The group, in a sense, returns to this stage after it has taken actions and thereby generated additional shared concrete experiences.

Observe and Reflect

Level 1: Through the reflective inquiry process, group members examine their problem-solving and action strategies to begin assessing their degree of success.

Level 2: The learning coach asks the group to reflect on the quality of their decision making, group interaction skills, and individual learnings. New individual and team competencies are developed based on self-reflection and the perspectives offered by members of the group.

Generalize and Conceptualize

Level 1: At this stage the group determines if and how it can apply the proposed strategies and actions to other similar and dissimilar situations in the organization or in members' personal lives.

Level 2: The group identifies norms, principles, and strategies that will make it a better group as it works on this or future problems. In addition, individuals examine how these concepts may apply to other situations in their lives, to see if there might be what Mezirow (1991) describes as "transformative learning experiences."

Test and Experiment

Level 1: The group pilot tests its strategies to see how effectively they will resolve the problem. The group also may test the implications of its newly developed concepts in other contexts as well as discuss whether the new theories might work in future situations.

Level 2: The group reflects, with the help of the action learning coach, on whether its new and modified behaviors and values will enhance the groups' capabilities if it works on additional problems.

Types of Knowledge Created by Action Learning

In its efforts to generate as much knowledge as is needed to solve the current and future problems, the action learning group seeks to create and/or capture the following types of knowledge.

► *Know what:* identifying what knowledge is needed
► *Know how:* learning how the knowledge must be processed
► *Know why:* determining why specific information is needed
► *Know where:* knowing where to find needed information
► *Know when:* identifying the times when certain information is needed

All of these types of knowledge are gathered, selected, and then applied in a systemic and system-oriented manner at appropriate stages of the action learning process.

Tacit Versus Explicit Knowledge

Many organizations fail to tap the rich knowledge base or intellectual capital present in the brains of their own employees—what Nonaka (1994) calls "tacit knowledge" in contrast to "explicit knowledge," which already exists outside the internal knowledge of an individual.

Sources of tacit knowledge include an individual's expertise, memories, beliefs, and insights. This kind of knowledge is usually difficult to communicate or explain and, as a result, is used only by the individual; thus, its potential benefits to the organization are minimal. Action learning, however, through the reflective inquiry process, the focus on both action and learning, and the questioning approach of the coach converts this tacit knowledge to explicit knowledge so that it becomes available for the team and ultimately for the organization to utilize, resulting in tremendous new assets and capabilities for both.

Programmed Knowledge and Group-Created Knowledge

In addition to converting tacit knowledge into explicit knowledge, the action learning process interweaves the knowledge that each individual brings into the group (tacit or explicit) with the new knowledge created by the group as it reframes the problem, develops strategies, and takes action. The knowledge brought into the group (also referred to as *programmed knowledge*, or *P*, in action learning) is combined with *questions* (*Q*), which generates new knowledge. The *continuous reflection* (*R*) results in further and deeper learning and wisdom; thus the formula to show how learning and knowledge is created in action learning, $L = P + Q + R$.

Action learning elicits relevant information from group members and the context, rather than merely disseminating what a trainer or teacher thinks is important. Knowledge is likewise tapped at the points where it is needed. Experience itself, as we know, is a very slippery teacher. Most of the time we have experiences from which we never learn. Experience combined with group reflection, however, enables the group to throw a net around experiences and capture slippery but critical knowledge and learning (Smith, 2001).

Competencies Developed in Action Learning

The remarkable power of action learning is demonstrated by its ability to simultaneously develop learning and skills at the individual level (both for each individual's professional development and for the leader), at the group level, and at the organizational level. Action learning thus can help individuals to improve their lives; groups to better implement their functions; and organizations to leverage that knowledge, with increased staff, leader, and group competencies, to better achieve companywide success.

Action Learning to Develop Great Leaders at Microsoft

Over the past three years, hundreds of Microsoft managers from around the world have participated in action learning projects as part of their leadership development program. Microsoft uses both single-problem action learning and multiple-problem action learning (called Action Learning Circles) in developing their high-potential leaders. Large-scale action learning programs for leadership development have been held recently in sites such as Dubai, New York, Lima, Nairobi, and Paris. Shannon Banks, who developed and coordinated the programs, comments, "Microsoft has seen great value from action learning because it allows members to practice and develop leadership competencies, work together as high-potential teams, and learn to ask great questions as leaders, all while working on real, urgent business problems."

Leadership Development and Action Learning

A remarkable aspect of action learning is that every leadership skill can be practiced and improved. In this situation, a group of people are working on a problem for which there is no known solution. As they work together, everyone is equally capable of identifying the potential solution; this is what occurs in the action learning process.

Because every leadership skill can be developed deeply and quickly in action learning, more and more organizations around the world use action learning for the purpose of developing their leaders. Recent surveys by the American Society for Training and Development (ASTD) revealed that nearly 70 percent of organizations use action learning as part of their leadership development program. Since developing the leadership capabilities of each group member is critical not only for the long-term benefit of the organization, but also to better enable the group to become smarter and work better together, it is highly advised that leadership development be a formal and integral part of all action learning programs.

A powerful way to build leadership development into every action learning session is to have the action learning coach, at the beginning of each session, ask each member to identify the leadership skill that he or she would like to practice and demonstrate during the session. These skills are written on a flip chart. At the end of the session, the coach asks each person to summarize how he or she did on the chosen leadership skill and to provide some examples. She then asks if any of the other group members have additional examples of how this person demonstrated the skill.

This leadership activity within the action learning process has multiple benefits to the individual and the action learning group:

▶ Leadership skills are quickly and deeply developed since all four elements of skill building are occurring: namely, (a) importance of the skill to the person, (b) opportunity to practice the skill, (c) feedback from others experiencing and perceiving the skill, and (d) self-reflection on how well one has done on the leadership skill.

▶ It levels the differences among members relative to power and experience; everyone is acknowledging that they are not perfect and need to improve; anyone from any level can offer specific examples of how others have done; arrogance or superiority that one might normally exhibit is subtlely lessened or even eliminated.

▶ It provides an opportunity to say nice, positive things about each other, and thus build cohesiveness, trust, and good feelings toward each other.

Mintzberg (2011) noted that reflecting on your own experiences is a much more powerful tool than reflecting on someone else's experiences (as is done with case studies). Mumford (1995) states that the most effective way to gain insight into one's leadership style is to be placed under pressure in an unstructured, ill-defined, timed situation. Adding reflective inquiry and shared learning further accentuates the opportunities for increasing the awareness of and competency in leadership.

Action learning is built on a framework designed to capture and build on what exists in the real world rather than in the pure, detached, analytical, and rational world of what should be. Smith (2001) writes that in action learning, we "promote cogitation and insightful inquiry with perceptive partners in situations where solutions are not always obvious, and by leaving responsibility for implementation of the solution in the participant's hands, it is particularly suited to enhancing leadership capabilities" (p. 36).

Action Learning Develops the Critical Leadership Skills for the 21st Century

Most organizational theorists and practitioners agree that new leadership skills are needed for the 21st century. Leadership styles and skills that may have worked in stable, predictable environments are no longer adequate. What are the critical competencies needed by leaders in today's organizations? First and foremost, today's leaders must be able to handle complex adaptive systems and be able to work in conditions of rapid change and chaos.

Organizations need leaders who have strong interpersonal and communication skills as well as the ability to solve problems and take action. They seek leaders who have the ability to create opportunities and learn from failures. Leaders need to be able to define the problem and understand the environment before attempting to engineer a solution. Collins (2001), in his bestselling classic *From Good to Great*, discovered that leaders of great companies are both humble and persistent.

Forester (2011) points out the need for today's managers to have a high aptitude for both action and reflection. He notes that self-awareness and astute understanding of one's personal motives is the most critical of all leadership skills. Equipping people to become reflective practitioners will help them become better leaders. Argyris (2010) believes that the ability to reflect is a key leadership skill. He noted that too few leaders have the skill or ability to reflect in action (reflecting while doing) and reflect on action, a skill that is continuously practiced and developed in action learning.

Emotional Intelligence and Action Learning

Emotional intelligence (EQ) is seen as critical for today's leaders (Goleman (2000, 2006), and unlike IQ, EQ can be improved and developed. Emotional intelligence consists of five primary abilities:

1. *Self-awareness:* the ability to observe oneself and recognize the feeling as it happens
2. *Managing emotions:* the ability to handle feelings so that they are appropriate; realizing what is behind a feeling; finding ways to handle fears and anxieties, anger, and sadness
3. *Motivating oneself:* the ability to channel emotions in the service of a goal; emotional self-control; delaying gratification and stifling impulses
4. *Empathy:* sensitivity to others' feelings and concerns and taking their perspective; appreciating the differences in how people feel about things
5. *Handling relationships:* the ability to manage the emotions in others; this competence includes social competence and social skills

Developing Global Leadership Competencies at Boeing

The Global Leadership Program using action learning debuted in 1999 as one of several tools to enhance Boeing's ability to operate as a global company and to develop leadership competencies within the executive population. The action learning program is targeted to develop executive skills within three categories of global competencies: (1) most-critical competencies (adapting, thinking globally, building relationships, inspiring trust, leading courageously, aligning the organization, influencing, and negotiating), (2) very important competencies (shaping strategy, fostering open and effective communication, attracting and developing talent, driving for stakeholder success, demonstrating vision, using sound judgment), and (3) important competencies (driving execution, inspiring and empowering, working cross-functionally, focusing on quality and continuous improvement, applying financial acumen).

Action Learning Versus Other Leadership Development Programs

Action learning differs from normal leadership development programs in that it requires members to ask appropriate questions in conditions of risk, rather than to find answers that have already been defined by others—and that do not allow for ambiguous responses because the examiners have all the approved answers (Revans, 1982b). Dilworth (1998) notes that leadership development, as practiced by most organizations, "produces individuals who are technologically literate and able to deal with intricate problem-solving models, but are essentially distanced from the human dimensions that must be taken into account. Leaders thus may become good at downsizing and corporate restructuring, but cannot deal with a demoralized workforce and the resulting longer-term challenges" (p. 49).

The limitation of most management development programs is that they typically focus on a single dimension, unlike action learning, which derives its power from the fact that it does not isolate any dimension from the context in which the managers work; rather, it develops the whole leader for the whole organization. What leaders learn and how they learn cannot be dissociated from one another, for how one learns necessarily influences what one learns.

Most leadership development programs occur away from the organizational environment, and participants work on case studies that offer more information than real-world cases. If individuals make mistakes, there are no real consequences. Also, fellow learners are relative strangers who have limited stake and commitment to provide honest and frank feedback.

Bass (2008) points out that changes in attitudes, assumptions, and values require reflection on the leader's own mental models. Without a change in these models, it is impossible for a leader to change. Densten and Gray (2001) assert that reflection assists the development of leaders by enabling them to gain insight and to take into account the complexities of situations. The habit of seeking insight is the basis for the ability to retool the most basic element of leadership development, that is, ourselves. An important factor in any difficult decision is the character of the manager who makes it; since all managers are unique, development of the individual cannot be taught but must be learned, which is a unique strength of action learning.

Only through the reflective inquiries of the coach are one's limitations explored. Normally, we do not want to discuss limitations, and thus they are not addressed and do not change. But if people enter the session with the expectation that they need to grow, they can diminish their blind spots and enhance their leadership capacities. In action learning, there are many opportunities for self-reflection as well as supportive feedback from peers who are committed to helping us develop. Everyone is available to help each other develop a "team of leaders."

Learning cannot be solely the acquisition of programmed knowledge. Managers also need to improve their abilities to search out the unfamiliar. Action learning is the Aristotelian manifestation of all managers' jobs: they learn as they lead, and they can lead because they have learned—and go on learning. Dilworth (1998) notes that action learning provides managers with the opportunity to take "appropriate levels of responsibility in discovering how to develop themselves" (p. 37).

Mumford (1995) believes action learning is effective in developing leaders because it incorporates these key elements in management development: learning occurs more as a result of taking action than merely diagnosing and analyzing or recommending action, as most leadership development programs do; working on significant meaningful projects of the managers themselves creates greater learning; and managers learn better from one another than from instructors who are not managers or who have never managed.

Building a Team of Leaders in a Global Consulting Firm

CHUCK APPLEBY, EXECUTIVE DIRECTOR, GREAT ENTERPRISE CONSORTIUM

Rapid growth in the information assurance business created an unprecedented need for development of key leadership skills in a major management consulting firm. Top management sought a high-impact development methodology and chose action learning. Eight newly promoted managers were selected for a pilot action learning program that included eight sessions over a six-month period, with one-on-one coaching during the intervals between the meetings. Each meeting focused on the challenge of one of the eight members. The sessions also included discussion of supplementary leadership issues that were identified through feedback from customers and other managers.

Participants and top management were very pleased with the program and believed that action learning had indeed made a difference. The eight participants described the benefits of action learning not just in terms of the development of innovative solutions, but in the power of peer pressure in ensuring that they implemented the strategies developed by the group. The in-between coaching sessions helped them to explore and reflect further on some of the difficult issues raised in the sessions. Everyone felt that action learning created a supportive peer network. Top management in the firm noted significant improvement in participant performance in leading, working in teams, and solving problems.

Individual and Professional Development in Action Learning

The growth of each individual is important to the ultimate understanding and solving of the problem that has been given to the group. As Revans (1980) noted, if the group members are unable to change themselves, they will not be able to change what goes on around them. He writes: "One cannot change the system ... unless one is also changed in the process, since the logical structure of both changes is in correspondence with each other. The change in the system we call action; that in the self we call learning, so that learning to act effectively is also learning how to learn effectively" (p. 277).

The action taken on a problem changes both the problem and the people acting on it. O'Neil and Marsick (2007) point out that it is the action that generates the learning. While the group is working on the challenge via the action learning process, it develops its internal capacity to learn as well as to learn how to learn. The more we understand ourselves, our mind-sets, our strengths, and our areas needing improvement, the better we are able to reason and solve problems. Morris (1991) notes that "action learning provides moments of truth that stick in the memory, and may provide a turning point in one's life and the life of the organization" (p. 74).

In action learning, individuals gain not only valuable and valid knowledge, but also develop the skills and competencies that are most relevant to and needed by the organization. Such skills include critical reflection, inquiry and questioning, systems thinking, active listening, self-awareness, empathy, problem solving, decision making, presenting, and facilitating. Other valuable competencies developed by action learning are the ability to focus simultaneously on the problem/action and learning, the ability to give and receive feedback, self-discipline, and self-management.

Self-knowledge is critical for any aspect of professional development. As we all know, learning about ourselves can feel threatening, and we resist it if it tends to change our self-image, especially in a less than positive way. In action learning this threat is reduced to a level at which the fear no longer acts as such a strong barrier to gaining self-insight. This occurs because action learning provides safe "practice areas," along with the guidance and reflective questioning of the coach, that emphasize both personal responsibility for learning and also a supportive and challenging environment with fellow group members.

Action learning is concerned with empowering people to become critically conscious of their values, assumptions, actions, interdependencies, rights, and prerogatives so that they can act in a substantially rational way as active partners in producing their reality. Action learning creates an emancipatory kind of learning as it obliges group members to become aware of their own value systems, thereby leading people, as Revans (1983) notes, to "undeceive themselves."

An important part of self-learning is becoming aware of, and changing as necessary, one's beliefs, values, and basic assumptions. A tenet of action learning is that the individual knows more than anyone else what he has learned. And if given time and support, he will discover and develop that learning. In addition, the individual receives comprehensive feedback from other group members and from the results of the problem-solving actions.

Sveiby (1997) defines knowledge as "the capacity to act" (p. 37). True knowledge, according to Davenport and Prusak (1998), is action oriented. Individuals who have experienced action learning are encouraged, enabled, and expected to put their newly acquired knowledge and skills into action in their daily lives and throughout their organizations.

Learning and skills acquired by individuals in an action learning group are easily and frequently applied to day-to-day activities. For example, after interacting with a customer on the telephone, the person who has experienced action learning will begin to reflect: "How did that conversation go?" "What went well?" "How could I do better next time with this customer as well as with other customers?" Or, as he is interacting with a fellow employee, the seasoned action learning person may ask his colleague, "Is this meeting achieving what we want it to?" "What have we done well thus far?" "How can we improve it?" The changes and improvements in individual behavior of those who have participated in an action learning program can be quite remarkable.

Team Learning and Development in Action Learning

Action learning quickly forges groups into high-performing work teams who are able to think, create, act, and learn as a powerful entity. Unlike most groups that begin and often remain at a low level of productivity, action learning groups improve their level of teamwork as well as their team thinking and team learning every time they meet. The team growth commences at the first meeting, when members are advised of the importance of learning as a team, a necessity for the group to become smarter and better able to successfully and innovatively solve the problem or problems they must overcome as a team.

Earlier we identified eight ingredients of a successful, high-performance work group. Let's briefly analyze how action learning creates and reinforces those features.

Shared commitment to solving a problem. In action learning, the group is formed to accomplish a specific purpose, namely, to solve a particular problem. The members realize that they are accountable and that they must work together if they are going to be successful.

Clear and common goal. In action learning, the team never assumes that there is clear agreement on the goal for the group, and thus the first step is to jointly clarify the goal and achieve agreement on the group's purpose. Members realize that consensus on a goal is possible only if they ask questions of each other. To confirm the consensus, the action learning coach will check with the group regularly before allowing them to begin working on solutions.

Willingness to work with others to develop strategies. In action learning, the group members often are thrust into problems and situations entirely new to them, as the organization has sought individuals who may have fresh questions in addition to individuals who have experience with the issue. Thus, no one in the group has all the information, resources, or political power necessary to solve the problem. Everyone's perspectives, knowledge, and experience are needed to understand the issues and develop possible strategies.

Courage to question others. In action learning, everyone is expected, even required, to ask questions of each other. No one has all the answers, and asking fresh questions is critical for the group's ultimate success. Taking risks is one of the skills developed in this setting.

Clear and accepted norms. Action learning groups begin with the most powerful and positive group norm that is powerful in every group: statements can be made only in response to questions. Additional norms are explicitly developed by the group whenever they respond to the action learning coach's question ("what can we do better as a group"); such norms typically include building on each other's questions, making a commitment to take actions between sessions, being present at all meetings, listening, and so on.

Respecting others and supporting their ideas. As a result of the interplay of the six components of action learning, particularly as members share their learnings and help each other develop their leadership skills, action learning groups generate a positive and healthy regard for one another. They care for and respect each other. They become interested in the well-being of their team members and support them whenever possible.

Willingness to learn and help others to learn. When action learning groups begin, members are reminded that the group has two purposes, namely, to work on the issue and to learn. Throughout the program, time and energy will be spent on learning about the self, the team, and the organization. Accepting the responsibility to learn and to help others learn generates a helping and sensitive atmosphere within the group.

Cohesiveness and trust. A strong bond is built in action learning groups as members jointly focus on reframing problems and developing strategies. Interconnectedness is also built by the egalitarian nature of the groups, in which the quality of questions rather than the ability to provide answers is important. Finally, high levels of trust are built when people share their vulnerabilities.

Team and Organizational Learning at GE

General Electric began using action learning in the 1980s. Action learning has enabled GE people to learn and apply new skills while working on real problems—skills such as team building, conflict resolution, problem solving, coaching and facilitating, and understanding change management methodologies and tools, as well as communication methodologies. Over the past thirty years, GE has used action learning to help it become a learning organization in which the following results have been achieved.

▶ Boundaryless behavior in which employees work more easily across borders and business units

- ▶ Greater speed in decision making and implementation
- ▶ Accountability at appropriate levels with less controlling leadership
- ▶ Involvement of employees and resulting improved morale
- ▶ A management willing to take more risks
- ▶ Reduction of the culture of analysis paralysis
- ▶ More open dialogue and increased trust among staff
- ▶ Reduced impact of the burdens of hierarchy

Organizational Learning and Action Learning

Action learning is perhaps the quickest and most effective means of building a learning organization. Action learning groups model learning organizations because learning is a continuous, strategically used process that is integrated with, and runs parallel to, the work of the group. In order to survive, organizations, like action learning groups, must be able to continuously adapt, renew, and revitalize themselves in response to the rapidly changing environment. Learning organizations seek to learn faster and more efficiently from failures as well as successes. Zuboff (1988) notes that productivity and learning in the workplace are becoming one and the same, that "learning is the new form of labor" (p. 395).

A learning organization is constructed around four primary components: (a) increased learning skills and capacities, (b) a transformed organizational culture and structure, (c) an involvement of the entire business chain in the learning process, and (d) enhanced capability to manage knowledge (Marquardt, 2011; Waddill and Marquardt, 2011). Members of action learning groups transfer their experiences and new capabilities to the organization to build these four components.

Increased Learning Skills and Capacities

Within the action learning process, the group members develop their metacognition skills, that is, their ability to learn. They learn the principles and theories of effective learning, the ways in which learning can be augmented and applied, the different types of learning (anticipatory, adaptive, generative), as well as the key skills of learning (testing personal mastery, understanding mental models, systems thinking). In action learning individuals learn how to learn as a team, an opportunity made possible by the reflective questions of the action learning coach. Finally, the action learning process enables people to discover and experience how organizational learning occurs through the shared insights, knowledge, and mental models of members of the organization and by building on the past knowledge and experience of the organization (i.e., policies, strategies, explicit models).

Transformed Organizational Culture and Structure

Action learning develops values important for the culture of a learning organization, a culture in which learning is seen as essential for corporate success, where learning becomes a natural part of all organizational functions. Members of action learning groups come from all levels and units of the organization, thus enabling them to work more comfortably and confidently with groups from across organizational departments and functions. Strategies are used that build the learning capacities of its members. Learning organizations operate with minimal hierarchies, structures, and bureaucracies. Like action learning groups, they are fluid, flexible, and streamlined, and they maximize communication flow and innovative action.

Involvement of the Entire Business Chain in the Learning Process

Learning organizations involve not only staff in the learning process, but also customers, suppliers, vendors, and even the community. Organizational learning requires that we examine the organizational system as a whole. In action learning, members are always on the lookout for people both within and outside the organization who may possess the knowledge, power, or passion necessary to successfully reframe the problem, develop strategies, and take action. Gaining the perspectives and wisdom of fresh faces opens up the boundaries of possible learnings and actions.

Enhanced Capability to Manage Knowledge

Action learning models and allows members to practice and apply each of the aspects of knowledge management.

Acquiring knowledge. In action learning sets, members recognize not only the importance of acquiring information from external resources, but also the value of tapping the tacit, internal wisdom and experience of each other. The internal networks developed in action learning sets heighten the awareness of organizational resources, facilitate exchanging and sharing of ideas, and generate new knowledge.

Creating knowledge. Nonaka (2008) suggests that information creation is a fundamental requirement for the self-renewing (i.e., learning) organization. Participants in action learning programs understand that they should seek new ways of solving old problems, that the old knowledge may no longer be sufficient. Thus, members are constantly searching for novel strategies, taking risks in a supportive setting, pilot testing alternative solutions, and so on.

Storing knowledge. Knowledge needs to be categorized and stored according to learning needs, work objectives, user expertise, and function so that it can be found quickly and accurately. Through their ongoing reflection on learning and the knowledge acquired, action learning groups develop the ability to make meaning of the data collected and to store it within the group's memory or in the organization as appropriate. The action learning coach regularly checks out what knowledge is being stored and why.

Transferring and testing knowledge. Action learning groups continuously seek ways in which they can transfer the learnings, wisdom, and experience gained within the group to the organizations and communities in which they work. The knowledge is tested by determining whether it does indeed work.

Action Learning Incorporates Adult Learning Principles

Adult education specialists over the past century have identified a number of principles and practices that increase the speed, understanding, quality, and application of learning, particularly for the workplace. Action learning builds upon the following adult learning principles:

- ▶ Adults are motivated to learn as they experience needs and interests that learning will satisfy.
- ▶ We learn not so much when we are motivated to learn, but when we are motivated to achieve something.
- ▶ Experience is the richest resource for adults' learning, and thus the core methodology of adult education is the analysis of experience.
- ▶ Learning intensifies when we reflect on what we have experienced; and the more recent the experience we reflect on, the greater and more intense the learning.

- ► Learning is deepest when it involves the whole person, mind, values, and emotions.
- ► We learn more when we are responsible and accountable for applying the learning.
- ► Significant learning occurs when one is forced to sort through the past for relevant concepts, put ideas together in unique ways, and seek new information.
- ► Learning increases when we are asked questions or ask questions of ourselves.
- ► The strongest learning occurs when there is both an urgency and sufficient time and space to deal with the urgency.
- ► Critical, transformative learning occurs when we are able to question our assumptions.
- ► We learn when we receive accurate feedback from others and we are encouraged and supported in our deliberations.
- ► Group responsibility for learning empowers members and enhances learning of the entire group.
- ► Working on unfamiliar problems in unfamiliar settings causes us to unfreeze some of our previous ways of doing things and develop powerful learnings since we are faced with challenges and difficulties that are difficult to address.
- ► We learn best when we can see results and are allowed to take risks.

Action Learning and Knowledge Harvesting at British Airport Authority

British Airport Authority (BAA) is the world's largest airports operator, with a dominant UK position and global programs in the United States (Pittsburgh, Indianapolis) and in Melbourne. Action learning was introduced in the 1980s as part of a knowledge-creating and knowledge-sharing culture called Project Harvest. Some fifty managers were involved in five different projects. With the first wave of managers, more than two hundred new items of knowledge were generated from tackling real business challenges, including the forecasting at Southampton Airport and managing the construction of Heathrow Express rail service.

As a part of the action learning program, there were concentrated efforts to augment learning by encouraging action learning groups to cascade knowledge gained to those around them, with a special focus on program outcomes and their effects on profit and loss with the enterprise. The real challenge was to share this knowledge with those others within the organization who could act upon it in their own roles and in response to their own challenges. A comprehensive database was created, an important part, but only a part, of the answer to knowledge management. Key benefits of the action learning were the macro-level analysis and dissemination of the knowledge to achieve Project Harvest. (Christie and Sandelands, 2000)

Action Learning Incorporates Principles and Practices from All Five Schools of Learning

Action learning utilizes the theories, principles, and practices of each of the five schools of adult learning, namely, the cognitive, behavioral, social, humanist, and constructivist learning schools. Unlike most learning programs that tend to follow one approach or another, action learning bridges the schools and consequently builds a uniquely powerful learning opportunity for individuals, teams, and organizations (Marquardt and Waddill, 2003). Let's examine how action learning applies the best practices of each of the five schools.

Cognitive Learning

Cognitive learning theorists (Bruner, Argyris, Schön, and Piaget, among others) are concerned primarily with how the brain processes information and experience, and then converts it into knowledge, skills, and values. Action learning incorporates key elements of cognitive psychology through its focus on metacognition skills and learning how to learn; the internal process of acquiring and retaining information; using the problem as a trigger for the internal mental process of learning; looking for patterns, insights, and understandings while reflecting; and thinking about doing while doing.

Behavioral Learning

Behavioralists such as Skinner and Tolman believe that creating the proper environment and stimuli will create the ideal conditions for maximizing learning or any other behaviors. In action learning, the strong stimuli are the urgent, critical problem that needs to be resolved and the pressure on the group to develop effective solutions as well as to improve individual, team, and organizational behaviors. There is also pressure from the group and the coach to observe the norms. A specific group size (four to eight members) provides the optimum number for decision making and the active involvement of all members. Group members are required to ask questions, which causes synapses to be open and prevents domination of any individual. The action learning coach also causes behavior modification through her interventions.

Social Learning

Social learning theorists such as Dewey, Bandura, Lave, and Wenger emphasize the social nature of learning, the importance of the context or environment in which learning occurs and that causes learning to occur. For them, learning requires social interaction and collaboration.

Learners seek to connect past and present experiences, and learning is facilitated through "communities of practice," a social context in which action and learning are important. An effective way to learn is through modeling competencies, skills, and learning. The individual makes sense of an experience by conceptualizing it and generalizing the replicable points, and plans for future actions based on the learning gathered. The group provides the forge in which an individual's actions are shaped through contemplation and the insightful questioning of fellow group members.

Humanist Learning

Humanists (e.g., Rogers, Maslow, Knowles) believe that everyone has untapped abilities to contribute, to learn, and to act. Learning requires support and caring among fellow group members, so there is a comfort and freedom for asking fresh questions. Learning to seek what is unique to each situation as well as what is significant for each individual is an essential element of humanist learning theory. This school also emphasizes that the best learning occurs when the whole person (affective, cognitive, psychomotor dimensions) is involved. Everyone is responsible for his own as well as others' learnings. Creativity and innovation are encouraged. Each of these principles is inherent in action learning.

Constructivist Learning

For constructivist learning theorists such as Weick, Vgotsky, Illich, Friere, and Mezirow, knowledge and learning are context bound. Individuals and groups construct learning, as well as norms and meaning, from the action or experience. Being forced to deal with an unfamiliar problem or setting generates transformative learning and innovation. People need to inquire of each other's perspectives. Constructivists posit that learning optimally occurs by the interaction with the environment in a problem-anchored and learner-centered approach. Action learning's focus on learning with real problems with real applications thus incorporates the key elements of constructivist learning theories.

Learning from Experience

B. F. Skinner, a leading proponent of behavioralism and behavioral learning, stated that the "major difference between rats and people is that rats learn from experience." Most of us are members of groups that never seem to improve in their efficiency or effectiveness. Staff meetings are a prime example. How many of our staff meetings ever improve? Are they any better than they were six months ago or six years ago? Yet we continue to attend them. A rat attends a bad meeting only one time, and then it stops attending. Humans keep on returning—we don't learn from experience. In Johnson and Blanchard's (1998) bestseller *Who Moved My Cheese?* the mice in the story move to other parts of the land when the cheese is finished at one site, whereas the humans keep returning to the same place, expecting the cheese to somehow magically reappear. The mice learn from experience.

Intensity and Power of the Action Learning Experience

Wilfred Bion (1991), a noted British psychologist, observed that individuals, teams, and organizations could and, in fact, did have the ability to change their behavior quickly and permanently when faced with an intense experience to which they responded with the proper attitude and discipline—for example, a tremendous external environmental threat, the birth of a child (for parents), or surviving on an island (for a group). Action learning does, in fact, provide that intensity (a problem, comrades in adversity who need to hang together or hang separately, the requirement to take action with no certainty of success, with people who may be unfamiliar to us or to the problem); that attitude (working as a team, the need to learn, seeking innovation and success); and that discipline (statements only in response to questions, listening to each other and the action learning coach, being present at each session).

"The most powerful form of learning, the most sophisticated form of staff development, comes not from listening to the good words of others but from sharing what we know with others. Learning comes more from giving than from receiving. By reflecting on what we do, by giving it coherence, and by sharing and articulating our craft, knowledge, we make meaning, we learn."

—Roland Barth (1981)

The Power of Learning in Action Learning

Because action learning is built on and applies so many dynamics of the field of learning, it generates an amazing speed, depth, and breadth of learning.

Speed of learning. In action learning, the participants go through all cycles in a continuous and seamless fashion. The speed of the learning is what enables action learning groups to quickly develop as individuals and as a team.

Depth of learning. Since questions are continuous and challenge one another's assumptions and perspectives, there is significant depth of learning. Reflective questions raised in dialogue create double-loop (reasons why) and triple-loop (systems behind the whys) levels of learnings.

Breadth of learning. Through the guidance of the action learning coach, new learnings and knowledge transfer across teams and organizations.

The potency gained from this learning transforms individuals, teams, and organizations. The resultant power allows for rapid and meaningful success in personal and organizational arenas.

Checklist for Learning at the Individual, Group, and Organizational Levels in Action Learning

- ▶ What is the quality of our learnings?
- ▶ How are we optimizing our learnings?
- ▶ How is the action learning coach effectively helping us learn?
- ▶ What questions have been most effective for guiding our reflections and learnings? Why?
- ▶ Are we growing as individuals? How?
- ▶ Are we developing our leadership skills?
- ▶ How are we helping each other to learn?
- ▶ How are we learning as a team? How can we improve ourselves as a team?
- ▶ Are we interweaving learning and action in the workplace?
- ▶ Have we transferred knowledge to other parts of the organization? Why or why not?
- ▶ Are we applying our new skills in the workplace?
- ▶ In our team, do we have an environment where it is safe to take risks?
- ▶ How are we learning from what we have done well and what we could do better?
- ▶ Have we applied the learnings between sessions?
- ▶ Is our environment one that is collaborative, supportive, and concerned about learning?
- ▶ Are we taking time to focus on our learning?
- ▶ Are we questioning our basic assumptions?
- ▶ Are we taking responsibility as a group for our learning?
- ▶ Are we learning from reflecting on our experience in the group as well as from actions taken outside the group?

The Action Learning Coach

The action learning coach is the catalyst who optimizes the power of action learning as well as the questioner who accelerates the learning. She is the synergizer who helps to bond the group members. The action learning coach is the servant leader who enhances the group's ability to learn and to take vigorous action. She is the mirror who enables the group to reflect on its experience and convert that reflection into learning opportunities and results. The learning coach models the listening, learning, and questioning skills needed by high-performance work groups and great leaders. Her enthusiasm for learning and her commitment to helping the group succeed is a key value that she should hold and exhibit.

The key role of the coach is to optimize the group's ability to learn and thereby become more capable to quickly and innovatively solve the problem. The focus of the coach must always remain on the learning, not the problem. Learning will provide the leverage for continuously improving group performance. The more the coach is able to improve the speed and quality of learning and the growth of the group, the more successful the group's work will be.

Through the use of reflective questions, the coach helps group members to examine their actions and interactions and thereby improve their ability as a group not only to solve the current problem, but also to better solve future problems they will encounter as a team or as individuals. Her questions should be open and supportive and should enable the group to

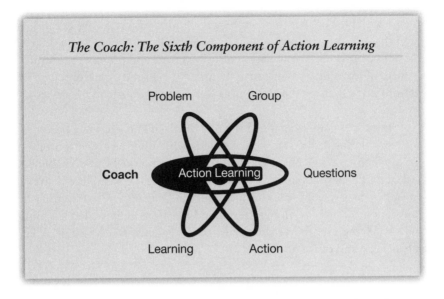

The Coach: The Sixth Component of Action Learning

Problem   Group

Coach   Action Learning   Questions

Learning   Action

reflect on how they are doing as a group, how they can improve, what they are learning, and how their learning can be applied to their lives and to their work in the organization.

Why Is One Person Designated to Focus on the Learning?

Although it certainly would be possible for any group member to focus on the learning and to ask the questions assigned to the action learning coach, the reality is that these tasks are rarely performed unless someone is designated to concentrate on them. In the absence of a designated action learning coach, the reflective learning questions are usually not asked, and if they *are* asked, this is rarely done with the quality and timing that accelerates learning and action.

To maximize individual and group learning, one person must be designated to focus exclusively on that task. Problem solvers (i.e., the group members) are focused, as they should be, on the urgent problem. The urgency of the problem always overwhelms the importance of learning. Thus, a person who has power must be assigned this important role, or else it gets lost because of time pressure (the tyranny of the urgent).

Action learning is dependent on two simple rules and processes. The action learning coach ensures that these are followed. Unless he is empowered to see that the members are asking or answering questions and that the group is given the time to learn, learning will be neglected or not occur at all. The coach is critical to create and promote the atmosphere of learning and reflective inquiry. To expect a group member to competently manage the learning as well as the problem-solving actions is unrealistic.

Thus, if no one is assigned the role of coach and everyone becomes responsible for it, the learning questions will either be asked too often in too many ways or not at all. And the questions asked will probably be asked for purposes other than to help the group learn. In addition, group members may resent or may be uncomfortable with anyone in the group at any time arbitrarily assuming the role and functions of the action learning coach. Taking over this responsibility in a spontaneous way will likely be challenged and resisted.

Benefits of a Skilled Action Learning Coach

Although any group member or outside person could possibly serve as an action learning coach, the role is too critical and requires too much skill for it to be done well by someone who has not been trained for this particular role. The ability to enable a group and its members to learn while they are seeking to solve a complex, urgent problem can be overwhelming if one does not have the competence and confidence to handle the diverse aspects of the role.

As a result, the value of having a person trained and skilled in carrying out the important but challenging role of the action learning coach is becoming more and more recognized around the world. A skilled and experienced coach can significantly enhance the speed and quality of action and the learning of the group.

Thus more and more organizations employ an internal or external person who has trained in the coaching of action learning groups. Like Microsoft, Panasonic, and Goodrich, many companies either contract for an external certified action learning coach or develop a cadre of internal certified action learning coaches (see sidebar titled "Coaching Certification"). Constellation Energy has a trained coach at each of its manufacturing sites available to managers whenever they would like to use action learning to solve a problem or achieve a critical goal.

Coaching Certification with the World Institute for Action Learning (WIAL)

Over the past ten years, the World Institute for Action Learning has trained and certified hundreds of action learning coaches around the world. The certification program of WIAL, a nonprofit educational institution with affiliates around the world, includes providing six days of intensive training/practice as well as guiding the coaches through their initial experiences as coaches. The certification program incorporates much of the content and principles contained in the book. For more information about training locations and dates, the reader can view the WIAL website (www.wial.org).

Coaching of Multi-Problem Action Learning Groups

Although we strongly encourage companies to have a skilled and experienced action learning coach for in-company, single-problem action learning programs, which results in strategic benefits and high ROI, this option is less critical and may be economically less viable for multiple-problem action learning groups, because the problems presented are usually less complex. Thus, in these situations, the role and responsibilities of the action learning coach may be rotated among the group members. For example, at each session, or for each problem presenter, a different person would serve as the coach. There are a number of benefits accrued by rotating the role of coach:

▶ Everyone in the group develops this leadership competency of helping people learn and develop.
▶ Serving as an action learning coach enables members to understand the value and appreciate the importance of the coaching role when they return to working on the problem.
▶ While serving as the coach, each person develops new skills in asking solid, learning-inducing questions.
▶ The group or organization saves the time and cost of an outsider.
▶ Confidentiality becomes less of an issue if the content of the problem and solutions must remain only with the select group working on the problem.
▶ The coach usually sees options and insights not apparent to others in the group who are involved with the details of solving the problem;

this helicopter perspective can then be brought into the group when the coach rejoins as a group member.

Developing a Cadre of Internal Action Learning Coaches

A growing number of organizations around the world have developed an internal cadre of action learning coaches so as to increase their capacity to implement numerous action learning programs as well as to be able to quickly establish a coached action learning group to handle crises as they arise. These organizations include Microsoft, Samsung, Goodrich, Constellation Energy, Humana, SmithKline Beacham, Kirin Brewery Company, National Bank of Dominica, Krones, and Panasonic.

The Power of the Coach to Intervene

As noted in Chapter 1, the second ground rule of action learning is that the coach has the power to intervene when she sees an opportunity to help the group improve its performance or to help individuals improve their leadership skills. So when a coach decides to intervene, the group pauses from working on the problem and listens to the questions raised by the coach. The coach only asks questions (although occasionally, as will be shown later in this chapter, she may make an observation followed by the question). The group listens and responds to the coach's questions until she indicates to the group that it should now resume working on the problem.

In addition to helping the group learn and thereby better and more quickly complete its task, the coach is also responsible for managing the time. She therefore indicates how much time may still be available to work on the problem before she does her end-of-session intervention to confirm the actions and to capture the learnings.

The reason the coach needs to have this power to intervene is to ensure that the group achieves both important actions and significant learnings at every session. We all know from our experiences that, without an intervening mechanism, the *importance* of learning will be overshadowed by the *urgency* of the problem. Therefore, power must be given to the person in charge of what is important so that he can overrule the natural tendency to go with the power of what is urgent.

If time for reflection and learning is not taken when the coach requests it, then it simply will not happen. Experience and research show that this aspect of group work is abandoned unless it is the chief and sole responsibility of a designated person. The coach must be given this power, particularly if he is seen as a lower-level person in the organization. Unfortunately, if he is perceived as someone with less knowledge or experience or power, he will be ignored and/or overruled by other members of the group—unless he has specifically been given this authority. Thus, it is critically important that when the coach announces that he is intervening, the group immediately stops (or completes the sentence or thought begun) and listens to the questions of the action learning coach.

As long as the coach is within her intervention, she has control of the discussion. It is important that she not lose that control and allow the group to jump back into the problem before she has indicated that members may resume, for once a group ignores the coach, it will be difficult to regain that authority in future interventions. If she can successfully and comfortably retain control during the first intervention, she will be more easily able to retain it for the rest of the life of that group.

How the Coach Introduces Action Learning and the Role of the Coach

It is very important that the action learning coach clearly and concisely describes action learning and explains his role to an action learning group that is meeting for the first time. The process of action learning may be very different from any problem-solving process that they have used in the past, and it is unlikely that they have ever experienced a person with the role and power of an action learning coach. A number of key points should be covered in the first few minutes. Here is an example of what I might typically say at the beginning of a new action learning project.

> Thank you for being here to help (Person X or Organization X) to solve an urgent and important problem. We will be using a process called *action learning* in which we will be learning while we work together to solve this problem. Thus, we have two objectives: one, to develop a breakthrough strategy on the problem; and two, to develop our individual leadership competencies. There is one simple ground rule in action learning; statements can be made only in response to a question. Anyone can ask a question of anyone at any time. A question may generate many responses from members of the group, or, if it is a great question, there may only be silence as we all may need time to reflect on it. There are three reasons why questions are emphasized in action learning: one, they will help us be more creative and able to achieve breakthrough thinking and problem-solving; two, they will keep us

focused and productive; and three, questions will help us develop our leadership skills. Does everyone understand the ground rule?

Let me also identify my role in action learning. I will be serving as the action learning coach, and will not be directly involved in solving the problem. Rather, I will be focused on improving the performance of the group and helping you to develop your leadership skills. I will only ask questions, and I will manage the time so that we complete the actions and the learnings by the end of the session. Does everyone understand my role?

You will note that the coach does not ask for approval of the two ground rules, but rather checks to be sure that they are understood by all members of the group. If the benefits of these norms are clearly elaborated, the group is eager to apply them, or at a minimum, is willing to try them out to see if they will work—and they always do work!

Building the Learning Climate of the Group

The action learning coach helps to set the climate of learning, openness, trust, and being nonjudgmental. He should demonstrate frank, targeted questioning and reflecting skills. Although he may be tempted to get involved with the problem, he must always focus on the process and interactions and continuously strive to find opportunities for developing the group and enhancing the leadership skills.

The coach should not be put in the role of being the expert, controller, teacher, or chairperson. However, since she is more knowledgeable and experienced in action learning than the other members of the group, she is responsible for orienting and preparing group members on the fundamentals of action learning, including the six components and two ground rules (as shown in the sample introduction earlier in this chapter).

The coach should not use statements to tell group members what to do. Rather, through her questions, she assists them in discovering what they need to do for themselves. She does not teach, but seeks to create an atmosphere wherein members can learn for and from themselves, develop confidence in themselves, reflect, and develop new ideas (Lawlor, 1997). The role of the coach is not to correct or to be critical, but rather to raise the group's consciousness about what is happening. Also, statements from the coach, unlike questions, will cause people to become defensive, defiant, and/or dependent on the coach; all these reactions are contrary to the spirit and power of action learning. If this occurs, the coach will be seen as not objective, insensitive, controlling, or manipulative.

The coach must always be cognizant of the fact that significant learning occurs as a result of getting the group to reflect, and significant reflection occurs as a result of good questions. He must also help the group members to assume responsibility for learning and for taking their knowledge and learning back to other parts of their lives. He initiates all of these essential processes through questions—the right ones at the right time.

Questions: The Modus Operandi of the Coach

The action learning coach only asks questions. Why is it so important for the coach to only ask questions? First, questions are always more powerful and valuable than statements in helping others to reflect and to learn. Since a primary role of the coach is to enable group members to reflect and learn, then it is appropriate that he do this through questioning.

As noted in the first ground rule, we expect group members to ask questions, and to make statements only in response to questions; therefore it is important that the coach model the behavior that he expects from the group. Questions also empower the group to consider perspectives other than that of the coach.

The coach should not be seen as taking sides on issues or making judgments about the behavior or attitude of group members, which statements will invariably do. Good reflective questions are nonjudgmental. The person responding will make his own judgments. Thus the members need not be afraid that the coach will be jumping in and pointing out an idea or behavior that may have been detrimental to the group or indicative of a negative personality trait.

A final reason why it is best for the coach to ask questions is that it allows the group to reflect and make their own decisions. For example, if the coach perceives an action as being negative or positive, and makes a statement to that effect, then the group may accept his statement as the truth, even if that judgment is incorrect. As a result, the group may be totally misdirected in its work and its learnings.

Coordinating and Managing the Action Learning Sessions

The action learning coach needs to know before a session begins or at the very beginning how much time will be available so that he can ensure that there will time allocated for learning as well as actions. In a single-problem session, the coach may advise the group when they have approximately thirty minutes left to work on the problem, since he is reserving the last fifteen minutes for final reflections and learnings. If the coach does not provide a time warning, members may be surprised and even upset that they had to stop working on the problem. They may push for a little more time, the result of which is that there is little or no time left for the final learnings, which is when the most significant developments generally occur. The power and value of the coach will be diminished, and the group may continue to erode his time and power as they may feel that it is not as important as solving the problem.

The coach will need to confirm the timing of the different stages of the session in a multiple-problem set so that there will be an equal amount of time allocated for each person. He needs to be sure that there is reflection/learning time after each session as well as a more comprehensive learning time at the end of the program. Table 5 shows a sample schedule for a multiple-problem group with five members.

Interventions and Questions of the Action Learning Coach

In addition to knowing what questions to ask and how to ask questions, knowing when to intervene is an important skill for the action learning coach. Interventions should occur at the beginning of each session, one or

TABLE 5

Sample Schedule for Multiple-Problem Session, Five Members

9:00	Welcome and planning of session
9:10	Presenter 1 (20–30 minutes)
9:35	Action learning coach, capturing of learnings (5–10 minutes)
9:40	Presenter 2 and learnings
10:10	Presenter 3 and learnings
10:40	Break
10:50	Presenter 4 and learnings
11:20	Presenter 5 and learnings
11:50	Final reflections and learnings
12:00	Adjourn

more times during the session, and at the end of the action learning session. Let's briefly examine how the action learning coach intervenes at each of these stages and the types of questions she asks during those interventions.

Intervention and Questions at the Beginning of the Session

The coach's first intervention (although technically not an intervention since it occurs before the group begins its work) occurs at the very beginning of the first session of the group. At this time, the coach checks that all the group members are familiar with the principles and norms of action learning. Once he has been assured that the members understand the action learning process, the coach asks the problem presenter(s) to state the problem/challenge. In subsequent meetings of the group, he will ask the individual (in the case of multiple-problem sets) or the group (in single-problem sets) what actions have been taken since the previous session of the group and what has been the impact of those actions as well as learnings gained. Following are examples of questions the coach might ask at the beginning of a session.

- ▶ Is everyone familiar with how action learning works? With the role of the action learning coach? The importance of questions?
- ▶ At the first session of a multiple-problem set (addressed to the problem presenter): What is the problem (task, challenge, issue) that you would like the group to help you with? Could you take a few minutes to briefly summarize the key elements of the problem?
- ▶ At the first session of a single-problem set (addressed to the entire group): What is the problem as we understand it?
- ▶ At subsequent sessions: What actions have been taken since our last session? What has been the impact of those actions? What actions did not occur? Why not? What can we learn from these experiences? What would we do differently? What learnings can be applied to this project? To other parts of our lives or of the organization? How can we transfer these learnings?

Interventions and Questions During the Session

There is no set point at which the coach makes his interventions during sessions. He may sometimes intervene within the first few minutes and at other times not until twenty or even forty minutes have elapsed. He may intervene as many as four to six times during a session or as few as one or two times. He should always intervene at least once, for, in addition to providing the group with some breathing space, it helps members to become more aware of what they are doing well and what they might do better to identify and continue their positive interactions, and to improve upon the obstructive and unproductive behaviors.

There are always some more comfortable and natural times to intervene, for example, when the group is not working well or there is struggling or uncertainty as to what to do next. Enabling the group to be more conscious of the factors that may be causing the difficulty will allow them to address it directly and intentionally and thereby identify actions to remedy or overcome it.

An interesting phenomenon occurs while the coach has the group reflecting on the quality of the group's work. While the group consciously works on what it is doing well, what can be improved, and so forth, it subconsciously continues to work on the problem. After the group has finished working on the learnings and improvements, it returns refreshed and invigorated and ready to work on the problem. Amazingly, instead of being sidelined and delayed by the coach's intervention, the group discovers that its subconscious has been thinking about the problem and now generates new ideas and solutions that might never have occurred if the group had continued focusing only on the problem.

A wide variety of questions may be asked during the action learning sessions. Generally, they will fall into five major categories: problem framing questions, action strategy questions, group effectiveness questions, leadership questions, and application questions.

The first question that is asked by the action learning coach at her first intervention is, "How are we doing as a team—okay or not okay?" This is an excellent question in that it allows an easy transition from the intensity of working on the problem to beginning to reflect on the group's process and productivity. Remember that it is difficult for people to move from the urgent problem into a reflective stage in which the focus is on the process and the learning. It is important to obtain everyone's response to this question so that one opinion or a few people's opinions do not determine what the whole group feels or thinks. This question provides an opportunity to get everyone involved, especially the quiet person who may have said little or nothing thus far. This is referred to as a "gut question" because the coach is exploring people's feelings about the quality of the group work to this point.

Once the coach has a sense of how each member feels about the group, he moves from the emotional level to the cognitive or intellectual level by asking the second question, "What have we done well thus far?" Even if everyone answered the first question by saying "not okay," the coach knows that the group has done some things well. For example, at a minimum, everyone is asking questions because of the ground rule, but people are also probably listening, gathering information, and working on the problem. The coach wants the group to identify those positive behaviors so that they continue. In this way, the coach is applying the positive focus of appreciative inquiry (Cooperrider, Sorensen, and Yaeger, 2001), which energizes the group and causes people to be more satisfied and confident when they resume work on the problem.

The coach's next question, "What could we do better?" is also always asked, even if everyone said the group was doing well, because, again, the coach knows that every group has some behaviors that can be improved. The responses to these two questions—"What have we done well?" and "What could we do better?"—begin to form powerful and positive norms that enable the group to immediately improve the manner in which it operates. The group is thus able to avoid the traditional forming-storming-norming-performing pattern and move to the much preferred norming-performing-norming-performing pattern that occurs in action learning groups (see Chapter 3 for a discussion of these stages).

Note the use of the word *we* by the coach when she is asking the questions. This conveys to the group that she is a full member of the group and anxious for its success, even though her role is to focus on a complementary element of improving the skills of the group and each individual in the group. If the coach instead asked "How are you doing?" she would imply that she is separate from, maybe even above, the group and thus able to avoid responsibility for any failures or weaknesses of the group.

There are many possible questions the coach can ask to help the group ask better questions, listen more carefully, work better together, and become more creative. Questions about the quality of the questions being asked by group members are important, since the quality of their questions will ultimately determine the speed and quality of their actions (see Chapter 4). Following are examples of the types of questions that are asked by coaches during action learning interventions.

- ▶ How are we doing as a team thus far—okay or not okay? (Some people prefer to use numbers, so the coach may provide the alternative: How are we doing as a team thus far on a scale of one through ten, with one being terrible and ten being terrific?).

▶ What are we doing well? Can you give an example of what we have done well? Any other examples? What was the impact of that?

▶ What could we do better? Any other ways we could improve our work together? Can you be specific?

▶ Do we have clarity and agreement on the problem? (Ask everyone to write it down.)

▶ What is the quality of our questions?

▶ Are we building on each other's questions and ideas? Examples?

▶ What is the balance between questions and statements?

▶ Could you turn that into a question?

▶ How creative have we been? How could we be more creative?

▶ What questions have been the most helpful?

▶ What is the quality of our ideas? Our strategies?

▶ Any learnings thus far about the problem content? Leadership? Teams?

The action learning coach should keep the time consumed by his interventions to no more than five to ten minutes so that the group can quickly return to working on the problem. Some interventions may last for a few seconds (e.g., "Could you put that statement into a question?") or for less than a minute (e.g., "Jim, what do you think is the impact of your question [or statement] on the group?"). The coach therefore must carefully consider and choose questions that best enable the group to improve its capacity as a group and thereby more quickly and effectively handle the problem it is seeking to solve.

Intervention and Questions at the End of a Session

The intervention and questions at the end of each action learning session provide immensely valuable opportunities for significant and transformative learning for individuals as well as the group. To adequately prepare for the end-of-session intervention, the action learning coach alerts the group about the time frame for the meeting. He might say, for example, "This two-hour session is scheduled to end at 4:00. Since we will need the final fifteen minutes to help us confirm our action, capture our learnings, and identify ways to apply our knowledge, we will need to complete our work on the problem at 3:45." The coach may then provide a fifteen-minute alert at 3:30 and remind the group to begin focusing on actions that they will be taking between this and the next session. Then at 3:45, the coach moves forward and begins asking questions such as the following.

The first set of three questions is always asked to the problem presenter in a multiple-problem set, or to the entire group in a single-problem set.

▶ What actions are you (we) going to take as a result of this session?
▶ Were you (we) helped? How?
▶ How did we do as a team? Okay, not okay, great?

Some of the following questions are then addressed to all group members.

▶ What did we do best? What could we do better?
▶ What do we think about the quality of our problem solving? Of our proposed actions?
▶ How could we improve our team and individual efforts for our next session?
▶ What helped us make progress? What hindered us?
▶ Which questions were most valuable?
▶ How did each of us do on the leadership skills that we have chosen to work on?
▶ Could you provide some specific examples of how Jim demonstrated his leadership skill?
▶ How do you intend to apply your new leadership skills in your work?
▶ What have we learned about teamwork, problem solving, company policies, customers, systems thinking (depending on the problem/issue)?
▶ What have you learned about yourself?
▶ How can we apply these learnings to other parts of the organization or to our lives?
▶ What helped us learn?

In multiple-problem sets, each person will have approximately twenty to thirty minutes to receive help and guidance on his or her problem. The coach will tee up each round by letting everyone know the amount of time available for this problem and at what time she will initiate her final intervention. A five-minute reminder may be provided to ensure that action steps are identified before she asks her final questions.

The action learning coach directs the first set of questions to the entire group for single-problem sets or, in multiple-problem sets, to the individual who has just presented the problem. Asking the question "What action are you (we) going to take?" forces the individual or group to articulate specific action steps. No session should end without a determination and selection of specific actions, ideally by what date and by whom. Being able to respond to this question allows the group some degree of satisfaction that they have indeed helped or begun to help the individual and/or organization. The question "Were you helped?" (which almost always receives an enthusiastic "yes") solidifies the fact that the group has been helpful and valuable. It is rare for an individual or group not to be helped by having received questions asked from a variety of perspectives. At a minimum, the problem has become much clearer.

The question "How were you (we) helped?" shows the group how various questions and ideas coalesced and resulted in these useful strategies and possible solutions. It also sets up the group for the second series of questions that focus on how well the group has done, what it has learned, what skills have been developed, and what knowledge can be applied. The "how" question is also a systems question as it causes the individual or group to reflect on how they were helped organizationally, emotionally, cognitively, and so on.

The action learning coach needs to choose well which questions will be most valuable and helpful for the group as a whole and for the learning of each individual. Her time is limited, so she should select three or four questions that she believes will accomplish the most learning and provide the greatest leverage for the future.

Intervention and Questions at the End of the Final Meeting

Action learning projects may involve a crisis that needs to be handled with one meeting and then the group never meets again. However, most action learning groups meet anywhere from two times to ten times over a period of one week to one year. In any case, at the last meeting of a group that has met more than a few times, the coach's intervention should be more substantial and may last from thirty minutes to two hours. This is the opportunity to capture the most significant learnings that occurred during the many hours the group deliberated on the problem and implemented actions. It is also a time to reflect deeply on how the group members have developed their leadership skills and applied these skills over the past several weeks or months within their lives and their organizations.

The action learning coach facilitates this final session through a systematic exploration of the overall learnings of the group, seeking to identify and apply the most valuable individual learnings and the greatest areas of skill development. She should be sure to capture the key information and competencies that were or could be transferred to the organization, and the elements and processes that most helped this group to succeed. Following is a list of the types of questions asked at the end of the final meeting.

- ► How well did we solve the problem and achieve our goal?
- ► What is the quality of our strategies?
- ► What did we do best? What could we have done better?
- ► What have been your most significant learnings?
- ► What have been the most valuable learnings of the group?
- ► What made us successful?
- ► What did we learn about teams?
- ► Which learnings and skills could be or have been applied to the organization?
- ► What is the quality of our individual development and learning? Of our team development and learning?
- ► Has a systematic analysis of the learning been applied to other parts of the organization?

Follow-up Questions

A script of the beginning, middle, and ending questions listed in this chapter can effectively serve as a guide and starting point for the action learning coach. Valuable and powerful information and change will accrue as the group members respond to these questions. The greatest power and impact, however, generally derives from the follow-up questions raised by the coach. Follow-up questions will quickly elevate the competency level of the group and/or individual. Follow-up questions (sometimes just a "Why?" or "Can you give me an example?" or "How?") create deep levels of learning, as well as double-loop (causes for) and triple-loop (systems behind) learning. Often a follow-up question simply builds on the response to the previous question. Careful listening is needed for great follow-up questions.

Here is a simple illustration of follow-up questioning.

Coach: What could we do better as a group?

Response: We could be more creative.

Coach: How could we be more creative?

Response: (None)

Coach: Why do you think we are not being creative?

Response: I do not think we are building on each other's ideas.

Coach: Why not?

Response: Don't know.

Coach: Anyone else have any thoughts as to why we are not building on each other's ideas?

Response: I think we are more interested in getting our own ideas into the mix rather than listening to someone else's ideas.

Coach: Any other ideas as to why we are not building on each other's ideas?

Responses: (May be several)

Coach: What is the impact of not being interested in someone else's ideas?

Response: We show that we do not think much of their ideas.

Coach: What are some ways in which we could be more creative?

Responses: (May be several)

Coach: Okay, let's resume working on the problem.

As that scenario illustrates, the coach follows a fairly simple procedure in the asking of follow-up questions. She addresses the first follow-up question to the person who has answered the initial question. After this response, she looks to see if others may have different perspectives and responses or additional comments to the question. If the person addressed does not have a response, the coach quickly turns to the other members of the group for their response(s).

Note that the coach does not have to agree or confirm the response. His responsibility is to help the group become aware of its behavior and the positive or negative consequences of that behavior, and how to improve. Once a group recognizes what is happening and why, it will quickly and almost automatically adapt its behavior to achieve what the group has determined is valuable. In the scenario shown here, which is taken from a real situation, the group, somewhat to its surprise, started asking innovative questions within ten minutes and came up with great strategies by the end of the session. This positive change in the group's interactions occurs naturally and automatically because the coach has helped the group set new norms, and subsequently their desired behaviors are converted into real actions. Also, questions from the coach go deep into the subconscious of the group and each individual, and this subconscious alertness soon changes the behaviors of the individual(s) and/or group.

The Art and Skill of Questions Asked by the Action Learning Coach

Although inexperienced coaches may initially be concerned about their ability to ask questions, there is generally little to fear since the power is primarily in the question, not in the person asking the question. Using the questions listed in this chapter can provide the starting point. Listening carefully to the response will provide the clues for the follow-up questions. As people gain experience in serving in the role of the action learning coach, the questions flow more easily and they become more relaxed and confident in introducing the next questions.

It is best if the coach phrases her questions positively, using what Cooperrider, Sorensen, and Yaeger (2001) refer to as *appreciative* inquiry. Instead of asking what went wrong, the coach asks questions that focus on what has gone well, what can be done, how it can be improved. The approach will guide the group in seeking what might be rather than what is not. The focus remains on improvement and continuous learning rather than complaining and venting.

It is important and comforting to know that the coach accomplishes much of his objective simply by asking the questions. The subconscious of the group members will wrestle with the coach's questions while working on the problem, and changes will begin to occur simply because the question was asked.

Although the action learning coach is not directly involved in working on the problem, it is important that he show his deep interest in the problem and his sympathetic concern that the group is successful and is working well as a team. He can demonstrate this by body language that communicates his support for the group. It is also helpful for him to jot down notes and possible questions to ask at the time of his intervention. Observe when the energy level of the group is rising and falling. When someone says, "That is a great question!" be sure to write that question down and later ask about it. The key to an eventual innovative solution has its seeds in that question.

Coaches should be comfortable when there is silence or there is no immediate response to a question. Allow group members to reflect and let them know that you are comfortable with the silence. If the person who is asked a question is unable to answer it, after a few seconds ask the question of the rest of the group. Sometimes there will be no response. That is okay, as the question will continue to incubate in people's minds, and a number of responses will emerge when that same question is asked at the next intervention. Remember that the power and value are often more in the question and the reflection that it causes than in the responses that it generates. Also, the coach has prepared the subconscious to reflect on the questions asked during previous interventions, and the next time he asks the same question, the responses will be greater and richer.

The Power of Questions Asked by the Action Learning Coach

What makes the questions of the learning coach so powerful? Why do they generate rapid and significant change in the culture and behavior of the group? The intensity of the situation and the quality of the questions produce this effect. Bion (1991) notes that if something is done intensely and well, it needs to occur only once for behavior and values to change. In action learning, group members know that their success depends on each other, that together they are accountable for the solution to the problem. In addition, as they have identified areas for learning and growth, they have shared their vulnerabilities. The magnitude of the context combined with the role and power of the learning coach causes the questions to go to both the consciousness and, even more strongly, the subconsciousness of each member of the group. The resultant responses trigger a natural biological need to change the individual's and the group's behaviors.

It is also valuable to note again that while people are focusing on learnings as a result of questions addressed to them by the coach, their subconscious minds are working on the problem. The reverse behavior occurs once the coach allows the group to return to working on the problem; namely, the subconscious is now working on the learning while the conscious mind is working on the problem. Reflection, which is critical for the generation of innovative ideas, is made intentional by the coach and results in the interweaving of emotional and cognitive mind-sets. The questions of the coach cause members to return to the experience and replay it. This helps them to capture and acknowledge the feelings associated with the experience.

How the Coaching Process Accelerates Learning

A significant amount of research has been undertaken in the past fifty years to identify ways and means to enhance the speed, quality, and retention of learning. Some of the best known and respected research was conducted by Heiman and Slomianko (2004), who identified the four actions that were deemed most critical for increasing the speed and quality of learning. These are:

▶ Asking questions (which cause the synapses to open, and allows the brain to better receive data and learn)
▶ Breaking up complex ideas and tasks into understandable, specific parts
▶ Being asked to identify what and how one has learned
▶ Connecting and applying the learning to specific goals or actions

We can see that all four of these actions are an integral part of action learning. The coach explicitly and purposefully executes each of these actions on a regular basis. Through his questions, he helps to bring to the consciousness of the group what is happening and what people are learning. They become more aware of how they are learning and how they can apply it elsewhere.

Research has also shown that deep learning can only occur in response to reflection, since reflection is necessary for someone to understand and internalize external data. And, as we noted in Chapter 4, an individual can only reflect from a question, a question either addressed to her from another person or a question that she asks herself. Thus, every question asked by the action learning coach causes the individual or the group to reflect, and therefore to experience deep learning as an individual and/or as a group.

Coaching versus Facilitation

Although there is certainly much overlap between the role and actions of a facilitator and a coach, there are also clear differences in terms of emphasis and philosophical beliefs. To illustrate some of the differences, let us briefly examine the two roles. Table 6 summarizes these differences.

The facilitator's primary role is to help the group improve its functioning. He does this by observing and occasionally making statements and offering advice on what the group could do better. This is expected from the group, since this person has been trained to be a facilitator and that is his role. The members depend on him to guide them, and they hope that their individual behaviors, if not productive, are not publicized or blown out of proportion by the facilitator. The expertise and role of the facilitator can lead to dependence and, in some cases, resentment.

The primary role of the action learning coach is to enable the members to take responsibility for themselves to learn how to develop as a team, to increase their awareness of how they are doing, and to generate norms and processes that will improve their effectiveness. The job of the action learning coach is to get the group from today to tomorrow (unlike the therapist, who seeks to get the individual or group from yesterday to today). The focus is on learning and connecting that learning to action, and the means

TABLE 6
Facilitator's Role versus Learning Coach's Role

Facilitator	Learning Coach
Focus on group process	Focus on learning and improving team
▶ Team norms	▶ Performance and actions
▶ Decision making	▶ Making learning explicit
▶ Communications and feedback	
Statements	Reflective questions
What happened	Why and how it happened
▶ Focused on desired outcomes	▶ Aligning intentions and action
Dependence	Independence
Single-loop learning	Double-loop and triple-loop learning
	▶ Connecting learning to business
	▶ Skills of learning
Focus on the present/past/future	Focus on the future/present
Focus on the facilitation tools	Focus on the why
Generates reaction	Generates reflection
Depends on expertise and experience	Depends on perspective
Values participation	Values wisdom
Asks questions and occasionally facilitates with statements	Only asks questions
Generates discussions	Fosters critical thinking
Focus on success of group	Focused on success of individual, group, and organization

to achieve that learning is reflective questioning. Action learning groups become increasingly confident in their own internal ability to manage their group process and to successfully complete their tasks.

Dos and Don'ts of an Effective Action Learning Coach

Arthur Freedman, a leading team theorist and a certified Master Action Learning Coach (MALC), offers the following advice for action learning coaches:

- ▶ Remain neutral in the problem reframing and strategy selection. Refrain from advocating particular solutions.
- ▶ Ask open-ended or closed-ended questions, but not leading questions.
- ▶ Rely on the team members to create and/or apply problem-solving methods rather than suggesting your own.
- ▶ Focus on achieving results and learnings, and not just on solving the problem.
- ▶ Use conflicts as an opportunity to help groups learn.
- ▶ Use resistance as information as opposed to being ignored.
- ▶ Enable the group to work on the total system and not just on the immediate problem, such as how the problem is influenced by the environment and how the possible solutions impact the environment.
- ▶ Don't get involved in the solution.
- ▶ Don't take on responsibilities, roles, or knowledge that the action learning group can manage or obtain for itself.
- ▶ Avoid making judgments, as they will cause the group to become dependent, defensive, or defiant. Rather, encourage independence and self-determination.
- ▶ Raise questions that will test assumptions and the validity of conclusions reached by the action learning group.
- ▶ Do not immediately rescue the group if it is in trouble, as the struggle can be a great opportunity for learning.

Why the Action Learning Coach Should Not Be Involved in the Problem Solving

Although there are times when the coach would like to focus on the problem because of an idea or insight he may have, in general this is discouraged for several reasons.

Loss of objectivity and fairness. If the coach becomes involved in the discussion, his viewpoint may be seen as being supportive of one group member or another. Then, when reflective questions are asked by the coach at the end of the session, the member(s) who may have felt slighted might not see the coach or his questions as being objective or open or fair. As a result, their reflections or responses may not be objective, and might even include a negative reaction to the coach.

Problem is seen as more important than the learning. In action learning, we place so much importance on learning that we designate an individual to focus her entire attention on it. If the coach becomes involved in the action, she is indicating to the group that the problem is more important than the learning. It becomes difficult later to recapture the sense that the coach truly believes the learning is so important that it needs her entire attention.

Coach is unable to focus on learning or timing of interventions. If the action learning coach is involved in the problem, he may miss examples of questions, statements, or behavior that will be important in helping the group to learn. He will not be able to properly prepare questions to ask or to make the best decisions on the timing for his interventions. If the appropriate time to intervene is right after he has asked a problem-related question or answered another person's question, his intervention may be seen as self-serving, exploitive, or controlling.

Imbalance of power or expertise. Because the action learning coach has been granted authority when intervening on issues of learning, she has an aura of power and expertise that may unduly influence the decision making and participation of other members of the group. Her participation in the problem solving may be seen as the "appropriate" or "best" answer, and the group may defer to her (or become defiant).

Loss of coaching power. If the coach becomes involved, his power may dwindle as he uses more and more airtime. He will tend to lose the credibility and neutrality he should have while serving as the learning coach. His few moments of "wisdom" and servant-leadership behavior will now be seen as more ordinary.

Lack of confidence in the group. If the coach feels that unless she intervenes the group will miss an important insight or solution, she is indicating to group members that she does not trust them, that they need her to save them. The group will become either more dependent or more resentful as time goes on.

There may be situations and occasions when the learning coach does need to involve herself in the problem, such as if she and only she has critical data that the group is missing or when the group has only two or three members and the diversity value of the coach may be needed. However, she should become involved with caution and be fully aware of how this involvement lessens the power and benefits provided by a coach who is focused only on the learning.

Coach Seeks to Empower the Group Members

An important nuance in implementing the role of the action learning coach is understanding the distinction between motivating and empowering the group. Motivation relies on the external, whereas empowerment believes in the internal capacity of people. The action learning coach seeks to empower whenever and in whatever way she can. She believes that each and every member is needed and can contribute to the group. The group and its members have a variety of internal capabilities and talents. People can and should discover what they must change and learn, and should be held accountable for their decisions and actions. Internal expectations and fulfillment rather than external threats or rewards should be what stimulate and inspire them.

Table 7 summarizes the distinctions between the motivating and empowering approaches.

Values of the Action Learning Coach

Due to the intensity and intimacy of the action learning process, group members will quickly perceive and recognize the mind-set and attitude of the coach toward them. A positive, humanistic confident attitude will

TABLE 7

Assumptions for Motivating Versus Empowering

Assumptions for Motivating	Assumptions for Empowering
Something is wrong with people	People need new perspectives; the solution is within
People need to be told what to do	People can learn and change in action
People need to be threatened or rewarded	People need to be held accountable
People need to be comforted	People need appreciation and respect

result in the coach being both more effective and more enjoyable to work with. With the right attitude and right questions, the coach becomes highly valued and appreciated by the group. Carter McNamara (2002), a leading action learning theorist and practitioner, recently identified several values and attitudes that the coach should embrace relative to how he perceives the members of action learning groups.

- ▶ Members have great or even unlimited potential.
- ▶ They must develop first and primarily from within themselves.
- ▶ Learning and development include the whole person—thoughts, feelings, head, and heart.
- ▶ People can develop a great deal by asking the right questions and by closely examining their assumptions and perspectives about themselves and the world around them.
- ▶ The goals and direction of coaching come from the nature and needs of the group members.
- ▶ The role of actions and experience are critical to learning and development; without practice, there is no knowledge.
- ▶ Coaching is a way of working with people that should leave them more competent, more fulfilled, and more able to contribute to their organizations and to find meaning in what they do.

How the Coach Handles Group and Individual Dysfunctional Behaviors

During the sessions, a number of pitfalls and difficulties may emerge, such as some of the following issues.

One Member Dominates the Group

This problem does not normally arise in action learning groups, since an individual should be making statements only in response to a question. New questions are not raised until the previous question has been answered. If a person begins to try to take over the group, the coach can simply ask the group, "What is the quality of our questions at this time?" Everyone, including the person who may be dominating the group, will quickly recognize that the group norm and action learning ground rules are being violated, and the group's balance will quickly be restored.

Conflict Exists Among Group Members

In any problem-solving situation, with individuals with different personalities and different perspectives, and with a problem that has multiple possible solutions, there will inevitably be some disagreements and even hostile feelings expressed. Because of the intensity within the context of action learning, there will be times when emotions run high. However, if they become too high, the resulting stress will cause people to back off, and they may become concerned about offending someone inside or outside the group.

Problem- or strategy-based conflicts are fine as long as they are legitimate and are openly examined. Personality conflicts, on the other hand, are not beneficial for a group. These types of conflict, however, can be overcome, since the coach brings above the table what, in most groups, stays below the table. The coach merely asks, "How are we doing as a group?" One or more individuals will say, "Not well." Asking for examples and why this conflict is occurring will enable the group to recognize how the conflict contributes to and detracts from the effectiveness of the group, how to best deal with the conflict, and how to reinforce earlier agreed-upon norms and/or introduce new norms. Upon resumption of work on the problem, the group will return to high levels of performance.

Members Are Late or Cannot Attend

Of course, serious emergencies can arise when busy people attempt to fulfill commitments made weeks or months in advance. If someone is late or not able to attend an action learning session, the coach should help the group to decide how to most effectively use the session with this person being absent. The group should also discuss how to update and assist the absent member in "re-experiencing" what the group did at this missed session.

Members Interrupt or Engage in Side Conversations

It is important that all members be fully engaged in the work and learning of the group at all times. Interruptions and side conversations are disruptive and demonstrate that the individual's self-interests are more important than the group's. The coach should intervene with an observation (e.g., "I am observing an interruption or side conversation"), followed by questions that will enable the individual and the group to recognize the impact of this behavior and to identify ways in which new or stronger norms can be developed to handle this behavior in the future (e.g., "What is the impact of this behavior on the work of the group?"; "What could the group do to prevent this behavior from re-occurring in the future?").

Low Energy or Frustration Exists in the Group

There will be times when the group has worked long and hard, but it would be unwise to end the session yet or take a break. The coach can simply note that the group appears to have low energy (or to be frustrated) and help the group to become aware of this and to identify what they could do through questions such as the following: Why are we low in energy? What would enable us to be more energized? Or, why are we frustrated now? How can we best overcome our frustration?

Members Do Not Use Questions, or They Provide Extraneous Information

If a member is making statements rather than using the questioning format, the coach can simply ask the person, "Can you put that in the form of a question?" Likewise, if a person provides information not sought by the questioner, the coach should ask, "What question are you answering?" Group members quickly recognize that the coach is being friendly but firm in enforcing the norm of "statements can be made only in response to questions."

Additional Roles of the Action Learning Coach

In addition to the coaching role that occurs with action learning groups, the coach may be called on to serve a variety of other roles to ensure the success of action learning in the organization.

Trainer/Teacher

Often the action learning coach is responsible for orienting and preparing individuals and the organization as a whole for action learning. She should brief them on the basic principles and benefits of action learning, including the six components and two ground rules. Such training may occur before large groups prior to the establishment of an organization's action learning programs (see Chapter 8 for more details on introductory workshops). At the beginning of the first learning sessions, the coach introduces or reviews the fundamental components of action learning, particularly her role as the coach.

The teaching role may arise during sessions when the coach is asked by group members to explain what action learning is or why there are the six dimensions or the two ground rules. However, when the coach is asked questions relative to the problem or for direct feedback on their group dynamics, the coach should indicate that, although he appreciates the question, his role is to focus on how to help the group learn, and that their ideas/opinions are more important. He should then turn the question back to the questioner: "What tool, resource, or idea would be helpful here?" or "How do you feel we are working as a group?" or "How do you think you could improve?"

Administrator

In some organizations, the action learning coach may also serve as the administrative coordinator and manager of the action learning program. He is involved in arranging the sites and dates of the sessions and serves as a bridge between the group and top management. He maintains contact with key people outside the groups to ensure their continued support, and he updates appropriate people as necessary. He may need to work with the sponsor to assure her that the group is progressing well or to confirm that she will support the action being proposed by the group. He may serve as a link with and provide support for the organization's action learning champions. Between meetings of the groups, the coach may send reminders of upcoming sessions, of agreed upon actions, and of the importance of applying the learnings in other parts of the organization. If the group is composed of people from different organizations, he may need to serve as the key link and contact point among the various organizations.

Action Learning Coaches at DuPont

PAULA TOPOLOSKY, DUPONT GLOBAL SERVICES BUSINESS

DuPont's coaches should have the following attributes:

- ▶ Familiar with group processes
- ▶ Able not to take control of the group's work
- ▶ Comfortable being an invisible observer
- ▶ Helps team learn from its mistakes
- ▶ Knows how to create a learning environment
- ▶ Creates energy for learning and growth

Skills and Values of a Competent and Confident Action Learning Coach

The action learning coach, because of the power given him, should be cognizant of how his values and skills as well as his actions impact the group and the action learning process. His presence alone has a significant effect on the group; the members know that the coach may raise questions at any point that will challenge their thinking and actions. Therefore, there are a number of important skills and values that are needed to be successful as an action learning coach. Let's briefly examine ten of them.

(1) Ability to Ask Questions

A critical skill of the action learning coach is her ability to ask good, hopefully occasionally great, questions. Her questions should make people think and feel challenged; they should be supportive and positive rather than critical. To ask good questions consistently, the coach needs to have a strong and sincere belief in the power of questions and the critical role of the action learning coach in asking questions. The manner of introducing questions should be gentle and never arrogant. The coach should screen herself and determine whether her question will be truly helpful to the group. She should be looking at how questions can create possibilities for significant learnings and breakthrough actions.

(2) Courage and Authenticity

Asking questions is not always easy, especially asking the tough follow-up questions or questions that require deep and intensive soul searching. The action learning coach needs to be courageous and authentic. He needs to be strong and not intimidated by the rank, expertise, or character of the person to whom the question is posed. He should trust his doubts to confirm if agreement and/or clarity truly exist.

(3) Confidence and Trust in the Action Learning Process

It is important for the coach to have confidence in her role and to demonstrate this confidence by her comfort in the action learning process. She should have confidence that the process will work because it is built on theories and principles (the six components and two rules) that are already in place, and that every group has the right and needed people, and will be successful. With a strong confidence in the ultimate success of the process, the action learning coach is able to tolerate and handle the bumps along the way because she recognizes that she will soon see the group learning, maturing, and becoming remarkably efficient and effective.

(4) High Positive Regard for All Group Members

The action learning coach respects each person and has a concern for the well-being of all members. He sincerely believes that the group has all the necessary abilities to solve the problem; his job is merely to bring out and capitalize on these strengths. He wants them to succeed with the project and to learn from so doing. His ability to empathize and be supportive is very important. He should see members as having great potential and recognize that their potential will be realized during the action learning sessions.

(5) Open and Nonjudgmental

The effective action learning coach is open to different perspectives and personalities of group members. Of course, she will have opinions about the strategies being offered, but she should not be taking sides. While she may like certain personality types better than others, that should never be shown nor should it affect her questions, commitments, or objectivity. This attitude of openness and being nonjudgmental will generate much goodwill and ultimate team cohesiveness and dialogue among members.

(6) Humble yet Confident

Like the Level 5 leader described by Collins (2001), the action learning coach should be humble, yet confident in herself and in the group. She should be cognizant of both her strengths and limitations. Her self-confidence enables her to be authentic and resilient. Her humility demonstrates that she is willing and able to learn. She should be seen as someone who can be trusted, and who can handle rivalries, distrust, and anger.

(7) Sense of Timing

Finding the ideal time to intervene is an art for the action learning coach. If he intervenes too early, the group or individual may not have sufficient data to adequately respond, and thus there may be a missed opportunity for understanding. If the intervention is too late, there may also be a missed opportunity for learning as well as frustration on the part of the participants because the group has been struggling too long. Experience will help the coach grow more comfortable and confident in intervening at the right time with the right questions.

(8) Ability to Multitask

The action learning coach has a variety of roles to perform while serving as an action learning coach. She needs to monitor the questioning-responding dialogue within the group, observe the demonstration of leadership skills, develop and sequence questions for asking during and at the end of the session, manage time to ensure action and learning, handle any dysfunctional behavior that might harm an individual or the group as a whole, and so on. In many ways, the action learning coach must be a model of a person who is learning while acting, and thus able to competently handle a number of tasks simultaneously and improve every time a similar task is required.

(9) Ability to Listen and Reflect

Successful coaches possess strong listening skills. They are able to hear what is not said as well as what is said. Careful observation and good note taking allows them to be in tune with who is saying what, how, when, and to whom. Active listening requires a great deal of attention. Strong listening skills enable coaches to acquire a "helicopter" perspective, a holistic view, which enables them to see the big picture and how each and every group member is acting and learning.

(10) Strong Commitment to Learning

Action learning coaches are eager to help people learn, and they become excited and proud when group members develop and improve. As tempting as it may be to become involved in problem solving during a session, coaches recognize that the learning is so much more important, and is therefore committed to use all their time and energy to help the individual and the group learn. They know that one great learning may result in a changed life, a changed problem, and a changed organization.

"In two hours, I accomplished more through the action learning process than I would have achieved in six months."
—Doug Park, Director, Microsoft Xbox Support

Powerful Impact of an Effective Action Learning Coach

The action learning coach has the power to build great individuals, great teams, and great organizations. His service to the action learning group can enable that group to solve very complex problems in short periods of time. His interventions, observations, and questions can help group members to become terrific leaders and wonderful human beings. The groups coached by action learning coaches are a joy to be in; folks who normally do not enjoy groups at all love to be in action learning groups. In a recent group in which I served as a coach, a person noted that this action learning group was the first group in his twenty-five years in the company in which the group was quickly achieving its goal, everyone was learning, and it was lots of fun. The action learning coach is a true catalyst whose strategic and timely interventions can lead to momentous and powerful business results and learning successes.

Checklist for Action Learning Coach

- ► Has the coach been able to guide us in reflecting?
- ► Has a learning and action climate been established?
- ► Are the interventions timely and appropriate?
- ► Does the coach model good questioning and listening skills?
- ► Does she demonstrate confidence in the action learning process?
- ► What is her attitude toward group members?
- ► Does she avoid getting involved with the problem?
- ► Did the coach recognize learning opportunities when they occurred?
- ► What other roles does the action learning coach need to play? Teacher and trainer? Administrator? Promoter? Adviser? Champion?
- ► Is the coach committed to helping us learn and develop?
- ► Did the coach enable us to get consensus on the problem? On the strategies?
- ► Does the coach handle dysfunctional behaviors effectively and promptly?
- ► How could the coach be more effective?

Twelve Steps for Sustainable Action Learning

8

Introducing, Implementing, and Sustaining Action Learning in Organizations

Action learning can be introduced into an organization by any individual or business unit that would like to use this marvelous tool for solving problems and enhancing development. To successfully and systematically introduce, implement, and sustain action learning programs throughout an organization, follow the twelve steps listed in table 8 and detailed in this chapter. These steps will enable you to optimize the power of action learning and promote its extension throughout the organization. The careful launching of the program will ensure its success and continuation as well as help the organization to overcome the barriers and pitfalls that might derail action learning along the way.

Step 1: Gain and Maintain Support of Top Management

The first step, and certainly one of the most critical steps in establishing powerful and successful action learning programs in an organization, is to gain the support of top management. The leaders in the organization will become invaluable in launching action learning throughout the organization

TABLE 8
Twelve Steps for Introducing, Implementing, and Sustaining
Action Learning

1. Gain and maintain support of top management.
2. Develop an action learning management team.
3. Conduct an Introduction to Action Learning workshop.
4. Hire and/or prepare action learning coaches.
5. Determine participants of the action learning group.
6. Choose problems and projects for action learning.
7. Orient group members and set up the action learning project.
8. Reframe the problem, establish high-level goals, and develop strategies.
9. Present the strategies developed by the action learning groups.
10. Implement the action strategies.
11. Assess, capture, and transfer the individual, group, and organizational learnings.
12. Make action learning part of the corporate culture.

and assuring the action learning groups that their efforts, strategies, and learnings will be championed and promoted by the organization.

To gain this support, the leaders themselves must first be convinced that action learning will successfully and quickly solve the complex and urgent problems of the organization. They must be willing to acknowledge that some of their existing challenges and problems have been intractable and not well resolved by the existing approaches, such as task groups, training, and outside consultants. These leaders should therefore be open to trying a new approach that will generate quantum improvements for their business and prepare their workers for the challenging and competitive environment surrounding them.

It is very important that top management has a solid understanding of action learning processes and principles. Otherwise, they may not select the appropriate problems, people, or resources for action learning. Or they may withdraw support at the first sign of difficulty or resistance. It is valuable to highlight the fact that action learning enables the organization to have more time in the long term by resolving present problems that are obstructing success in the short term.

If top management becomes convinced that action learning will develop and improve the organizational capacity to provide better products, services, and profits, they will be willing to assign their most critical and urgent problems to the action learning groups and to commit themselves to implementing the solutions and strategies developed by the group. Ideally, they will allow, encourage, and enable the group itself to carry out the solutions it has identified.

Top management should be aware of the fact that if proposed solutions from the group are rejected or ignored, the energy and efforts of members will quickly dissipate, and much of the power and potential growth of action learning will be impaired. Managers must also understand that if the action learning process is to build leaders and teams, they must allow time and provide appropriate resources (e.g., an action learning coach). Time for learning and development needs to be an integral part of the company's action learning programs. An important question, even at this early stage, is whether the organization will be using internal or external action learning coaches.

A tremendous boost to action learning is to have top management commit to assigning senior managers to action learning groups or to become members of groups themselves. They can also reinforce action learning by allowing groups to use company time to work on organizational problems. Such actions clearly demonstrate their commitment to the program. It is important that leaders maintain management support even when some projects do not achieve immediate success.

What is the best way to secure the support of top management for instituting action learning, and who should introduce action learning to top management? Usually, one or more staff members have heard about or experienced action learning at a conference or in another organization and decide to approach management on their own. These people may emerge as internal action learning champions who offer to submit their own problems and staff to the initial action learning programs. Or they may decide to use action learning at their staff meetings so that they can then show top management how it has been working for them.

Some action learning proponents have found that a more effective approach is to bring an external source—either a leader from another company who is a strong proponent or an experienced action learning coach—into the organization to introduce the principles and benefits of action learning. Often leaders are uncomfortable trying a new system or tool unless they know that other companies have had success with it. Thus, it is valuable to provide examples of companies that have used action learning with wonderful results.

Maintaining Senior Management Involvement and Support

Sustained involvement and support by senior management is an important success factor for action learning. There are many instances where action learning was readily adopted and initially supported by senior leadership, only to lose momentum and vital support as the process unfolded. Factors that erode support include (a) competing demands and (b) unexpected business challenges.

It is important that top management be prepared for these possibilities and provide the support. They also need to clearly communicate that the action learning programs are critical to the success of the organization, and that not remaining committed or undercutting the action learning programs will not be acceptable.

Checklist for Gaining and Maintaining Top Management Support

▶ Is top management committed to action learning?

▶ Do managers understand the benefits and expectations of action learning?

▶ What information or endorsements would enhance their support?

▶ Will they support the action learning groups with time and resources?

▶ Are they aware of and supportive of cultural changes created by action learning?

▶ Is there agreement on overall objectives for the program?

▶ Do they want leadership development as part of the action learning programs? Team building? Organizational culture change?

▶ Have the program and its objectives been discussed with potential participants and their managers?

▶ Do managers and participants understand the time factor involved?

Gaining Top Management Support for Action Learning at Samsung

Action learning at Samsung was introduced to the top leadership by the Samsung HRD department, which had learned about action learning through benchmarking at sites such as GE as well as from attending action learning forums of the World Institute for Action Learning (WIAL). Top management was persuaded to adopt action learning as a strategic tool to develop business leaders. The action learning programs were designed to last five months in both offline and online training, and would culminate in a final presentation in which all key executives, including the CEO, would participate. Samsung senior executives are responsible for assigning strategic problems to the action learning teams. Samsung's action learning programs require the top management's engagement from issue selection to final evaluation to make sure that proposed solutions are actually put to work. The CEO is involved in selection of problems, selection of action learning participants, interim strategy development reporting, and evaluation of the action learning programs.

Step 2: Develop an Action Learning Program Management Team

To ensure the successful introduction and implementation of action learning in the organization, there are four support systems that are most valuable: (1) a steering committee, (2) an action learning champion, (3) an action learning program manager, and (4) supervisors of the members of the action learning teams.

1. Steering Committee

An action learning steering committee is a senior-level executive group that has the final authority for approving the business goals, learning strategies, and budget for the action learning program. Just as important, the executive committee plays an important role in shaping the organizational learning environment. Active executive sponsorship may encourage greater risk tolerance and openness. All learning requires a certain amount of courage, and a risk-tolerant environment facilitates learning and performance by encouraging team members to engage in experimentation and actively challenge assumptions. Because action learning proposals may challenge currently accepted management orthodoxy, an open environment supported visibly by an executive steering committee sets the stage for true inquiry (Marquardt et al., 2009).

2. Action Learning Champion

Top management should identify someone who is the action learning champion, someone who will be responsible for acquiring and maintaining support for action, who serves as the cheerleader for action learning. This person promotes action learning to top management and throughout the organization, recruits problem sponsors, and regularly updates those affected by the action learning groups. The champion serves as the key link between top management and the action learning projects, and continuously looks for new action learning opportunities for the organization. The champion is the organizational person who ensures that action learning programs are given high visibility and acceptance in the organization. She is someone who understands the nature of the program, thinks it is important, and can be influential in making sure the group gains access to the necessary resources. She will work with key leadership in the organization to be sure that action learning programs are supported and implemented. This person seeks to ensure that appropriate company people cooperate in providing time, answers, and resources to the action learning members, both in the group setting and occasionally in one-to-one situations.

3. Action Learning Program Manager

The program manager's role is to plan, monitor, and measure the impact and effectiveness of the action learning intervention. This includes the development of a program design that links program goals with business, talent, and learning strategies. An action learning program plan—which addresses scope, quality, and change issues; staffing requirements; communication plans; risk; evaluation strategies; and budget requirements—is also an important responsibility of the program manager. The program manager is responsible for overall program quality, smooth functioning, and responding to the steering committee, program champion, or team member requests. The program manager arranges for sponsor, team member, and steering committee education. He manages budgeting, events, and communication.

4. Supervisors of the Action Learning Participants

Often overlooked, but highly important, members of the action learning support team are the supervisors of the participants. Participation in action learning requires time away from the core job. This time is an investment by both the participant and the supervisor and should be acknowledged as such from the very beginning. Some of the additional organizational support factors provided by managers include timely, relevant, and specific feedback as well as appropriate and meaningful consequences. The supervisor may also be involved in nominating his or her participant for the process. It is advisable for the supervisor, the action learning coach, and the participant to meet prior to the start of the action learning program to select the individual's development focus as well as to identity how learnings and ideas from the action learning sessions can be applied to his work and benefit the organization.

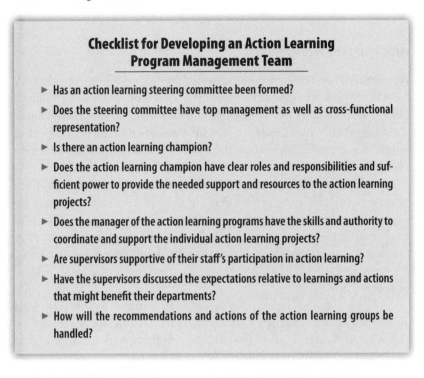

Checklist for Developing an Action Learning Program Management Team

► Has an action learning steering committee been formed?

► Does the steering committee have top management as well as cross-functional representation?

► Is there an action learning champion?

► Does the action learning champion have clear roles and responsibilities and sufficient power to provide the needed support and resources to the action learning projects?

► Does the manager of the action learning programs have the skills and authority to coordinate and support the individual action learning projects?

► Are supervisors supportive of their staff's participation in action learning?

► Have the supervisors discussed the expectations relative to learnings and actions that might benefit their departments?

► How will the recommendations and actions of the action learning groups be handled?

Step 3: Conduct an Introduction to Action Learning Workshop

Once top management has given its support to introducing action learning into the organization and has created a support team, it is important to get the rest of the organization aboard. The best way to accomplish this goal is to conduct an Introduction to Action Learning workshop that orients everyone to the principles and benefits of action learning. This workshop can also be an opportunity to demonstrate that top management supports the use of action learning in the organization. Some organizations extend time for the workshop to allow for one or two action learning sessions so that staff can experience action learning for themselves in addition to observing it. The workshop should generate enthusiasm from staff members for action learning, encourage them to participate in the program, and, in some cases, encourage them to establish action learning groups in their own business units. Therefore, it is critical that the workshop is well delivered, exciting, informative, and thorough so as to build momentum and commitment throughout the organization for action learning.

Arranging the Workshop

A number of key decisions must be made in preparing for the introductory workshop. First, who should conduct the workshop? Is there an internal person who has sufficient knowledge and experience to lead and facilitate the session? Or is it preferable to seek an outside action learning expert or contact an organization such as the World Institute for Action Learning (*www.wial.org*)?

To determine the initial interests and concerns of the organization, you may wish to do an informal survey of some of the staff to ascertain the expectations, biases, previous experiences, and misconceptions they may have about action learning. This will allow the planner(s) and presenter to develop the most responsive content and to identify the cases and issues for the workshop that best demonstrate the concerns as well as the benefits of action learning.

Logistics are also important. Provide a convenient and quiet place with sufficient space for the action learning workshop. Arrange for adequate time (ideally two to three hours), not so late or early that people are arriving late or leaving before the workshop has been completed.

You may wish to identify a possible problem or task beforehand that is of interest to most of the attendees and can best demonstrate action learning in a short period of time. If this is not possible, you will need to seek a volunteer to offer a problem during the workshop itself.

This is sometimes risky, as often no one wishes to volunteer a problem, or the one posed is either too complex to be handled in the abbreviated time period or is unimportant to many of the people attending the workshop.

Ideally, everyone in the organization should have the opportunity to attend the workshop. If there is limited space and only a limited number of people can attend, be sure to recruit the decision makers and those who can quickly put the program into action. It is important to market the workshop extensively to get people to willingly attend. Capture their curiosity. Highlight the benefits. And even if management is requiring everyone to attend, it is still valuable to develop the pre-workshop enthusiasm via word of mouth and/or flyers and in-company media.

Before conducting the workshop, it is beneficial to have top management, or at least some managers, identify problems or tasks around which they would like to use action learning groups in the near future. This will harness the momentum created by the workshop, and the energy can be quickly put to use. Other possible pre-workshop issues include deciding whether to seek volunteers or appoint action learning group members, determining time frames for action learning groups, and selecting the action learning coaches.

Content of Workshop

The two-hour workshop has three distinct segments: overview of action learning, demonstration of action learning, and questions and next steps.

Overview of Action Learning (30–45 minutes)

During the first segment of the introductory workshop, the attendees should receive a clear picture about the following topics.

- ► What action learning is and what it is not (i.e., how it is different from quality circles, task forces, outdoor adventures, other problem-solving groups)
- ► The benefits of action learning, namely, the solving of complex and urgent problems and the development of leaders, teams, and organizations
- ► The six components of action learning and two ground rules
- ► The single-problem and multiple-problem types of action learning
- ► Basic principles and procedures of action learning

Demonstration of Action Learning (30–45 minutes)

Action learning should always be demonstrated; nothing explains how and why action learning works or confirms its power and benefits as well as seeing and experiencing the real thing. If the organization has already identified the problem, then the problem is announced and four or five volunteers are requested. If no problem has been identified, the presenter indicates a need for four or five volunteers, one of whom would be willing to share a problem or challenge for the group to work on.

The volunteers should assemble on a stage or in a center space so that the entire audience can observe and hear the interactions of the volunteers as well as the questions and comments of the action learning coach. The volunteers may need to be reminded to speak loudly, even though they are talking to someone a few feet away, so the audience can hear their words.

The presenter/consultant should serve as the action learning coach, as only someone who is experienced and skilled in this role can adequately demonstrate it. The success of the demonstration will depend to a large extent on the competencies of the action learning coach.

The coach indicates, in the interest of time, that she will be condensing the stages of action learning and jumping more quickly to subsequent stages so as to go through all the stages in the allotted time frame. She also indicates that she will be serving both as the action learning coach and as a teacher who will be highlighting action learning principles and describing events to the audience as they occur. Thus, she will be more active and vocal than she normally might be in the role of action learning coach.

To maintain the interest and learning of the audience, the coach asks these observers to note the changes in group dynamics of the action learning group, the impact of the action learning coach on the group, examples of leadership skills, and great questions that have been asked. Audience members should not be allowed to ask their questions during the demonstration, as that would destroy the cohesiveness and direction of the group, as well as consume much more time than can be allocated to the demonstration.

During the demonstration, the group should quickly go through the stages of reframing the problem, identifying the goal, and developing strategic actions, with perhaps one or two interventions by the coach. After the group has worked for fifteen to twenty-five minutes, the coach will advise the group that it has another five minutes to work on the problem and strategies before she concludes the demonstration with some reflective questions for them. During the course of the demonstration, there will be a number of strategies that will have been developed by the group and that the problem presenter or organizational representative will be asked to consider.

When the group has completed its work, the coach asks the problem presenter what action he is going to take based on the ideas and strategies that have arisen. After he has identified his proposed actions, the problem presenter is asked if he has been helped and, if so, how. Inevitably, he has been helped, since he has had the problem clarified and reframed, a result that always occurs when a problem is talked out and explored from a variety of perspectives.

The coach uses the final five to ten minutes to ask the action learning group a number of questions to develop their individual, team, and organizational learning, concurrently alerting the audience as to why she asked the questions that she asked, and the intended impact of those questions.

Questions and Next Steps (15–30 minutes)

The organization's presenter and/or the action learning coach should then ask the audience what observations they have made about the group and the coach relative to questions, learnings, and actions. She should also answer any questions they might have about any principles and practices of action learning that were unclear. It is important that this discussion period focus on the process of what happened, not the content of the problem, since the problem could have been resolved in a number of ways, and members of the audience, because of their different perspectives, might have considered other alternatives. To debate what someone might consider a better alternative would be nonproductive and inconclusive and would miss the point of the demonstration, namely, how and why action learning works.

Another option at this point would be to form a panel at the front of the room composed of a senior leader of the organization, the action learning coach, and the champion of action learning in this company. Following questions and discussion about action learning in general, the panel may begin ascertaining the audience's understanding and commitment to action learning, as well as specific actions and steps that the organization will take to establish an action learning program.

Opportunity for All Participants to Experience Action Learning (2–4 hours)

Many organizations recognize the value of immersing as many staff members as possible into action learning (especially senior managers). This participation can far surpass merely observing it. Thus they extend the introductory program for an additional two to four hours so that the attendees can experience one or two action learning sessions. These sessions can reinforce the power and speed of action learning to solve problems as well as develop the leadership skills of those participating.

Introduction to Action Learning Programs at Fraser & Neave

Recently, Fraser & Neave, a global corporation headquartered in Singapore, scheduled seven full-day Introduction to Action Learning workshops, each attended by fifty senior leaders. Thus a total of 350 managers discovered and experienced the power of action learning and began utilizing action learning to solve problems in their respective business units. In July, 2011, an Action Learning Showcase Conference was held at which the top action learning projects were presented and recognized, thus encouraging an even greater awareness of and commitment to action learning throughout the entire organization.

Benefits of Introduction to Action Learning Workshop

The introductory workshop can serve many purposes. Not only does it enable the organization and potential group members to understand action learning, how it works, and how it benefits individuals and the organization, but also it can begin the screening process to determine which managers now believe sufficiently in the tool to initiate an action learning program in their department. It may also identify individuals who would like to join an action learning group as well as those who might like to become action learning coaches. The impetus created by this workshop should quickly be converted into one or many learning groups.

Checklist for Planning and Assessing Preparatory Workshop

▶ Is top management in support of and present at the workshop?

▶ Are the facilities adequate for presenting and demonstrating action learning?

▶ Is there sufficient time available?

▶ Are all the appropriate people attending?

▶ Are the basic elements of action learning being well covered?

▶ Is the demonstration well organized and set up?

▶ Has the organization identified an appropriate problem or challenge for the demonstration?

▶ What is the level of organizational/employee enthusiasm for action learning?

▶ Has a training workshop been developed and conducted that ensures that the participants will have (a) a solid understanding of the basic concepts and mechanics of action learning and (b) an appreciation of the value of reflective questioning and continuous learning?

▶ Are outside resources and linkages needed?

▶ Has a time frame been established for setting up the action learning programs in the organization? (This is optional, but it is important for participants to have a sense of the level of commitment to action learning by the organization.)

Action Learning Lessons at Oxford University Press

As a result of the numerous action learning programs at Oxford University Press, the following lessons have been learned that will ensure greater successes for future programs (Marsh and Wood, 2001):

- ► Ensure that you have top management support and that sponsors of projects fully understand their vital role. We insist not only on briefing sponsors, but also on training them alongside their participants before the project work begins. You must have the best people tackling the projects and people who will manage their time effectively to complete the work.

- ► The project content is vital. Pick inappropriate projects and the program is doomed to failure. The projects must be big, but not so big as to overwhelm a project leader and the team working on it for six months.

- ► The brief for the project may need to be renegotiated a number of times. It must also have some finite results. Beware, too, of continuous improvement fatigue. Participants, and the organization generally, can tire of the same messages being circulated. The projects need to be marketed effectively and presented imaginatively.

- ► The purpose of an action learning program is that action should take place. Participants should always be encouraged to act and to make decisions, not just recommend courses of action. This is the very essence of the action learning program.

Step 4: Select and Prepare Action Learning Coaches

The overall success of the action learning program is dependent on the quality of coaching, particularly at the initial stages. If coaches perform their roles competently, the program will likely achieve the goals of innovative problem solving as well as individual, team, and organizational learning. The organization should make the following three key decisions relative to action learning coaches.

Should Coaches Be from Within or Outside the Organization?

The organization needs to decide whether it is interested in and has the resources to bring in skilled (ideally certified) outside coaches. If the organization chooses to have internal coaches, it will need to determine who will select the coaches and what the selection criteria will be. Additional questions such as "How many coaches should we have available?" and "Should we choose only from our HRD staff or from among our managers or other staff?" must be addressed.

Whether the coaches are internal or external, it is critical that they have a solid understanding of the role, responsibilities, and attributes of the action learning coach. They should be comfortable in asking reflective questions and have confidence and trust in the power of questions rather than their own power. It is important that they have the self-discipline to not involve themselves in the problem, a challenge especially for internal coaches, who, because of their familiarity with the problem or their desire to get a solution that they find favorable or desirable, are tempted to jump into working on the problem rather than focusing on the learning.

Growing Leaders and Coaches at the U.S. Department of Agriculture

The U.S. Department of Agriculture, in its search for an efficient, cost-effective tool to train its leaders in specific leadership competencies, chose action learning. In order to build an internal capacity to continue action learning without contracting for an external action learning coach, the department created a parallel program to develop two internal coaches who were first provided training in action learning coaching and then gradually assumed greater and greater responsibility for the coaching function during the initial two leadership programs.

Should Coaching Be Rotated Among Members of the Group?

The action learning coach may serve in that role permanently for a particular group, or the role may be rotated during the life of the group (i.e., a different person in that role at each session). The benefit of rotating the coaching role is that it develops some key leadership skills that naturally and effectively occur within that role. For example, when a person serves as a coach, she often will see things that are missed by those involved in the details of the problem solving. Rotating coaches within the group also lessens the time and cost of bringing in outside people. On the other hand, the advantage of an outside person is that the entire group can devote all its attention to the problem.

If an external action learning coach is contracted, she will need to become familiar with the organization—its culture, mission, structure, and so on. If internal people are chosen, whether on a rotating or permanent basis, it is important that they be properly trained. Whether internal or external, rotating or permanent, coaches should be skilled and prepared to serve in that role. In Chapter 7, we examined the qualities and competencies needed to successfully coach an action learning group.

If Internal People Serve As Coaches, How Can We Train Them?

The best way to prepare someone to work internally as an action learning coach is to work with an organization such as the World Institute for Action Learning. Candidates can either attend public workshops to receive training and practice in becoming a certified action learning coach, or they can arrange for the training to be done internally. Numerous organizations, including Microsoft, Goodrich, Nationwide, Fuji-Xerox, Samsung, Humana, and Panasonic, have sent employees to external programs for coaching training; potential coaches have also received in-house training.

If the organization would like to informally prepare an internal staff person to become a coach, the following three stages are appropriate.

Participate in an Action Learning Group

Before serving as a coach, one should experience being a member of an action learning group to feel how it is to be asked reflective questions from a coach as well as to participate in the action learning stages and the learning process.

Shadow an Experienced Action Learning Coach

The next stage would be to shadow and observe a learning coach in action. After a session has ended, the coach will ask the observer-coach what happened and the impact of the questions of the coach. The coach will also ask the candidate what he learned from watching the session as an outsider.

Co-Coach

The third stage would be for the person to co-coach an action learning session. The two coaches would agree beforehand on who would intervene during and after the session. At the conclusion of the session, the "senior" coach would ask the aspiring coach how she felt she did, what she did well, what she could do better, and what she learned. The senior coach would then turn to the other members of the group and ask them what the co-coach did well, what she could have done better, what made her effective, and what questions were the most effective.

Selection and Training of Coaches at Boeing

At various points in the Boeing Global Leadership Program, action learning coaches work with the teams to help members reflect on how they could improve their capabilities as a team and how they could transfer their learnings to other aspects of Boeing operations. The action learning coaches receive an intensive two-day training course prior to serving in that role. In addition, the coaches receive coaching guidance during the initial facilitations of the Boeing teams. Both HRD staff and Boeing managers with no previous group facilitation background have served as action learning coaches.

Checklist for Selection and Preparation of Action Learning Coaches

► Will we use internal or external action learning coaches?

► Do we want the coach to be certified?

► If using internal staff, how will we train them?

► Will members of an action learning group rotate as coaches, or will a person be appointed to serve as the full-time coach?

► What attributes and criteria are we seeking for coaches?

► Are the learning coaches knowledgeable? Experienced? Comfortable with and trusting of the manner in which the action learning coach facilitates?

► If using internal coaches, how can we sustain and improve their skills?

Step 5: Determine Participants for the Action Learning Groups

After the organization has been oriented to action learning and selected the problem(s) for the group(s) to resolve, then decisions need to be made relative to the membership of the action learning groups. The following issues should be considered at this point.

Who Will Determine Membership in the Groups?

Membership in groups may be by self-selection or members may be determined by the organization, in which case the decision may be made by the sponsor, champion, and/or top leadership.

What Will Be the Number of Members in Each Group?

Action learning is most potent and efficient when the group size is five to six members. If at all possible, membership should not exceed eight members or be less than four. (See Chapter 3 for discussion of group size.)

What Will Be the Criteria for Membership?

The selection of participants should be vigorous to allow for a match between individuals' experiences and project needs. In addition, the organization should seek diversity of perspectives, with people from different business units, different age groups, different disciplines, and so on. Diversity of team members is essential for fresh questions and to capture a wide variety of perspectives. It also helps to break down silos and build a learning culture.

Membership should be a combination of those who are familiar with the problem and/or context and those who are not. If all are familiar with the problem or context, the group may have difficulty seeing "beyond the box" and being aware of their assumptions regarding the situation and the solutions. They will tend to say "no" or "we have already tried" too quickly and too often. The organization may feel that it takes too much valuable time to help an outsider "catch up" with people already familiar with the problem. However, as discussed in Chapter 3, the action learning process enables an outsider to quickly contribute to the group through his fresh questions and different perspectives and experiences, all of which can lead more easily to breakthrough problem solving.

Will Members Be Appointed, or Can People Volunteer?

In general, members of single-problem/organization-supported action learning groups are appointed, whereas multiple-problem action learning groups are usually composed of people who have voluntarily chosen to join this particular action learning group. The organization may choose to appoint people to be members of specific action learning groups for a number of reasons.

- ▶ The organization wishes to mix people from different business units for building corporate culture.
- ▶ The organization is eager to have certain individuals become familiar with particular settings or issues (many executive development programs choose this approach).
- ▶ Certain individuals are being considered for potential future leadership positions, and this is an opportunity to assess their true potential.
- ▶ Top management recognizes the importance of fresh perspectives or diversity and appoints people from different parts of the organization with different backgrounds and experiences.
- ▶ As a matter of convenience and cost, the organization takes advantage of the availability of certain people.

On the other hand, if employees have the option of volunteering to join action learning groups, their choice may be determined by the following factors.

- ▶ They care about the problem and/or people in the group.
- ▶ They have knowledge of and interest in the issue.
- ▶ This problem may have relevance to their work/problems.

Will Action Learning Include Members from Outside the Organization?

There are significant benefits to including people from outside the organization (e.g., customers, individuals from noncompeting companies, dealers, or suppliers). However, urgency of the problem, availability of the outsiders, and costs of using external members must be considered. Of course, the organization must weigh the advantages of gaining fresh ideas and different perspectives versus the potential loss of confidential internal information. Outside perspectives, however, can be helpful in developing and launching new programs. Novartis, for example, formed action learning groups with several noncompeting companies to solve problems submitted by the various companies (see case study in Chapter 2).

Checklist for Selection of Members for Action Learning Groups

- ► Will membership be by choice or appointment?
- ► What will be the size of the action learning group?
- ► Will we include members from outside the organization?
- ► How will timing and frequency of the action learning sessions affect potential members?
- ► Are the most appropriate people in the group?
- ► How can we best get diversity of ideas?

Step 6: Choosing Organizational Problems/ Projects for Action Learning

Choosing the projects or problems that learning groups will work on is absolutely critical for the ultimate success of action learning in the organizations. Urgent, complex problems and projects in need of innovative solutions will demonstrate the organization's commitment to action learning and help ensure that the action learning program will result in great actions as well as great learnings. Thus, whether chosen by an individual, by the business unit, or by the organization's top leaders, the problem should be urgent, important, and worth resolving, and it should have a definitive time frame for taking action.

A number of important decisions relative to the choice of the action learning problem need to be made at this juncture.

What Types of Problems Should Be Chosen?

Any problem that is important to the organization and requires breakthrough strategies to solve can be considered. Problems may be connected to operations, strategic planning, personnel, management, marketing, or customer relations. They may be significant and complex problems that require several months to complete or quick, urgent, and minor problems that need to be resolved before the end of the day. Examples of potential action learning problems include the following.

- Create a new performance appraisal system
- Develop a global strategy for the manufacturing division of the company
- Handle a disgruntled employee
- Build a global solution brand business
- Improve information systems
- Cut operational costs by $1 billion

Whatever problem is chosen, it must be one for which the group has been given the power and responsibility to solve and to develop strategies. When the problem is given to the group, the members need to be informed whether their task is to only develop the strategies or if they are also the ones who will implement the strategies.

Who Should Choose the Problem?

The problems in single-problem action learning groups are generally chosen by the organization, be it by a department manager or the CEO. The higher the level at which the problems are chosen, the more importance the project will be perceived as having. In multiple-problem action learning, usually all members select a problem that they would like to receive help for.

Choosing Action Learning Projects at Boeing

In the Global Leadership Program at Boeing, the problems were initially chosen by HR staff. However, as the Boeing Executive Council recognized the high quality of strategic actions developed by the action learning groups, the Council soon decided that it should choose future projects that were much grander in scope and provide even greater benefits for Boeing.

Who Will Present the Problem/Project at the Initial Session?

There are a number of options in how a problem is presented to the action learning group.

1. *Problem owner presents directly to action learning group.* The problem presenter is the person who has the problem or shares this problem with others. If the problem being considered is an organizational one or is one from a business unit, and two or more members of the group are familiar with the problem, then either a few or all of them can collaborate in presenting the problem and answering questions about the

problem. Of course, for the problem owner(s) to be part of the action learning group indicates a strong interest in solving the problem and a stronger commitment to implementing the solutions proposed.

2. *Problem owner's representative presents to the group.* There may be instances, however, when the problem owner is a manager who is unable to commit herself to attend every meeting of the group (as noted in Chapter 3, attendance at every session is essential for successful problem solving and learning), or she feels her presence would lessen the spontaneity and courage of the group in seeking fresh answers or examining root causes. In these circumstances, she may designate a representative to present the problem and to ensure that the group's proposed strategies will be implemented.

3. *Written document is prepared by the organization or problem presenter and distributed to the group prior to or at the beginning of the first action learning session.* Organizations may choose to spend considerable time to identify a key organizational problem and then prepare a document that provides some of the background of the problem, its importance, some desired objectives, and a time frame for solving the problem. If the problem owner is not able to be a full-time member of the group, he should try to be available at the first session to answer questions from the group. He should also be available between sessions to answer questions and to indicate his support or uncertainty relative to strategies being considered (particularly since the problem owner may be the "who knows, who can, and/or who cares" person). When possible, it is valuable for someone who prepared the document to be available at the first meeting to provide the initial description of the problem and to answer questions from the group. This will help the group reframe the problem as well as assist members in identifying and clarifying the business issue and deliverables.

4. *If it is a problem experienced by the group itself, no one presents the problem; rather each person is asked to write down the problem as he or she understands it and then share with other members of the action learning group.* Oftentimes, the problem to be worked on by the action learning group is a problem that is experienced by all or most of the members of the group. Thus, instead of having one person present the problem (which would only include one perspective, and likely not be agreed to by other members of the group), it is best to simply give each person an equal opportunity to describe the problem as he or she experiences it. For example, an internal organizational problem may be seen as a problem of morale by one person, a problem of poor leadership by another,

a problem of corporate culture by another, and a problem of poor skills by the fourth person. By allowing all members to present their own perspective, the group can then begin the session by asking all members to explain why they saw the problem in the way that they did.

What Aspects of the Problem Should Be Presented?

There is a fine balance between providing too little information about the problem (leaving the members wandering aimlessly) and too much information (thus limiting the range of options that the group considers). To frame his presentation, the problem presenter should take into account the following areas:

- ▸ What is the background of the project?
- ▸ How will the organization measure the success of the project team?
- ▸ What is the critical information you can provide to the team relative to
  - ▸ Business/strategic plans?
  - ▸ Marketing plans?
  - ▸ Competitive information?
  - ▸ Financial results and plans?
  - ▸ Benchmarking data?
- ▸ Who are the key people within the business/function that the team should meet with? Who will be responsible for scheduling people to meet with the project team (e.g., marketing, financial, manufacturing, legal, sourcing)?
- ▸ How can you help the project team have access to key stakeholders? Who will schedule these meetings?
- ▸ What key people outside the company should the team engage— customers, suppliers, competitors, trade associations, government agencies?

How Quickly Must the Problem Be Resolved?

Problems usually come with deadlines by which decisions need to be made and tasks need to be completed. If a problem needs to be solved this afternoon, the action learning group will be able to meet only one time. If the decision is due next week, the organization may arrange for the group to meet either on a part-time or full-time basis. If the final action date is a month or six months from now, then the group will probably meet on a part-time basis.

What Authority Should the Problem Presenter Retain?

Many managers are unable or unwilling to delegate power and decision making to a group that might come up with actions with which they are not fully comfortable. It is very difficult to sustain action learning programs if the teams soon recognize that they are merely offering suggestions that may or may not be implemented by the organization. Possible ways of overcoming this resistance include the following.

- ▶ Relate case studies from organizations such as Samsung, Novartis, Microsoft, or Boeing that have successfully used action learning over a number of years.
- ▶ Select a problem that is important but has primarily internal impact and for which there is sufficient time for interim testing and actions.

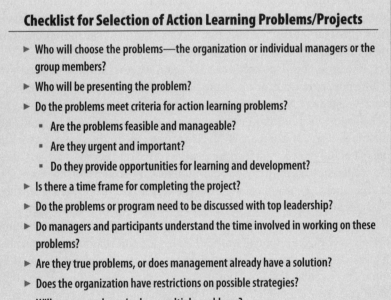

Checklist for Selection of Action Learning Problems/Projects

- ▶ Who will choose the problems—the organization or individual managers or the group members?
- ▶ Who will be presenting the problem?
- ▶ Do the problems meet criteria for action learning problems?
  - ▪ Are the problems feasible and manageable?
  - ▪ Are they urgent and important?
  - ▪ Do they provide opportunities for learning and development?
- ▶ Is there a time frame for completing the project?
- ▶ Do the problems or program need to be discussed with top leadership?
- ▶ Do managers and participants understand the time involved in working on these problems?
- ▶ Are they true problems, or does management already have a solution?
- ▶ Does the organization have restrictions on possible strategies?
- ▶ Will groups work on single or multiple problems?
- ▶ Will the group have the authority to implement its recommendations?
- ▶ Will proposed solutions first need to be presented to higher management for implementation? If so, to whom will the group present its recommendations?

Step 7: Orient Group Members and Set Up the Action Learning Project

Before or during the first action learning session, a number of logistical and clarifying tasks should be handled before the group begins working on the problem. These tasks include the following.

Arrange and/or Confirm Meeting Dates, Times, Frequency, and Locations

It is important that members attend each meeting of the group. If a member has a conflict that has arisen since the dates were established prior to the group's first meeting, the remaining members of the group should examine how they can help that person rearrange his schedule or priorities, or rearrange the schedule so that meetings are not held when someone cannot attend. It is better to have the group meet less frequently with everyone in attendance than to hold meetings with someone missing. Remember, action learning groups are unique in their "teamness" and in the potency amassed from that teamness; therefore, that quality of time is far more important than the quantity of time spent by the group.

The group needs to confirm once again whether it will be meeting on a full-time, part-time, or one-time basis, a decision that may be made by top management before the group has its first meeting.

Meeting full time may be necessary when the organization must quickly make a decision or immediately develop strategies for an issue or crisis. The benefit of full-time action learning groups is that the members are less likely to be interrupted by other job responsibilities. It is important, however, that the members not be pulled out of the group and that they concentrate their energies and efforts on solving the problem and developing strategies.

Many problems allow for the action learning group to meet on a part-time basis over a longer period of time. Meeting part-time has many advantages. It allows for members to carry out their regular, on the-job responsibilities; thus, the organization does not need to deploy other resources to cover their absence. (Although it is certainly possible for action learning sessions to occur outside working hours, this would indicate that the organization is not very committed to action learning.)

Meeting part-time also gives members the time and opportunity to gather information and/or apply strategies between sessions. In addition, individuals and the organization itself can more easily see growth and development as leaders, team members, and professionals.

More and more organizations are creating full-time action learning programs, especially as part of their leadership development efforts. Companies such as Boeing, Unilever, DuPont, and Baxter place high-potential leaders in one- to three-month action learning projects to work on major company challenges as well as to develop key leadership competencies. Some organizations, such as GE, establish one- to two-day weekday or weekend action learning programs. Others prefer projects to last for one to two months. Of course, the scheduling of sessions is determined by both the problems of the organization and the developmental needs of the group members.

Some action learning groups meet for one time only, as the problem has an urgent time frame and the issue is clearly defined. The availability of preferred group members (distance, other commitments) make the time and resource availability a now-or-never proposition.

Organizations should be careful not to overly restrict the time available for the group to work on the problem. Too short a time period may result in a less than stellar understanding of—and therefore poor solutions to— the problem. Gaining a systems perspective and identifying the points of greatest leverage require time during and between sessions.

Part-Time Action Learning Projects at Bristol-Myers Squibb

Bristol-Myers Squibb, a global leader in personal and health care, has used part-time action learning projects for nearly ten years to resolve its most complex challenges. Action learning groups meet for two to three hours a week or a month over a period of two to six months. Action learning projects have included development of marketing strategies, examination of plant closures, and means to increase customer support.

Specific Learning Purposes of the Action Learning Sessions

Organizations and the group members can identify both the specific individual and organizational learning purposes for the group. Most groups have a goal to develop the individuals' competencies, whether leadership competencies that are expected of all leaders in this organization (e.g., Boeing, Microsoft) or the specific competencies identified for this individual (e.g., U.S. Department of Agriculture). Individual members may ask the rest of the group to help them develop some specific personal skills, such as handling conflict, being a better listener, or tolerating ambiguity. Organizations may also seek goals that change the culture and competencies of the organization or develop team building and membership skills. The organization may also be expecting the learnings to be systematically transferred throughout the organization, and thus, time and effort to accomplish those goals need to be arranged by the action learning coach.

The individual's leadership goals are determined either before or at the beginning of the first session. The value of identifying the leadership skills or the organizational culture's goals up front is that everyone will be consciously or subconsciously thinking about them and therefore better able to provide specifics when the coach asks for examples of leadership behavior or opportunities for application.

Beginning the First Session

Before beginning the first session, all members of the group should understand the overall principles, the six components, and the two ground rules that serve as the foundation of action learning practice. Otherwise, they will not understand why they are to focus on asking and listening to questions, or why the action learning coach does what he does and with what authority. Members who are not properly oriented may soon become frustrated. They may feel the group is spending too much time clarifying the problem and not getting quickly enough to the solutions.

Also, never assume that group members understand and/or remember the principles and rules of action learning. Even if everyone attended the preparatory workshop (step 3), they may remember it differently or have forgotten some key elements. Therefore, someone in the group, usually the action learning coach, should take a few minutes at the beginning of the first session to clarify the elements of action learning and determine if there are any questions or confusion.

Confidentiality of Action Learning

For action learning to work, all group members must feel confident that their comments about the organization, customers, employees, and each other are kept in the room. Without confidence in the confidentiality of the group, problem presenters and members may not be willing to share the crucial information that they possess and may not be honest and frank in responding to questions. The quality of the problem solving and the group's development, accordingly, will be severely hampered. The importance of confidentiality can be addressed organization-wide if the company establishes this norm for all its action learning programs: any information shared within an action learning session is considered confidential and may be shared outside the group only with the approval of all members.

Checklist for Orientation and Preparation of Action Learning Groups

- ▶ Are the members clearly oriented to the principles of action learning?
- ▶ Are they aware of how action learning is different from task forces and other problem-solving groups?
- ▶ Is the role of the action learning coach clear and accepted?
- ▶ Are there any specific organizational or individual learning goals?
- ▶ Is there agreement on ground rules relative to confidentiality, starting and stopping on time, being supportive, and taking action between meetings?
- ▶ Have members agreed on future dates for set meetings and committed to attending them regularly?
- ▶ Do we have access to the necessary outside resources and knowledge?
- ▶ Is there a sense of ownership and responsibility for the problem?
- ▶ Has necessary time been reserved at the end of meetings for reflections, learnings, and applications?
- ▶ Are members interested in and committed to solving problems?
- ▶ Do members listen to, respect, and learn from others?
- ▶ Has sufficient time been allocated for learning?
- ▶ Is everyone committed to attending each meeting for the entire meeting?
- ▶ Is there a balance between problem solving/strategizing and reflection/ learning?
- ▶ Are participants practicing new kinds of behavior, for example, tolerating ambiguity, continually rethinking decisions and looking at probes from a new angle, taking risks, challenging others, searching out rather than receiving information, reflecting?
- ▶ How are we handling conflict, domination by an individual, member absence, and discomfort in sharing information (if these occur)?

Step 8: Reframe the Problem, Establish High-Level Goals, and Develop Strategies

Based on decisions made earlier relative to the time frame and deadlines for making decisions and taking action, the group may meet either on a full-time or part-time basis. The frequency of part-time meetings may thus be daily, weekly, or monthly. For example, if external events require an earlier decision point, and the problem is urgent, the group could establish a new schedule. The length of meetings may range from one to three hours (usually the minimum for multiple-problem groups) to a full day. Of course, the frequency and length of sessions can be adjusted if it is determined that more frequent or longer meetings are necessary.

Action learning groups are more valuable when there is more than one session and a reasonable amount of time between sessions, since the group can go only so far in reframing the problem and developing action plans during the session. Information and support from resources outside the group may be needed before the group can go any further. In addition, the group and/or individual members may need to carry out actions developed by the group, report back to the group at the next session, and only then plan further actions based on the results of earlier actions. Also, individuals need time to ascertain whether their competencies are being developed to have more opportunities for developing these preselected skills.

If, however, there is too long a time between meetings (i.e., more than one month), there may be missed opportunities for developing and implementing the action, particularly if this is, as it should be, an urgent problem. In addition, momentum for working on the problem, as well as the cohesiveness of the group, may be lost. Prior decisions and learnings may be lost as well. Also, group members may return to their previous problem-solving culture of making statements and jumping to conclusions, of debating rather than dialoguing.

Normally, the first session(s) will focus on the stages of problem reframing and goal framing, and later sessions will be spent primarily on the stages of developing strategies and taking actions. Skip Leonard and Arthur Freedman, Master Action Learning Coaches, have developed the graphic shown in figure 5 to capture the flow and process employed by action learning groups as they go through the four stages of solving complex problems.

It is important for the coach to assert her responsibility for retaining sufficient time to capture learnings and assist the group in developing its problem-solving abilities. Although group members may have the natural tendency to devote all their time to working on the problem and to depart immediately after the next action steps have been determined, the coach needs to insist on having the entire group take time to examine its growth and to identify areas for improvement. This resistance is usually overcome

FIGURE 5
Stages of Effective Problem Solving

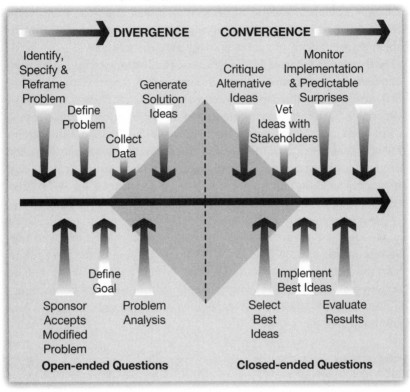

the first time the group sees improved performance as a result of the time they spent in "mining the learning."

Action learning groups have definitive time periods in which to produce clear results. Each group should take an appropriate and diligent amount of time to reframe the problem and establish the goal(s) that will have the most significant, long-term benefit to the organization or individual. It is important to remember that the group may often end up working on a goal not directly related to the originally presented problem, but one that is clearly the most appropriate goal for resolving the situation faced by the organization or individual in the most effective way.

The group knows it is accountable and responsible for resolving the problem. The reputation and future status of the organization, as well as the success of the organization itself, may depend on the quality of the group's strategies and the success of its actions. Thus, there should be full commitment to solving the problem. It is also important for the group to see each problem as unique, rather than as similar to a past problem and requiring a past solution. The group should avoid the tendency to jump to solutions too quickly or accept an easy, mundane solution.

As noted in Chapter 5, in a typical action learning project, the group considers three systems as it examines and solves the problem. These are *System Alpha*, or situation analysis; *System Beta*, the survey, hypothesis, experiment, audit, and review stage; and *System Gamma*, the mental predisposition of members and the organization to the situation. While group members are working on the problem and developing strategies, they need to monitor organizational support and commitment for participants and projects. It is important for the group to have clarity on the boundaries regarding what is open to change and what is not.

It is also important that specific actions to be taken are identified at the end of each action learning session. Clearly identify who will be responsible and by what dates. At the beginning of the next action learning meeting, the status and results of these actions should then be reviewed. Action learning groups take agreed-upon actions between sessions until the final decisions and overall actions have been determined and implemented.

Action Learning Programs at Boeing

The Global Leadership Program is divided into three phases: introduction, in-country, and report-out. The introduction consists of three days in a location within the United States and is filled with introductions, orientation, and guest speakers from within and outside of Boeing. The second phase of the program is spent entirely within the country selected by the corporate executive board as a strategically important country. The three weeks are spent traveling to major portions of the country, interviewing business leaders, hearing from country experts, and being immersed in the culture. After approximately ten days into this phase, the Boeing leaders are introduced to a specific business issue selected by the corporate executive board as an important and current issue for the company. The participants form action learning teams to develop solutions and recommendations to present to Boeing's corporate decision makers. The members of the action learning teams return to the United States for the final two days of the program. These days are spent reviewing, refining, and practicing the team's presentation before the executive committee at a regularly scheduled session. Boeing has incorporated many of the recommendations from Global Leadership participants, adding much to the company's global success.

Checklist for Reframing the Problem, Establishing High-Level Goals, and Developing Strategies

▶ What is the quality of problem framing?

▶ What type of problem is it—technical or adaptive?

▶ Have we identified the real problem versus the presenting problem?

▶ Are our goals specific, measurable, feasible, and beneficial to the organization?

▶ Are we asking fresh questions and taking risks?

▶ Have the obstacles been identified?

▶ What is our level of commitment to solving the problem?

▶ Are we committed to innovative, high-quality solutions and strategies rather than quick solutions?

▶ Have we looked for and linked up with the power, passion, and knowledge?

▶ Have we identified outside resources and links that may be needed?

▶ Are action plans specific and part of each meeting?

▶ Have the action to be taken been clearly identified at each meeting, including the responsible person(s) and the specific dates?

▶ Are strategic actions recorded and then reviewed at the next meeting?

▶ Are the best-leveraged solutions chosen?

▶ Have learnings from our actions been achieved?

▶ Have we considered the impact of our strategies?

▶ Is there sufficient time between meetings to allow for necessary information collection and action?

Step 9: Develop and Present the Action Strategies

There are three possible options for implementing the strategies and actions devised by the action learning group.

▶ The group may have already been given the power to implement the strategy as part of its original charter when it was formed. The group can therefore immediately apply the strategies and solutions it has developed.

▸ The group may need to take its plan and recommendations to top management for approval. If approved, the group will be expected to implement the strategy.

▸ The group presents its recommendations to top management. Top management then appoints or creates another group or business unit to implement the action strategies.

If the group is not taking, or cannot take, action before having it approved by an outside group (e.g., top management, the sponsor, a business unit director), then it should take the necessary time and effort to carefully craft a strategy for convincing the powers that be to take the recommended actions. This may involve both a rational and emotional presentation of the facts and figures behind the group's decision and recommendations. Some organizations (e.g., Boeing, GE) will want to hear about the group's learnings as well as their strategies.

Accordingly, as teams enter into the final phases of the action learning process, the looming deadline tends to increase the sense of urgency and move the members toward completing their work on the project. Teams are challenged to complete their collection of data, analyze test results, prepare recommendations, preview with stakeholders, and develop an executive report and presentation. Logistics for the presentation can be very complex. In some organizations action learning teams present their recommendations to executive sponsors individually at an agreed on day and time. At other organizations, like Chrysler, Smith, and Goodyear, all teams present to a panel of executives and the presentations are spaced out over the course of a day. With four or more teams presenting in a given day, it becomes challenging to orchestrate the process and ensure that each team's recommendations have a proper hearing (Marquardt et al., 2009).

Preparation of Teams

The individual or panel receiving the recommendations should provide the action learning teams with an outline of what they would like to receive, for example:

▸ *Who's on your team and its members* (including sponsor and coach). Acknowledge people who have provided important assistance to your team.

▸ *Your case for change:* State your case in a way that will address potential reluctance and that demonstrates the importance of this project vis-à-vis your organization's strategy, vision, or values. Answer this question: "Why should we be unhappy with the way that things are right now?"

▶ *A brief summary of the proposed solution.* It may include a statement of the solution purpose, the project goal(s), the scope of the project, a general time frame for completing the project, key project members, overall budget/cost estimate, and so forth.

▶ *Your business case for change.* ROI, cash flow, or other business impact calculations should be included here. Set specific measures of success for evaluating the proposal. Include a deadline for attaining the goal.

▶ *A realistic estimate of the cost and/or resources required.* The estimates should include human resource requirements in terms of roles, skills required, and time commitment, and any costs necessary to implement your solution.

▶ *Important milestone events.* Include time frame, staging, and accountability.

▶ *Concise conclusion.* Give a brief summary of the key messages.

Smith International provides presentation skills training two days before the presentation. After the training, each team is recorded practicing their presentation. Coaches review these videos with each team and assist the team in identifying areas for improvement. At Chrysler, all teams are provided an opportunity to conduct a trial presentation with a group of coaches prior to the final presentation. The coaches focus on a very specific set of criteria: Are the teams believable? Do they support one another? Is the argument compelling? Is the case for change clear? Are risks and benefits identified? What are the immediate action requirements? Each team receives feedback from at least one other team and a panel of three coaches.

Preparation of Executive Panel

Typically, executive panel members, sponsors, and coaches all receive preparation for their role as evaluators or feedback providers either during the face-to-face mid-course meeting or in a virtual meeting. On average, most teams receive thirty minutes to make their presentation, and then thirty minutes are allowed for question and answers posed by the executive panel.

Following the presentation, the executive panel gathers to share impressions and reactions to the various presentations. The coaches accompany the team back to the preparation/debrief staging room. The coach should ask the action learning team to reflect on two key questions: What did you learn about yourselves (triple-loop learning) as you went through the entire process? What did you learn about the organization (double-loop learning)? The coach asks each person to take a few minutes to respond. Lastly, the coach hands out reflection guidelines for the peer coaching wrap-up session to be conducted one month following the presentation.

While the team is debriefing, the executive panel members should complete their feedback session. One executive panel member should volunteer to be the executive sponsor responsible for action on the project. This volunteer takes notes regarding evaluation discussions amongst the executives and later delivers initial feedback to the action learning team.

Checklist for Developing and Presenting the Action Strategies

▶ Does the action learning group only make recommendations or do they have the authority to implement the action strategies?

▶ Has the action learning team been prepared and guided in making recommendations?

▶ Who is on the review team? Have their expectations been communicated to the action learning team?

▶ What is important to the decision makers?

▶ How will the group's recommendations be handled and implemented?

▶ What communications between the top management, the sponsors, and the group have occurred during the life of the action learning group?

▶ Will the action learning group be sharing learnings as well as the recommendations?

Step 10: Implement Action Strategies

Taking action is an important element of any action learning group's activities. If the group is merely making recommendations, there will be diminished commitment as well as diminished learning. There is less learning without action, since we cannot be sure if our ideas will work.

Since action learning is not only about developing a recommendation (as with many problem-solving groups), but also about taking action, the preferred option for the organization is to have the group implement its own strategies. There are often situations, however, in which this is not possible, and only another group or business unit has the authority to implement the solution. This might occur because

- ▶ The proposed solution requires the actions of people throughout the organization and/or around the world.
- ▶ Only top management has the power or connections to implement the strategy.
- ▶ The strategy developed by the action learning group involves people not originally seen as essential by top management and/or the group.

If the organization chooses to have someone other than the action learning group implement the solution, it is important that the results gained by the new group's implementation be referred back to the original action learning group so that they have a final opportunity to learn about the quality and impact of their action strategies.

Only by testing the group's ideas in practice will members know whether the proposed strategies are effective and practical and whether there are any unanticipated consequences of the actions. Action learning groups should, when possible, pilot test part or all of their strategies. This will enable them to fine-tune the strategy, gain greater confidence in their plans, and acquire support from the organization. It also allows the group to choose between possible strategies so as not to have too many strategies to implement. Finally, reflecting on the pilot testing continues the group's learning and enables them to improve the final plans and actions.

The actions undertaken should be monitored for unanticipated troubles or benefits of the strategy. For each action item, there should be a clear indication of who will be responsible for implementation, what the specific time frame is, and what the anticipated results at critical junctures are. Solutions should complement and build upon the other work going on in the organization. The positive changes generated by action learning must be consistent with organizational values and messages. Lastly, it is important to keep decision makers and implementers up-to-date on actions—both the successes and the failures.

Checklist for Implementation of Actions

► How can we pilot test the strategies?

► What have we learned from the pilot testing?

► Who will implement the strategies?

► If the action learning group is not implementing the strategies, how will it be informed of the results?

► Are the strategies for the actions clear, systems oriented, and time based?

► Are there unexpected difficulties in implementation?

► Were problems resolved and actions taken?

► How effective were the actions taken?

► Is there sufficient support from top management?

► Is there follow-up to the action learning actions?

"Action learning has significantly enhanced Johnson & Johnson's leadership development and has improved our business by developing new and exciting business opportunities."

—William Welden, Worldwide Chairman, Pharmaceutical Group

Step 11: Assess, Capture, and Transfer the Individual, Group, and Organizational Learnings Gained from the Action Learning Programs

Action learning projects exist for specific purposes and for a limited time period. When the group has accomplished its action and learning purposes, it is disbanded. To ensure that an organization is fully capturing the power and benefits of action learning, it is important that the action learning programs are regularly and systematically evaluated. Therefore, at the end of each project, the action learning coach, organizational champion, and other key organizational figures should conduct a summative assessment of the overall results of the action learning group. They should analyze what worked and what did not and why. The effectiveness of the proposed strategies, the most significant learnings, and the degree to which those learnings were transferred should all be scrutinized.

Assessing the Impact and Benefits of Action Learning Programs at Boeing

Boeing conducts extensive evaluations during and after each action learning project. The follow-up evaluations are conducted three months and one year after the projects, with the data compiled, analyzed, and reported to the Boeing Executive Council. Analysis is conducted by both internal and external Boeing evaluators. Based on these findings, the Global Leadership Action Learning Program has been considered a great success in helping Boeing executives develop the global competencies identified as critical in undertaking Boeing's business. The return to the company in the form of enhanced global competencies is considered a wonderful return on investment.

In addition, the action learning group, together with top management, should identify how future action learning programs could be more effective in selecting problems and membership, interacting with the organization, and implementing recommendations. Finally, there should be an exploration of how other learning and training programs in the organization can better connect with the learning and development inherent in action learning.

Transferring Learning at Samsung

SUNHEE YOO, DIRECTOR, SAMSUNG HRD CENTER

Action learning has become an integral part of the corporate culture at Samsung, and a tool and strategy that drives the future of the company. As action learning team members become future corporate leaders, they will transfer and model the methods and principles they learned in action learning. Their subordinates will learn through the inquiring and reflective management style of their mentors how to be more effective leaders and managers and will come to regard the challenging action learning processes as essential preparatory steps in their path toward future senior leadership positions. Action learning has also provided them invaluable opportunities to develop both a global and multidimensional mind-set.

Samsung's action learning programs have also provided momentum for change and innovation throughout the company, and have brought together people from all sectors of the organization. The significance of Samsung's action learning program lies in the fact that the program has trained 800 management leaders strategically and produced more than 150 solutions and strategies that are being applied worldwide.

Samsung's action learning program has fostered an ingenious management style built on reflection and questions, on seeking ongoing feedback following field execution. Notably, the creative methodologies developed in the action learning teams have resulted in new businesses or pioneered technological standards that have been applied to similar cases across the many industries and business units to secure market leadership for Samsung. Action learning at Samsung has become the strategic tool and methodology to transform Samsung into a first-class global organization.

Checklist for Capture and Transfer of Individual, Group, and Organizational Learnings

▶ Have the learnings been applied throughout the organization?

▶ What is the quality of individual development and learning? Of team development and learning?

▶ Are the greater, long-term benefits and leveraging of learning valued?

▶ Is there commitment to team and individual learnings?

▶ Has there been a review of the learning?

▶ Has there been a systematic analysis of how the learning has been applied to other parts of the organization?

▶ What were the major benefits to the members of the action learning program?

▶ Have verbal or written reports been prepared for clients, managers, and others interested?

▶ How can future action learning programs in the company be improved?

▶ What are the follow-up plans?

Step 12: Make Action Learning an Integral Part of the Corporate Culture

As the organization continues to have success with its action learning projects, top management will naturally seek to institutionalize the process and make it an ongoing, integrated part of the corporate culture. Whenever urgent problems or projects arise that require innovative, powerful, and rapid actions, action learning teams are quickly established. All high-potential managers are assigned to action learning projects to develop the critical leadership competencies needed by the organization. Internal or external coaches are available as needed to coach the action learning groups.

The principles and practices of action learning are incorporated in day-to-day actions. Questions are more a part of corporate communications. Following events such as a performance appraisal, the manager and staff person reflect on what went well and how the next performance appraisal could go better. Upon completing a phone call with a customer, the salesperson asks himself questions: How did that call go? What could I do better next time? How can I improve my telephone sales techniques?

The power and successes of action learning programs should lead to strong and visible commitment, as well as further participation, from top management. When properly initiated and implemented, action learning provides a unique and powerful tool for simultaneously and effectively accomplishing five benefits for the organization: (a) solving the company's most urgent and important problems, tasks, issues, and/or challenges; (b) transforming the company into a learning organization that adapts quickly to the changing environment; (c) developing leaders who can be effective in the 21st century; (d) building high-performing and self-directing work teams; and (e) generating enhanced and continuous learning and professional development of all employees. As action learning becomes more and more an integral fabric of the corporate culture, some of the following will occur with greater frequency and ease.

Problem Solving

As action learning groups achieve successes in resolving the problems and tasks assigned to them, the organization should begin seeing those skills and the "can-do" attitude transferred to the problems that are confronted on a daily basis. The organization should observe greater competencies to systematically resolve the most complex problems. Problems should be easily reframed, goals should become more strategic, and actions taken should result in problems staying solved rather than arising in a mutated form elsewhere in the organization. Finally, the organization should see more team-solved rather than individual-solved problems.

> **Action Learning Helps Constellation Energy Become a Learning Organization**
>
> Action learning is credited with helping Constellation Energy become truly a learning organization. The entire company understands that learning is the necessary precursor to higher performance. Every new manager is required to participate in a leadership training program that involves action learning. In this training, participants are encouraged to question everything. Action learning has been added to the arsenal of tools the employees have at their disposal as the company continually strives for better ways of doing business.
>
> Constellation has trained a cadre of fifty skilled action learning coaches. Every plant has a trained coach who can be called in to work with groups to solve problems that arise. The language of action learning has become a part of the everyday language of the employees. It is not unusual to overhear someone looking for a "pizza person" for his or her action learning session.

Learning Organization

The most powerful potential benefit of action learning is its ability to transform an organization into a learning organization, since learning organizations, in the words of Walter Wriston, former CEO of Citicorp, "will blow the competition away." Learning organizations have significant competitive advantages because they learn more quickly how to capture knowledge and convert it into products, services, and profits. As mini–learning organizations, action learning groups model and exemplify the essence of what makes learning organizations so powerful. Through action learning, the organization will incorporate these organizational learning values and principles:

- Learning is performance based and tied to business objectives.
- Importance is placed on learning processes (learning how to learn).
- Continuous opportunities exist to develop knowledge, skills, and attitudes.
- Learning becomes a part of all action and work, a part of everybody's job description.

Leadership

The new kind of leadership needed in the global, knowledge-driven 21st century will be prevalent within the action learning culture of the organization—that is, leaders with transformational abilities, learning skills, emotional intelligence, ethical standards, problem-solving and project management strengths, self-awareness and understanding, and servant-leadership qualities. Organizations that have implemented action learning should be able to see remarkable differences in how their managers lead and in the successes accruing from these new leadership attributes. Companies using action learning should have greater confidence that the future leadership of their organization will be in good shape.

High-Performing Teams

Teams are critical as organizations seek to handle the complexity of organizational life and respond to the growing expectations of customers. Action learning will produce ideal teams that have extraordinary capacities to quickly and creatively solve problems and work in an effective and harmonious manner. Organizations should assess whether their teams—be they business units, task forces, or committees—are now more effective and successful.

The World Institute for Action Learning annually recognizes organizations around the world that have made action learning an integral part of their overall culture. Recent winners of the WIAL Organization Award include Panasonic, Microsoft, Kirin, and Goodrich.

Continuous Individual Development and Learning

Employees who have experienced action learning demonstrate a new capacity to learn as well as develop the skills they need to be successful in their jobs. They are more confident, innovative, and willing to take risks. Experience with action learning enables them to have a systems perspective, be able to handle uncertainty and ambiguity, be more competent when working in teams, and be able to assume leadership roles when called upon.

At periodic junctures throughout the action learning program, the organization should carefully examine and assess how the program is succeeding in attaining these benefits. And, in its efforts to fully tap the benefits of action learning, the organization should continue to search for additional ways of expanding the use of action learning and thereby expand the organization's ability to solve problems and develop its people.

Checklist of Making Action Learning
Part of the Corporate Culture

▶ What are the most significant benefits provided by the action learning programs?

▶ Are organizational problems being better resolved?

▶ What other problems or parts of the organization can apply action learning?

▶ Are employees better at framing and solving problems?

▶ Is action learning more effective in solving problems than other mechanisms used in the organization?

▶ Has the organization become a learning organization?

▶ Is the learning culture, as practiced in action learning groups, permeating the organization and how people learn?

▶ Are we placing a high priority on learning in all of our operations and planning, as we do in the action learning sets?

▶ How are we documenting the learning in the action learning groups and the application of these learnings throughout the organization?

▶ Do we expand our learning via ongoing questioning and reflection?

▶ Is learning that is acquired in one situation applied throughout the organization?

▶ Have we created new resources and networks for improving our learning?

▶ Are we creating more organization-wide opportunities for learning?

▶ Is learning rewarded and measured?

▶ How are we acquiring, storing, transferring, and testing our knowledge?

▶ How has leadership developed?

▶ What is the quality of our teams?

▶ Are people working better together?

▶ Are we better able to work in teams? To manage group processes?

▶ Are we more effective in managing projects?

▶ Are we better at systems thinking? Are we taking more and better risks?

▶ Are we more innovative?

▶ Do we manage uncertainty and ambiguity more effectively?

▶ What were the major benefits to the employees who were members of the action learning program?

▶ How can the organization's future action learning programs be improved?

Optimizing the Power of Action Learning

Action learning has rapidly become one of the most popular and powerful tools used by organizations around the world. Its capacity to provide the tremendous benefits of problem solving and individual, team, and organizational development at minimal costs and in relatively short time frames makes it a cost-effective resource for corporate success. Action learning can truly be a rich treasure for your organization!

Adams, M. 2004. *Change your questions. Change your life.* San Francisco: Berrett-Koehler.

Argyris, C. 1982. *Reasoning, learning, and action.* San Francisco: Jossey-Bass.

Argyris, C. 1991. Teaching smart people how to learn. *Harvard Business Review* 69, no. 3: 99–109.

Argyris, C. 2010. *Organizational traps: Leadership, culture, organizational design.* Oxford: Oxford University Press.

Argyris, C., and D. Schön. 1978. *Organizational learning: A theory of action perspective.* Reading, Mass.: Addison-Wesley.

Bandler, R., and J. Grinder. 1982. *Reframing: Neuro-linguistic programming and the transformation of meaning.* Salt Lake City, Utah: Real People Press.

Bandura, A. 1977. *Social learning theory.* Englewood Cliffs, N.J.: Prentice-Hall.

Bannan-Ritland, B. 2001. An action learning framework for teaching instructional design. *Performance Improvement Quarterly* 14, no. 2: 37–51.

Barker, A. E. 1998. Profile of action learning's principal pioneer—Reginald W. Revans. *Performance Improvement Quarterly* 11, no. 1: 9–22.

Barth, R. 1981. In the eyes of the led. *Executive* 6, no. 3: 30–33.

Bass, B. 2008. *The Bass handbook of leadership. Theory, research and managerial applications.* New York: Free Press.

Battram, A. 1999. *Navigating complexity: The essential guide to complexity theory in business and management.* London: The Industrial Society.

Beaty, L., T. Bourner, and P. Frost. 1993. Action learning: Reflections on becoming a set member. *Management Education & Development* 24, no. 4: 350–367.

Bennett, R. 1990. Effective set advising in action learning. *Journal of European Industrial Training* 14, no. 7: 28–30.

Bennis, W., and R. Thomas. 2007. *Leading for a lifetime.* Cambridge: Harvard Business School Press.

Bierema, L. 1998. Fitting action learning to corporate programs. *Performance Improvement Quarterly* 11, no. 1: 86–107.

Bion, W. 1991. *Experiences in groups.* London: Tavistock.

Block, P. 2011. *Flawless consulting.* San Francisco: Jossey-Bass.

Boddy, D. 1981. Putting action learning into practice. *Journal of European Industrial Training* 5, no. 5: 2–20.

Boshyk, Y. and L. Dilworth. *Action learning and its applications*. Houndmill, Hampshire: Palgrave Macmillan, 2010.

Boud, D., R. Keogh, and D. Walker. 1985. *Reflection: Turning experience into learning*. London: Kogan Page.

Bowerman, J., and J. Peters. 2000. Action learning: The lessons for Workers Compensation Board. *Human Resource Management International Digest* 8, no. 2: 26–28.

Brooks, A. 1998. Educating human resource development leaders at the University of Texas, Austin: The use of action learning to facilitate university/workplace collaboration. *Performance Improvement Quarterly* 11, no. 2: 48–58.

Brown, J. S., and P. Duguid. 1991. Organizational learning and communities of practice: Toward a unified view of working, learning, and innovation. *Organization Science* 2, no. 1: 40–57.

Brown, S., and K. Eisenhardt. 1998. *Competing on the edge: Strategy as structured chaos*. Cambridge: Harvard Business School Press.

Bruner, J. 1974. *Toward a theory of instruction*. Cambridge: Harvard Business School Press.

Bryant, A. 2011. *The corner office*. New York: Times Books.

Bunning, R. L. 1993. Action learning: Developing managers with a bottomline payback. *Executive Development* 7, no. 4: 3–6.

Butterfield, S., K. Gold, and V. Willis. 1998. Creating a systematic framework for the transfer of learning from an action learning experience. *Academy of HRD Proceedings*, 490–496.

Byrnes, N. 2005. Star search. How to recruit, train and how on to great people. *Business Week*, no. 40, 71.

Casey, D. 1997. The role of the set advisor. In M. Pedler, ed., *Action learning in practice*, 3rd ed. Aldershot, England: Gower.

Christie, A., and E. Sandelands. 2000. The knowledge harvest: Ensuring you reap what you sow. *Journal of Workplace Learning* 12, no. 3: 83–88.

Cho, Y., and T. Egan. 2010 The state of the art of action learning research. *Advances in Developing Human Resources* 12, no. 2, 163–180.

Collier, J., and R. Esteban. 1999. Governance in the participation organization: Freedom, creativity, and ethics. *Journal of Business Ethics* 21, nos. 2/3: 173–188.

Collins, J. 2001. *Good to great*. New York: HarperCollins.

Confessore, G. J., and S. J. Confessore. 1992. *Guideposts to self-directed learning*. King of Prussia, Pa. Organization Design and Development, Inc.

Cooperrider, D., P. Sorensen, and T. Yaeger. 2001. *Appreciative inquiry: An emerging direction for organization development*. Champaign, Ill.: Stipes.

Corporate Executive Board (2009)(March 19). *What drives leadership bench strength? Learningand Development Roundtable* [Email sent to all members]. Washington, DC: CorporateExecutive Board.

Cusins, P. 1995. Action learning revisited. *Industrial and Commercial Training* 27, no. 4: 3–10.

Davenport, T., and L. Prusak. 1998. *Working knowledge: How organizations manage what they know.* Boston: Harvard Business School Press.

Dean, P. "Why Action Learning Is An Ethical Addition To Performance Improvement: You Can Ask And You Can Argue." *Performance Improvement Quarterly* 11, no. 2 (1998): 3–4.

Densten, I., and J. Gray. 2001. Leadership development and reflection: What is the connection? *International Journal of Educational Management* 15, no. 3: 119–125.

Dewey, J. 1933. *How we think: Restatement of the relation of reflective thinking to the educative process.* Boston: D.C. Heath.

Dewey, J. 1997 (1916). *Democracy in education.* New York: The Free Press.

Dilt, R. 2006. *Slight of mouth: The magic of conversational belief change.* Capitola, Calif.: Meta Publications.

Dilworth, R. L. 1995. The DNA of the learning organization. In S. Chawla and J. Renesch, eds., *Learning organizations.* Portland, Ore.: Productivity Press.

Dilworth, R. L. 1996. Action learning: Bridging academic and workplace domains. *Employee Counseling Today* 8, no. 6: 48–56.

Dilworth, R. L. 1998. Action learning in a nutshell. *Performance Improvement Quarterly* 11, no. 1: 28–43.

Dilworth, R. L., and V. Willis. 2003. *Action learning: Images and pathways.* Malabar, Fla.: Krieger Publishing.

Dixon, N. M. 1996. *Perspectives on dialogue.* Greensboro, N.C.: Center for Creative Leadership.

Dixon, N. M. 1998a. Action learning: More than just a task force. *Performance Improvement Quarterly* 11, no. 1: 44–58.

Dixon, N. M. 1998b. Building global capacity with global task teams. *Performance Improvement Quarterly* 11, no. 1: 108–112.

Drucker, P. 2006. *The effective executive.* New York: Harper Books.

Forester, D. 2011. Consider: Harness the power of reflective thinking in your organization. New York: Palgrave Macmillan.

Foy, N. 1977. Action learning comes to industry. *Harvard Business Review* 55, no. 5: 158–168.

Freedman, A. 2011. Unpublished manuscript.

Freire, P. 1973. *Education for critical consciousness.* New York: Seabury Press.

Froiland, P. 1994. Action learning: Taming real problems in real time. *Training* 31, no. 1: 27–34.

Fulmer, W. 2000. On the edge. *CIO* 13, no. 14: 202–212.

Garratt, R. 1997. The power of action learning. In M. Pedler, ed., *Action learning in practice*, 3rd ed. Aldershot, England: Gower.

Geertz, C. 1993. *Interpretation of culture.* New York: Basic Books.

Gharajedaghi, J. 2005. *Systems thinking: Managing chaos and complexity.* Boston: Butterworth-Heinemann.

Gibson, M., and P. Hughes. 1987. The supervisory process in action learning. *Management Education and Development* 18, no. 4: 264–276.

Goleman, D. 2006. *Emotional intelligence*. New York: Bantam Books.

Goleman, D. 2000. *Working with emotional intelligence*. New York: Bantam Books.

Gregory, M. I. 1994a. Accrediting work-based learning: Action learning—a model for empowerment. *The Journal of Management Development* 13, no. 4: 41.

Gregory, M. I. 1994b. Accrediting work-based learning: Action learning—a model for empowerment. *Industrial and Commercial Training* 26, no. 4: 41–52.

Hammer, M., and S. Stanton. 2009. *How process enterprises really work*. Cambridge: Harvard Business School Press.

Heifetz, R., Linsky, M., and A. Grashow. 2009. *The practice of adaptive leadership*. Cambridge: Harvard Business Press.

Heiman, M., and J. Slomianko. 2004. *Learning to learn: Thinking skills for the 21st century*. Cambridge: Learning to Learn Press.

Henderson, I. 1993. Action learning: A missing link in management development? *Personnel Review* 22, no. 6: 14–24.

Hergenhahn, B. R. 1988. *An introduction to theories of learning*, 3rd ed. Englewood Cliffs, N.J.: Prentice Hall.

Hofstede, G. 2010. *Cultures and organizations*. London: McGraw-Hill.

Illich, I. 1999. *Deschooling society*. New York: Marion Boyars.

Inglis, S. 1994. *Making the most of action learning*. Brookfield, Vt.: Gower.

Ingram, H., K. Biermann, J. Cannon, J. Neil, and C. Waddle. 2000. Internalizing action learning: A company perspective—establishing critical success factors for action learning courses. *International Journal of Contemporary Hospitality Management* 12, no. 2: 107–113.

Isaacs, W. 1993. Taking flight: Dialogue, collective thinking, and organizational learning. *Organizational Dynamics* 22, no. 2: 24–39.

Johnson, D., and R. Johnson. 1998. Learning together and alone. Upper Saddle River, NJ: Allyn & Bacon.

Johnson, S., and K. Blanchard. 1998. *Who moved my cheese?* New York: Putnam.

Jones, M. 1990. Action learning as a new idea. *Journal of Management Development* 9, no. 5: 29–34.

Jubilerer, J. 1991. Action learning for competitive advantage. *Financier* 15, no. 9: 16–19.

Kable, J. 1989. Management development through action learning. *Journal of Management Development* 8, no. 2: 77–80.

Keene, A. 2000. Complexity theory: The changing role of leadership. *Industrial and Commercial Training* 32, no. 1: 15–18.

Keys, L. 1994. Action learning: Executive development of choice for the 1990s. *Journal of Management Development* 12, no. 8: 50–56.

Knowles, M., E. Holton, and R. Swanson. 1998. *The adult learner*. Houston: Gulf Publishing.

Kolb, D. 1984. *Experiential learning: Experience as the source of learning and development*. Englewood Cliffs, N.J.: Prentice-Hall.

Koo, L. 1999. Learning action learning. *Journal of Workplace Learning* 11, no. 3: 89–34.

Kotter, J. 1998. 21st century leadership. *Executive Excellence* 15, no. 5: 5–6.

Kouzes, J., and B. Posner. 2002. *The leadership challenge*. San Francisco: Jossey-Bass.

Lanahan, E. E., and L. Maldanado. 1998. Accelerated decision-making via action learning at the Federal Deposit Insurance Agency. *Performance Improvement Quarterly* 11, no. 1: 74–85.

Lawlor, A. 1997. The components of action learning. In M. Pedler, ed., *Action learning in practice*, 3rd ed., Aldershot, England: Gower.

Lawlor, A., and G. Boulden. 1982. *The application of action learning: A practical guide*. Geneva: International Labor Organization.

Lenderman, H., F. Lastar, and R. Lenderman. 2003. *Performance-based degrees earned at work: The Sodexho University story*. Prestonpan, England: Prestoungrange University Press.

Levi, D. 2011. *Group dynamics for teams*. Thousand Oaks, Calif.: Sage.

Lewis, A., and W. Marsh. 1997. Action learning: The development of field managers in the Prudential Insurance Company. *Journal of Management Development* 6, no. 2: 45–56.

Limerick, D., R. Passfield, and B. Cunnington. 1994. Transformational change: Towards an action learning organization. *The Learning Organization* 1, no. 2: 29–40.

MacNamara, M., M. Meyer, and A. Arnold. 1990. Management education and the challenge of action learning. *Higher Education* 19, no. 4: 419–433.

MacNamara, M., and W. H. Weeks. 1982. The action learning model of experiential learning for developing managers. *Human Relations* 35, no. 10: 879–901.

Margerison, C. 1988. Action learning and excellence in management development. *Journal of Management Studies* 32, no. 5: 43–53.

Marquardt, M. J. 1993. *Global human resource development*. Englewood Cliffs, N.J.: Prentice-Hall.

Marquardt, M. J. 1994. *The global learning organization*. New York: Irwin Professional Publishing.

Marquardt, M. J. 1996. Action learning: The cornerstone of building a learning organization. *Training and Development in Australia* 23, no. 4: 7–12.

Marquardt, M. J. 1997a. *Action learning*. Alexandria, Va.: ASTD Press.

Marquardt, M. J. 1997b. Action learning: An essential tool for corporate success. *HRD Focus*, 6–8.

Marquardt, M. J. 1997c. Action learning in the classroom. *Performance in Practice* (Summer): 4–5.

Marquardt, M. J. 1998. Using action learning with multicultural groups. *Performance Improvement Quarterly* 11, no. 1: 113–128.

Marquardt, M. J. 1999a. Action Learning. In *The resource guide to performance interventions.* San Francisco: Jossey-Bass.

Marquardt, M. J. 1999b. *Action learning in action.* Mountain View, Calif.: Davies-Black.

Marquardt, M. J. 1999c. Action learning: The cornerstone for building a learning organization. *Sozialpsychologie und Gruppendynamik* 24, no. 2: 3–16.

Marquardt, M. J. 2000. Action learning and leadership. *The Learning Organization* 7, no. 5: 233–240.

Marquardt, M. J. 2001a. Action learning: Does it work differently in different cultures? In S. Shankar, ed., *Action learning and action research for practitioners: An Asia-Pacific paradigm.* Sydney: Southern Cross University Press.

Marquardt, M. J. 2001b. Action learning. In S. Thiagarjan and E. Sanders, eds., *Performance Intervention Maps.* Alexandria, Va.: ASTD Press.

Marquardt, M. J. 2004. *Leading with questions.* San Francisco: Jossey-Bass.

Marquardt, M. J. 2011. *Building the learning organization,* 3rd ed. Boston: Nicholas-Brealey Press.

Marquardt, M. J., and N. Berger. 2000. *Global leaders for the 21st century.* Albany, N.Y.: SUNY Press.

Marquardt, M. J., and T. Carter. 1998. Action learning and research at George Washington University. *Performance Improvement Quarterly* 11, no. 2: 59–71.

Marquardt, M. J., and L. Horvath. 2001. *Global teams.* Mountain View, Calif.: Davies-Black Publishing.

Marquardt, M. J., S. Leonard, A. Freedman, and C. Hill. 2009. *Action learning for developing leaders and organizations.* Washington, DC: APA Press.

Marquardt, M. J., and D. Waddill. 2003. The power of learning in action learning: A conceptual analysis of how the five schools of adult learning theories are incorporated within the practice of action learning. *Proceedings of AHRD Conference,* Minneapolis.

Marsh, P., and B. Wood. 2001. Pressed for results: An action learning project in practice. *Industrial and Commercial Training* 33, no. 1: 32–36.

Marsick, V. 1988. Learning in the workplace: The case for critical reflectivity. *Adult Education Quarterly* 38, no. 4: 187–198.

Marsick, V. 1991. Action learning and reflection in the workplace. In J. Mezirow, ed., *Fostering critical reflection in adulthood.* San Francisco: Jossey-Bass.

Marsick, V., L. Cederholm, E. Turner, and T. Pearson. 1992. Action-reflection learning. *Training and Development* 46, no. 8: 63–66.

Marsick, V., and J. O'Neil. 1999. The many faces of action learning. *Management Learning* 30, no. 2: 159–176.

Mathews, K. M., M. White, and R. Long. 1999. Why study the complexity sciences in the social sciences? *Human Relations* 52, no. 4: 439–462.

McGill, I., and L. Beaty. 1995. *Action learning: A practitioner's guide*, 2nd ed. London: Kogan Page.

McLagan, P. 2003. The change-capable organization. *T + D* 57, no. 1: 50–58.

McLaughlin, H., and R. Thorp. 1993. Action learning: A paradigm in emergence. *British Journal of Management* 4, no. 1: 1003.

McNamara, C. 2002. *Authenticity circles facilitator's guide*. Minneapolis: Authenticity Consulting.

Merriam, S. B., and R. S. Caffarella. 1999. *Learning in adulthood*, 3rd ed. San Francisco: Jossey-Bass.

Meyer, S. 2000. Action learning as a vehicle for organizational change culture. *Proceedings of Academy of Human Resources Development*, 594–599.

Mezirow, J. 2000. Learning as transformational. San Francisco: Jossey-Bass.

Mintzberg, H. 2011. The long view. *T+D* 65, no. 1, 69.

Moravic, M., and K. Wheeler. 1995. Mission possible. *Human Resource Executive* (special report), n.p.

Morris, J. 1991. Minding our Ps and Qs. In M. Pedler, ed., *Action learning in practice*. Aldershot, England: Gower.

Mumford, A. 1991. Learning in action. *Personnel Management* (July): 34–37.

Mumford, A. 1995. Developing others through action learning. *Industrial and Commercial Training* 27, no. 2: 19–27.

Mumford, A., ed. 1984. *Insights into action learning*. Bradford, England: MCB University Press.

Noel, J., and R. Charan. 1988. Leadership development at GE's Crotonville. *Human Resource Management* 27, no. 4: 433–447.

Noel, J., and R. Charan. 1992. GE brings global thinking to light. *Training and Development* 46, no. 7: 29–33.

Noel, J., and R. Dolitch. 1998. *Action learning*. San Francisco: Jossey-Bass.

Nonaka, I. (2008). *The knowledge-creating company*. Cambridge: Harvard Business Press.

Olson, E., and G. Eoyang. 2001. *Facilitating organizational change*. San Francisco: Jossey-Bass.

O'Neil, J. 1997. Set advising: More than just process. In M. Pedler, ed., *Action learning in practice*, 3rd ed. Aldershot, England: Gower.

O'Neil, J., and V. Marsick. 2007. *Understanding action learning*. New York: AMA Press.

Ormond, J. 1999. *Human learning*. Upper Saddle River, N.J.: Prentice-Hall.

Orr, J. E. 1990. Sharing knowledge, celebrating identity: Community memory in a service culture. In D. Middleton and D. Edwards, eds., *Collective remembering*. Newbury Park, Calif.: Sage.

Patrickson, M. 1998. Action learning. In F. Sofo, ed., *Human resource development: Paradigm, role, and practice choices*. Melbourne: Woodslane.

Pedler, M. 2008. *Action learning for managers*. London: Lemos & Crane.

Pedler, M. 1997. *Action learning in practice*, 3rd ed. Aldershot, England: Gower.

Peters, T. 2010. *The little big things*. New York: HarperBusiness.

Pfeffer, J., and C. Fong. 2002. The end of business schools? Less success than meets the eye. *Academy of Management Learning and Education* 1, no. 1: 78–95.

Putnam, R. 2000. *Bowling alone*. New York: Simon & Schuster.

Raelin, J. 2008. *Work-based learning*. San Francisco: Jossey-Bass.

Raelin, J. A. 1997. Action learning and action science: Are they different? *Organizational Dynamics* (Summer): 21–33.

Raelin, J. A., and L. Michele. 1993. Learning by doing. *HR Magazine* 38, no. 2: 61–70.

Revans, R. W. 1965. *Science and management*. London: Macdonald.

Revans, R. W. 1980. *Action learning: New techniques for management*. London: Blond & Briggs.

Revans, R. W. 1981. Management, productivity, and risk: The way ahead. *Omega* 9, no. 2: 127–137.

Revans, R. W. 1982a. *The origins and growth of action learning*. Bromley, England: Chartwell-Bratt.

Revans, R. W. 1982b. What is action learning? *Journal of Management Development* 1, no. 3: 64–75.

Revans, R. W. 1983. *ABC of action learning*. Bromley, England: Chartwell-Bratt.

Revans, R. W. 1986. Action learning in a developing country. *Management Decision* 24, no. 6: 3–7.

Rogers, C. 1994. *Freedom to learn*. New York: Macmillan.

Rotter, J. B. 1954. *Social learning and clinical psychology*. Englewood Cliffs, N.J.: Prentice-Hall.

Sandelands, E. 1998. Creating an online library to support a virtual learning community. *Internet Research* 8, no. 1: 75–84.

Sanders, T. 2010. *Strategic thinking and the new science*. New York: Free Press.

Schein, E. 2010. *Organizational culture and leadership*. San Francisco: Jossey-Bass.

Schön, D. 1986. *The reflective practitioner: How professionals think in action*. San Francisco: Jossey-Bass.

Schuman, S. 1996. The role of facilitation in collaborative groups. In C. Huxham, ed., *The search for collaborative advantage*. London: Sage.

Senge, P. 2006. *The fifth discipline*. New York: Doubleday.

Shively, W. 2009. *Power and choice*. New York: McGraw-Hill.

Skinner, B. F. 1971. *Beyond freedom and dignity*. New York: Knopf.

Smith, D. 1992. Company based projects: Using action learning to develop consultancy skills. *Journal of Management Development* 11, no. 1: 12–24.

Smith, P. 2001. Action learning and reflective practice in project environments that are related to leadership development. *Management Learning* 32, no. 1: 31–48.

Sundstrom, E., et al. 1999. *Supporting work team effectiveness.* San Francisco: Jossey-Bass.

Sutton, D. 1991. A range of applications. In M. Pedler, ed., *Action learning in practice,* 2nd ed. Aldershot, England: Gower.

Sveiby, K. 1997. *The new organizational wealth: Managing and measuring knowledge-based assets.* San Francisco: Berrett-Koehler.

Thorndike, E. L., E. O. Bregman, J. W. Tilton, and E. Woodyard. 1928. *Adult learning.* New York: Macmillan.

Tversky, A., and D. Kahneman. 1974. Judgment under uncertainty: Heuristics and biases. *Science* 18, no. 185: 1124–1131.

Vince, R., and L. Martin. 1993. Inside action learning: An exploration of the psychology and politics of the action learning model. *Management Education and Development* 24, no. 3: 205–215.

Waddill, D., and M. Marquardt. 2011. *The e-HR advantage: The complete handbook to technology-enabled human resources.* Boston: Nicholas-Brealey Press.

Waddill, D. and M. Marquardt. 2003. Action learning and the five schools of adult learning. *Human Resource Development Review* 2, no. 4, 406–429.

Weick, K. 2000. Making Sense of the Organization. San Francisco: Wiley.

Weinstein, K. 1995. *Action learning: A journey in discovery and development.* London: HarperCollins.

Wenger, E., R. McDermott, and W. Snyder. 2002. *Cultivating communities of practice.* Cambridge: Harvard Business School Press.

Wheatley. M. J. 2006. *Leadership and the new science.* San Francisco: Berrett-Koehler.

Yoong, P., and B. Gallupe. 2001. Action learning and groupware technologies: A case study in GSS facilitation research. *Information Technology & People* 14, no. 1: 78–88.

York, L., J. O'Neil, and V. Marsick, eds. 1999. *Action learning: Successful strategies for individual, team, and organizational development.* San Francisco: Berrett-Koehler.

Zuber-Skerritt, O. 1995. Developing a learning organization through management education by action learning. *Learning Organization* 2, no. 2: 36–54.

Zuboff, S. 1988. *In the age of the smart machine: The future of work and power.* New York: Basic Books.